Sharing Your Faith
with a
Muslim

Sharing Your Faith with a

Muslim

Abdiyah Akbar Abdul-Haqq

Bethany Fellowship INC.
MINNEAPOLIS, MINNESOTA 55438

Copyright © 1980
Abdiyah Akbar Abdul-Haqq
All rights reserved

Published by Bethany Fellowship, Inc.
6820 Auto Club Road, Minneapolis, Minnesota 55438

Printed in the United States of America

Library of Congress Cataloging in Publication Data

Abdul-Haqq, Abdiyah Akbar, 1920-
    Sharing your faith with a Muslim.

    1. Missions to Muslims. 2. Christianity and other religions—Islam.
3. Islam—Relations—Christianity. I. Title.
BV2625.A23   261.2'7   80-16020
ISBN 087123-553-6

About the Author

Abdiyah Akbar Abdul-Haqq is an evangelist with the Billy Graham Association. His father was a convert from Islam to Christianity. Haqq travels extensively as an evangelist and addresses large crowds of Christians and adherents of non-Christian religions in many parts of the world. In addition to English, he speaks Hindi, Urdu, and Punjabi. He also reads in Urdu, Persian, Arabic and Greek. His efforts to bring Christ to the world take him around the world three or four times each year.

Preface

The winds of God are blowing across the face of our planet in an unprecedented way. At the same time there is a worldwide eruption of infernal powers of spiritual confusion and moral chaos seeking to counteract the salutary ministry of the Holy Spirit to the hearts and minds of people of all sorts and conditions.

In the traditionally Christian countries of the West, despite the current born-again movement, there is a disquietingly high incidence of defection from the Church and alienation from the lordship of Jesus Christ. This phenomenon has created a perplexing home missionary situation for the churches concerned and a promising foreign mission field for religions like Islam, Hinduism, Buddhism, and the many cults based on them. Islam, for example, has already made unexpected gains among the spiritually disaffected in the occident. This initial success has imparted a euphoria to its missionary strategists so that they are now dreaming of and planning for the Islamization of the Western hemisphere. The time is not too far away when people on the American and European continents will be confronted with the challenge of Islam in a way unknown in history.

In the so-called Third World there are indications of the beginning of a ground swell of interest in Jesus Christ on the part of the non-Christian masses in general. Despite the upsurge of religious nationalism in several countries of the area, the predominant religions have not succeeded in satisfying the spiritual hunger and messianic expectations of the thoughtful and morally sensitive. To such, in particular, the appeal of the teaching, life and Gospel of Jesus Christ is great. In this context the Muslims are an interesting case. Their scripture, the Koran, depicts Christ as a prophet unique in His preincarnate nature, miraculous birth, miracles and moral stature. This remarkable testimony to His preeminance should have kept thoughtful Muslims down the centuries excited about Him and anxious to learn more about Him from the Bible—recognized and commended by the Koran. But such a logical necessity never materialized in a significant way. On the contrary, even the Christ of the Koran was veiled from the eyes of free-thinking Muslims, rather early in the history of Islam, by the use of traditions and commentaries on the Christological passages which were weighted in favor of the cult of Muhammad.

On the current religious scene, the Muslim masses are being exposed to the matchless person and claims of Jesus Christ through media evangelism like radio broadcasts, Bible correspondence courses, and literature distribution. It covers Muslim lands in the Near and Far East with their various degrees of accessibility. It has been instrumental, to a significant degree, in arousing the interest of an increasing number of erstwhile unreachable Muslims in the Gospel. Though hindered by their traditional attitude toward Christianity and notions about Christ, many of them today are possessed of a curiosity like the Hellenists of old who came to Phillip saying, "Sir, we would like to see Jesus" (John 12:21, NIV). A very small number of these find their way to Christian discipleship. But the majority of them remain on the level of inquirers highly fascinated by and drawn to Jesus Christ, yet not interested in the church or even negatively disposed toward it.

At the harvesting end there exists a bottleneck on the evangelistic front of the Third World. This is a development in the advance of the kingdom of God in our time which calls for the full attention of a Christian close to the heartbeat of the One who says, "Look on the fields, for they are already white to harvest." Harvest season is proverbially short. Time is of the essence in harvesting and bringing in the sheaves from the fields of Islam. This task requires divinely commissioned laborers in the fields with proper tools in their hands. *Sharing Your Faith with a Muslim* has been written by the grace of God in order to provide one more tool, among many, for the use of all those who are called to witness to Muslims. Also, it should prove helpful for the edification of Muslims who seek after God and the experience of His salvation in Jesus Christ.

This book has grown out of a paper that the author was called upon to read during the Pan African Congress on Evangelism held in Nairobi, December 13-19, 1976. Most of the quotations from the Koran are translations by G. Sale (The Koran) and M. Pickethall (The Meaning of the Glorious Koran).

The author seeks to acknowledge gratefully the guidance and constraint of the Holy Spirit in the writing and completion of the book and to dedicate it to the glory of Him "whom to know is life eternal." He is also indebted to his wife for her tireless encouragement and inspiration during the entire project.

Table of Contents

Chapter 1

The Christian Neighborhood of Early Islam

On the basis of their scripture and tradition, Muslims entertain definite opinions about Christianity. These, however, often exhibit a gross misunderstanding of the true Christian faith and the Gospel of Jesus Christ. This has led many Christian scholars to the unwarranted conclusion that Muhammad, the prophet of Islam, never came into contact with the mainline churches and that all his ideas about Christ and Christianity were derived from some obscure heretical sects. In the light of modern scholarship, however, such a position is no longer tenable. From the beginning Christians have been neighbors of Muslims. Christian life and thought have influenced Islam from its very inception and on through the early formative centuries. In summarizing available evidence in this area of research R. Bell observed:

> Islam did not arise in a backwater from some obscure Judaic-Christian sect, but arose in the full stream of religious life in Asia. (*Origins of Islam in Christian Environment*. London: Macmillan & Co., 1926, p. 9)

Tore Andre considered the Nestorian church to be a major source of Christian influence on Islam. S. Zwemmer writes:

> Professor Tore Andre, of the University of Upsala, has shown in his recent study of Christian origins of Islam . . . that the opinion hitherto current, of sundry heretical sects to which Muhammad was indebted for his Christian ideas, is a mistaken one. He directs attention to the great church of Asia, the Nestorian Church, as the prime source of Christian thought and life in pre-Islamic Arabia. There are many points of similarity between Muslim teaching and Nestorian christianity, but the circle of ideas most prominent and characteristic, according to Tore Andre, is eschatology with its extraordinary stress on the Day of Judgment. (Zwemmer: Foreword to *Nestorian Missionary Enterprise* by J. Stewart, T. & T. Clark, 1928, p. 8)

The religious and political influence of Christianity on Arabia came from various directions. In the south, Yemen had seen Abyssinian rule under the governorship of Abraha, on the eve of Islam. The church in that territory flourished under the leadership of Saint Gregentius, bishop of Taphar. Abraha himself was a zealous Christian ruler. He has been praised by Greek, Syrian, and Muslim writers alike. He built a magnificent church in the capital city of Sana. It was considered to be one of the seven wonders of the age. In the year A.D. 567, on the night before its dedication, the church was defiled by pagan Arabs from the north, alleged to be members of the tribe of Quresh in Mecca. They, perhaps, were afraid of the church becoming a rival in popularity to their own temple in Käaba. This act of sacrilege led to the well-known expedition of Abraha against Mecca and its pagan sanctuary. He led his troops, riding on an elephant—something of a novelty to the Arabs. He had to abandon his march toward victory, however, because an epidemic broke out in his camp. The year of his unsuccessful attack on Mecca is known as the year of the Elephant.

During the same year the prophet of Islam was born. The Arabs were in touch with Abyssinia—modern Ethiopia—throughout the Christian centuries preceding the rise of Islam. Even after the attack of Abraha on Mecca, this relationship between the Arabs and Ethiopians continued on, including the lifetime of the prophet Muhammad. Ethiopic, the ancient language of Abyssinia, is closely related to Arabic philologically. However, the modern language of Ethiopia, Amharic, is divergent, in many ways, from the ancient Ethiopic. The pre-Islamic Arabs were exposed to this language, and many words from it passed on to their own speech and poetry. Some of this Arabicized foreign vocabulary found its way into the Koran. For example, in Sura 4:54 there is the interesting word "Jabit" which occurs with another term of foreign origin "Taghut" ("they believe in Jabit and Taghut"). Muslims believe that the Koran was revealed in pure Arabic. Yet in regard to the vocabulary under consideration, some Muslim scholars have conceded that they are foreign. As-Suyuti in his "Itiqan" tells us that some of these scholars knew that the two words above, as well as words like "Maida" and "Hawariyun," came from the Ethiopic language.

In the north the Christian influence on Arabia came from Egypt and Syria, representing the Roman Empire. Uthman b. Al-Huwayrith is reported to have been appointed king of Mecca due to Roman intervention. The details of this incident, however, are obscure. According to the Muslim historian Waqadi, Hashim, the grandfather of the prophet of Islam, had concluded a trade agreement with the Roman emperor. During the pre-Islamic days the Roman or Byzantine influence was predominant both in Syria and Palestine. Through the Banu Ghassan confederacy the Byzantine influence prevailed in several parts of Arabia. Refugees from Arabia like the celebrated poet Imar al-Qais visited the Byzantine court. During this time Greek and Coptic words were also assimilated into the Arabic language and thus came to be used in the Koran as well. Similarly, Syriac vocabulary found its way into the Koran due to its currency in pre-Islamic Arabic and the prophet Muhammad's exposure to it (see Jeffery, *The Foreign Vocabulary of the Quran*).

On the northern flank the kingdom of Hira radiated Christian influence on Arabia. It also served as a buffer state between the mighty Persian Empire and the desert tribes. The court of the Lakhmids of Hira became a great center of literary activity. The Christian poet Adi b. Zaid lived long at this court. Some other famous poets like Al-Asha, Tarafa, Al-Harith b. Hilliza and Amar b. Kulthum were also related to the same court. Their poems are full of Persian words. Through them and other media Persian vocabulary became current in pre-Islamic Arabic and eventually found its way into the Koran.

J. W. Sweetman believes that it can be shown conclusively that Arabia came into contact with all three major sections of the Church, i.e., the Byzantine, Nestorian and Jacobite-Monophysite churches (Islam and Christian Theology. London: Lutterworth Press, 1945, Vol. I, p. 2). However, it is important to note that it was the Nestorian Church which exercised the most significant influence on Islam. In this connection J. Stewart informs us:

> Prior to A.D. 547 when the great Jacobite revival began, the only form of Christian faith known in the whole independent Arabia and Hirtha was that held by the "Church of the East," the so-called Nestorians, and it is practically certain that every presbyter and bishop in the whole of that area recognized and acknowledged allegiance to the patriarch of Seleucia. When therefore, mention is found of Christians in Mecca and Medina and even in the tribe of Koreish, one is warranted in assuming that all such, prior to at least, the middle of the sixth century, were in communion with the same patriarchate. When the sudden rise of Islam took place it was the Nestorians who suffered most from the impact. (J. Stewart, op. cit., pp. 71, 72)

On the eve of Islam the New Testament was known and respected as a divine book. Though, according to Barthold, inscriptions dating from the sixth century of the Christian era reveal that the Arabic language was in common use in many oriental churches, yet there is no clear evidence of an Arabic translation of the Bible before Islam. Apparently the Christian Arabs used their native language in worship service but their scripture continued to be in Syriac and Hebrew. The earliest known Arabic version of the Old Testament dates back to A.D. 900, while that of the New Testament was transcribed by a Coptic bishop in A.D. 1271 and published in 1616.

In Mecca, the first city of Islam, worship in the temple of Käaba was based on the patriarchal tradition of Abraham. According to Ibn Ishaq, there were pictures of Mary and Jesus on a wall of the Käaba. When the Prophet of Islam ordered all signs of idolatry to be removed from the Käaba, he made an exception in the case of the pictures of Jesus and Mary (*The Life of Muhammad.* Ibn Ishaq, tr. Guillaume, p. 552). During the rebuilding of the Käaba, forty years before Muhammad's call to prophecy, they found a stone with the following inscription:

> He that soweth good shall reap joy; he that soweth evil shall reap sorrow; can you do evil and be rewarded good? Nay, as grapes cannot be gathered from thorns. (Ibid., p. 88)

The last sentence of the inscription is a quotation from Matthew 7:16. Obviously the gospel according to Matthew was extant and popular with several pre-Islamic seekers after the true God.

There was also a group among the pagan Arabs who despaired of idolatry and longed for the living God. They were monotheists before the rise of Islam. They sought to rediscover the tradition and faith of Abraham who has been called a Hanif, one orthodox in faith and sincere in Islam, according to the Koran (3:60). Four such seekers after God have been mentioned by Ibn Ishaq: Warqa b. Naufal, Ubaidullah b. Jash, Uthman b. Al-Huwayrith and Zaid b. Amar. As to their position:

They were of the opinion that their people had corrupted the religion of their father Abraham, and that the stone they went round was of no account, it could neither hear nor see, nor hurt nor help. "Find yourselves a religion," they said, "for by God you have none." So they went their ways seeking the "Hanaffiya"—the religion of Abraham. (Ibn Ishaq, ibid., p. 99)

It is interesting that three of the four afore-mentioned seekers after the God of Abraham found the end of their search in Jesus Christ. Warqa, a cousin of the prophet's first wife, Khadija, embraced Christianity and began to study the Bible. He knew Hebrew and had written down the Gospels in Hebrew (Aramaic). Though he was the spiritual counselor of the prophet and a relative, yet he never accepted the new religion in preference to his own. After his death the prophet dreamed of him in white robes—signifying that Warqa was in heaven (*Shorter Encyclopaedia of Islam*, p. 631).

As for Ubaidullah, he continued to be a seeker till the arrival of Islam. He became a Muslim soon after and married Umm Habiba, daughter of Abu Sufyan. Both he and his wife joined the first band of Muslims who escaped religious persecution from pagan Meccans and found a refuge under the Christian king of Ethiopia. Some time after his arrival in Ethiopia, Ubaidullah gave up Islam and was converted to the Christian faith. He used to testify of his new-found spiritual experience to other Muslim refugees. Ibn Ishaq relates:

Accordingly Muhammad b. Jafar b. Zubir has related to me saying, "Ubaidullah b. Jash, when he became a Christian used to dispute with the Companions of the apostle of God who were there in Ethiopia, and he used to say, 'We see clearly and you are blinking,' that is "We are clear-sighted and you are seeking to see and do not see," and that because a whelp blinks when it strives to open its eyes to see. The word he used means "to have one's eyes open." (Ibn Ishaq, ibid., p. 99)

Ubaidullah lived and died as a Christian in the land of his sojourn. The prophet married his widow. The third "Hanif" Uthman b. Al-Huwayrith was a relative of the prophet's first wife. He went to the Byzantine court and while there he became a Christian. The emperor granted him a high office.

The fourth seeker, Zaid b. Amar, did not accept either Islam or Christianity. But he forsook the paganism of his people, for which he was reproached by his uncle. He continued to worship one God in the sanctuary of Käaba. He used to taunt the pagan Quraish by saying:

"O tribe of Quraish, by Him in whose hand is the soul of Zaid b. Amar, not one of you has attained unto the religion of Abraham except myself." (Ibid., pp. 99, 100)

This realization of the religion of Abraham on the part of Zaid was only a negative one, for we find him still seeking as to the right way to worship. He used to pray:

"O God, if I knew which manner is most pleasing to Thee, I should worship Thee in it; but I know it not." (Ibid.)

Ibn Ishaq goes on to relate that someone asked the prophet to pray for

Zaid. He agreed and said:

> "Yes, for verily he shall be raised up by himself as a religious sect." (Ibn Ishaq as quoted by W. Tisdall, *Original Sources of the Quran.* S.P.C.K., 1911, pp. 266, 267)

The word "Hanif" occurs twelve times in the Koran. Abraham is looked upon as a model of "Haniffiya." The Koran goes on to say that he was neither a Jew nor a Christian (3:67), and Muslims are commanded to follow his religion. The Arab poets of pre-Islamic days used the term "Hanif" for a pagan or idolator. Even Muslim scholars have recognized the word to be of foreign origin. Thus Masaudi in his "Tanbih" tells us that the term is Syriac. The Syrian Christians used it as an equivalent for pagan. The pagan Arabic poets borrowed it from Christians. During the early days of Islam the followers of the prophet soon preferred not to call themselves "Hunafa" in line with the patriarch Abraham. In view of the embarrassing connotation of the word "Hanif" in its Christian usage, they chose to call themselves Muslims.

It is important to bear in mind that the pre-Islamic "Hunafa" were pagan Arabs who had been exposed to Biblical ideas in general and its monotheism in particular. Consequently, they rebelled against their native idolatry with its cultic center in the famous temple of Mecca. They were a class of people very much like the God-fearers of the Book of Acts (10:2). They claimed that their monotheistic tradition dated back to the Friend of God, Abraham. It was handed down by those spiritually alive during the pre-Islamic history of Arabia. According to the Koran, the prophet Muhammad came only as a reformer and a warner to pagan Arabs, calling them back to Abrahamic monotheism. This picture of the original mission of the prophet is confirmed even by an early outside source. Margoliouth points out that the earliest written account about the prophet dates back to the Armenian "Chronicle of Sebeos" of seventh century A.D. It states that the prophet was an Ishmaelite who taught his countrymen to return to the religion of Abraham and claim the promises made to the descendants of Ishmael (Encyclopaedia of Religion and Ethics, "Muhammad," Vol. 8, p. 872).

Besides his contact with the "Hunafa," the prophet received inspiration for a renewal of the faith of Abraham through his acquaintance with Jews and Christians. There was a considerable community of Christians living in his own hometown so that they had a cemetery of their own. These Christians belonged to various denominations and were quite friendly with their neighbors. Once when the pagan Meccans were planning to rebuild the temple of Käaba, they decided to entrust the project to a Coptic Christian whom they described as "a friendly craftsman" (Ibn Ishaq, op. cit., p. 84). Among Christians who lived in Mecca there were slaves from Ethiopia and Arab tribals who followed the Byzantine and Coptic creed. Some Christians of the tribe of Banu Asad lived close to the temple of Käaba, in the heart of the city of Mecca. Other Christians lived in the suburbs. Most of the well-to-do families of Mecca possessed slaves, among whom there were several Christians. Abbas, an uncle of the prophet, had a Greek concubine. He presented his illustrious nephew with a Coptic slave named Abu Rafi.

Christian travelers and monks often passed through the city of Mecca. Thus an oculist monk is reported to have cured the prophet, when he was a child, with dust from Mount Sinai. Once, a handsome deacon visiting the city, caused a mild sensation among its citizens. The prophet must have made his acquaintance and established friendship with Christians of his hometown. He also had ample opportunity to meet other Christians in the course of his journeys away from Mecca. We learn of his visit to Syria, at age twelve, with his uncle, Abu Talib. He entered the service of his first wife, Khadija, when he was twenty-five years old. In this connection he made business trips abroad, during the course of which he must have met both Jews and Christians who were proud of being custodians of revealed Scriptures. Thus he must have picked up a lot of firsthand information about these people of the Book who were later referred to in the Koran itself. In the famous annual fair of Okaz, Muhammad had opportunity to witness contests between Arab poets of both Christian and pagan backgrounds.

There were Christians in the prophet's own family. As it has been pointed out earlier, Warqa b. Naufal and Uthman b. Al-Huwayrith were cousins of his first wife, Khadija. Warqa played a historic role at a crucial juncture of the prophet's life. This story deserves mention in some detail. Before his call to prophecy, Muhammad used to practice meditation and withdrawal from the world annually in a cave located on Mount Hira near Mecca. This manner of spiritual retreat was practiced originally by Syrian Christians. Through them it gained currency among the pagan Arabs as well. Once in the course of such a retreat at Mount Hira, the angel Gabriel is reported to have visited the prophet in a dream and asked him to recite the first revelation of the Koran. On waking from sleep, the prophet became quite agitated about the possible significance of his dream. He wondered what was happening to him. He used to hate poets and had no use for those possessed by the spirits of the air. Hence he was worried lest his own unusual experience be due to one of those abnormal visitations. He became so overwhelmed by these dark possibilities that he began to contemplate suicide. He relates his own story:

> I shall go to some high mountain cliff and cast myself down therefrom so that I may kill myself and be at rest. I went off with this mind, but when I was in the midst of the mountains I heard a voice from heaven saying, "O Muhammad, thou art God's apostle and I am Gabriel." (Al-Tabari: *Tarikh al-Rusul Wa al-Muluk*. Leiden, 1881, I, p. 1152)

After the angel Gabriel departed from the prophet, he hastened to his wife, Khadija, and related to her his strange experience, wondering at the same time if he had become a poet or a possessed person. Khadija tried her best to console him and assure him that all was well with him. But she also decided to consult her cousin Warqa who was more knowledgeable in spiritual things than she. Having heard her account, Warqa exclaimed:

> "Quddus, quddus! By Him in whose hand is Warqa's soul, if you are telling me the truth, O Khadija, (it means that) there has indeed come to him the great Namus," and by Namus he meant Gabriel, upon whom be peace,

who used to come to Moses, "so he will assuredly be the prophet to his own people. Tell him so and have him stand firm." So Khadija returned to the apostle of God—upon whom be God's blessing and peace, and informed him of what Warqa had said, and that eased somewhat the anxiety he felt. (Al-Tabari, ibid., p. 1152)

According to the account above, Warqa advised the prophet that his mission was to his own people only. While Khadija became the first convert to the prophet soon after his call, Warqa remained a Christian all his life.

In his own immediate family the prophet had ample opportunity to learn about Christianity. Khadija's hairdresser was a Christian from Ethiopia. The first husband of his wife, Umm Habiba, was a Christian, as it has been mentioned earlier. This was also true of the first husband of his wife Sawda. Zaid b. Harith was an adopted son of the prophet. He belonged to the Christian tribe of Banu Kalb from south of Syria. When he was still a young boy, he and his parents were waylaid. The marauders carried him away and sold him into slavery. He came into the possession of Khadija who gave him to her husband as a present. But the prophet developed such a liking for the young slave that he freed him. He took Zaid to the Blackstone of Käaba and said:

"Bear testimony, all ye that are present. Zaid is my son; I will be his heir and he shall be mine." (W. Muir, *The Life of Muhammad*, ed. T. H. Wair, p. 35)

In this way the freed youth came to be known as Zaid b. Muhammad. Though he was severed from his Christian home at an early age, yet he must have carried facts and stories about his ancestral faith in his memory. Both he and his adopted father must have often had occasion to discuss Christian beliefs and practices. One of the favorite concubines of the prophet was a coptic named Maria. Al-Baidhawi tells us that the prophet received information from two Christians, Jubra and Ysara, and that on that account the Quresh said, "It is only a mortal that teaches him" (Al-Baidhawi on Sura 16:103). According to other traditionists, the prophet used to stop and listen to these two Christians as they recited aloud the Books of Moses (Torah) and the New Testament (Injil) (T. P. Hughes, Dictionary of Islam, p. 53).

There is no doubt that the birth and infancy of Islam were attended by Christian presence. It is tragic, however, that the Christian witness was missing from the scene. Hence despite the contact of Christianity with Islam, her evangelistic light was hidden under a bushel. The main reason for the historic and monumental failure of the Church was her own spiritual decay. The evangelistic fervor and missionary fire of the Church of the earliest centuries began to cool off gradually as she started on a course of increasing secularization. A milestone in this downward trend was reached when persecution of Christians ceased and the Roman emperor Constantine became favorably disposed toward the Church. From that time onwards worldliness began slowly to corrode the life and witness of the Church.

It is recorded that when the emperor Constantine presided over the famous ecumenical Council of Nicea, the first decision he was called upon to make concerned the numerous petitions of bishops against their fellow bishops. The emperor himself, who influenced the course of events in Nicea, was not a baptized Christian at that time. The Council of Nicea marks the beginning of a period in history when the Church got busy with an official defense of her faith against heresies that kept appearing on the scene. But during this critical juncture in her history, she learned to lean increasingly upon secular power rather than to depend wholly on her God-given resources, which were once good enough to determine the canon of the Scripture and bring masses of people into the kingdom of God. During the reign of Theodosius, heresy became punishable by the state. The emperor commanded all his subjects to become orthodox Christians. Such an intimate alliance between the Church and state exposed the former to the vicissitudes of national and international politics. Thus countries at war with the Roman Empire felt opposed to its official religion also. Moreover, Christian minorities within these countries were always likely to be suspected of complicity with the official guardians of Christianity. For example, the Nestorian Church found a refuge in Persia from the persecuting zeal of their fellow Christians of the Roman persuasion. This predominantly Zoroastrian country was ruled by the Sassanian dynasty which was almost constantly at war with the Roman emperors. Whenever a war between the two empires was imminent or in progress already, the Persians often suspected Christians among them of being in league with Roman Christians. Such a suspicion fanned by the jealousy of fanatical Zoroastrian priests often broke out into violent persecutions of Christians. In this way hundreds of thousands of Christians were martyred in Persia under the Sassanians. Matters came to such a pass that the Nestorian Church had no choice but to declare severance of all relationship with the Church in Rome and so put an end to needless suffering and persecution of its own members. Thus the Church became permanently divided into two major sections along the lines of political rivalry between Persia and Rome, East and West. This cleavage between the two churches existed on the mission fields also. Hence in Arabia the two factions were present side by side. In their mutual rivalry, they were not able to present a united front to the pagan world around them. This sad lack of unity among Christians was bound to be noticed by onlookers like the prophet Muhammad. The Koran bears a record to this effect:

> And from those who say, we are Christians, we have received their covenant; but they have forgotten part of what they were admonished; wherefore we have raised up enmity among them till the day of Resurrection. (Sura 5:17, Sale)

The active antagonism between the mainline churches showed up in various ecumenical church councils succeeding Nicea and preceding the rise of Islam. Sweetman describes this sad period of Church history as follows:

> At one time Irenaeus could look to the bishops as guardians of sound faith and apparently expect some uniformity from them, but now it is the bishops

who seem to be irreconcilables and uniformity is far to seek. (Op. cit., Vol. I, Part I, p. 45)

To be specific, the rivalry between the Patriarchates of Alexandria and Antioch greatly determined the course of theological disputes in the great church councils after Nicea. After a difficult struggle against divisive and heretical tendencies the church leaders at the Nicean Council formulated a statement of the doctrine of the Holy Trinity that was sound and acceptable to all the mainline churches. It was a unanimous theological confession of the Church that God was in Christ reconciling the world to himself. It delineated the divine nature of the Saviour in a manner that satisfied all Christians and guarded against heresy. But the issue that engaged the attention of the churches next concerned the mystery of relationship between the divine and human natures of Jesus Christ. What happened after the Incarnation? Did His two natures fuse into one or did they remain distinct? The difference of opinion on this subject, within the Church, came to a head at the Ecumenical Council of Ephesus. Cyril of Alexandria championed the one-nature theory while Nestorians, representing the Antiochean position, stood for a distinction of two-natures. This dialogue involved the status of the Virgin Mary. Cyril held that Mary was Theotokos—the bearer of God because she bore the flesh which was indissolubly united with the Logos. However, Cyril used the expression "Mater Theo"—mother of God, for Theotokos. This became the practice under the monophysites (Encyclopaedia of Religion and Ethics, Vol. 9, "Nestorianism," p. 328). Nestorius was concerned about the possibility of a gross misunderstanding regarding this designation of Mary on the part of non-Christians and pagans. Therefore he protested:

> The form that received God let us honour as divine together with the Word of God, but the Virgin who received God let us not honour as God together with God. (*Nestorius and His Teaching*. Bethune-Baker, p. 15)

Despite the disagreement of some Church historians, it seems certain that the status of the Virgin Mary was an important consideration in the controversy between Cyril and Nestorius. Cyril, the champion of the title "Mother of God," was held in high esteem "by those to whom monasticism and the cult of the Virgin were dear" (Ibid., p. 56). In the works of Ephraim (4th century A.D.) there are many hymns to the Virgin Mary. Several prayers addressed to her are attributed to Rahhula, bishop of Eddassa, who was a contemporary of Cyril, his devoted friend and well known for his zeal against the Nestorians (Ibid., p. 56, note 1). Bethune-Baker remarks that the following words of Nestorius are a conclusive evidence that the status of the Virgin Mary was definitely involved in the great controversy:

> It is sufficient to honour Mary that she gave birth to the humanity which became the instrument of God. (Ibid., p. 56, note 1)

Nestorius proposed to call Mary "Christotokos," bearer of Christ, instead of "Theotokos" which was equated with "mother of God" by the Monophysites and those who cherished the cult of Mary. The fears of Nestorius regarding a possible misunderstanding of this title by non-Christians were amply justified in the case of Islam. Cyril of Alexandria won the point over Nestorius and the Council of Chalcedon affirmed his stand, by and large, in A.D. 451.

The two-nature controversy in the high circles of the ecumenical Church Councils does not tell the whole story about Christianity before Islam. The eminent Church historian Harnack reminds us that from the end of the second century there appeared an increasing distinction between *doctrina ecclesia* and *doctrina publica*. The latter was a secondary type of the religion:

> Subterranian, different among different peoples, but every where alike in its crass superstition, naive doketism, dualism and polytheism. (*A History of Dogma*, Vol. IV, p. 304)

In this degenerate form of popular Christianity the adoration of saints and martyrs was an important feature. In the course of time these new intermediaries between man and God came to occupy a position very much similar to gods and goddesses, the like of which the prophet of Islam rejected in pagan Arabia. These were looked upon as more trustworthy mediators with God than angels. In the matter of adoration of the dead, even some well-known Church leaders had succumbed to the popular superstitions. Thus in the fifth mystagogic Catechism Cyril wrote:

> Then also remember those who have already fallen asleep, the Patriarchs, Prophets, Apostles and Martyrs, that God through their prayers and intercession may accept our supplication. (Ibid., p. 312)

Such a degeneration of the true Christian faith did not go unprotested by voices within the Church. At the end of the fourth century we find Vigilantius who refused to believe in the intercessory powers of the saints. He had witnessed some of the evils of this superstition and saint-worship in the sacred shrines of Palestine. His criticism did not go unheeded. It helped delineate the official distinction, made by the Church, between the proper worship of God and the adoration of saints. However, such a theological refinement could not be expected to have any salutary impact upon the religious superstitions and practices of the ignorant masses. We learn from sources of the fifth century A.D. that there were saintly novels in the West and biographies of saints and martyrs of the Jacobites, Copts, and Ethiopians in the East. These helped perpetuate cultic superstitions and practices within the Church. It is interesting to note, however, that the heretical Ennomians—strict Arians—were backward in the matter of saint worship (Harnack, ibid., p. 313). It must be pointed out that the worship of angels was also practiced in the Church along with the cult of saints and martyrs. But here again, the Church made a distinction between this cult and the proper worship of God (Ibid., p. 311).

The Virgin Mary occupied a prominent place in the cult of saint worship. In the Symbol she was given a place next to the Holy Spirit (Ibid., p. 315). Ambrose was a champion of Mary worship. He held that she took an active part in Redemption and applied Gen. 3:15 to her (Ibid., p. 315). She was looked upon as bride of the Holy Spirit—a description that could easily be misconstrued by non-Christians. There were some Church fathers at the

Nicean Council who held the notion of the divinity of Mary. In this, their Mariolatry, they thought that there were two gods besides God the Father, i.e., Christ and the Virgin Mary. They were known as Marionites (Eusebius, as cited by G. Sale; *The Koran*, p. 25). According to Epiphanius there were certain women in Thrace, Scythia, and Arabia who were in the habit of adoring the Virgin Mary as a goddess and offered her a certain kind of cake. He calls them Collyridians and rebukes this heresy:

"Let Mary be had in honour, but let the Lord be worshipped" (Encyclopaedia of Religion and Ethics, "Mary," Vol. 8, p. 476). John of Damascus, who was a great theologian and dialogued with Muslims, believed in the incorruptibility of the body of Mary and thought that she had a prominent place in God's plan of Redemption. However, true to the position of the Greek Church, he never considered her free from the original sin. During the fifth century pictures of Jesus and Mary were worshipped already along with many saints. As it has been pointed out above, pictures of Jesus and Mary were to be found even in the pagan shrine of Käaba in Mecca. Hughes sums up the spiritual condition of the Church on the eve of Islam in the following words:

> Doubtless much of the success of Islam in its earlier stage was due to the state of degredation into which the Christian Church had fallen. The bitter dissensions of the Greeks, Nestorians, Eutichians and Monophysites are matters of history, and must have held up the religion of Jesus to the ridicule of the heathen world. The controversies regarding the nature and person of our Divine Lord had begotten a sect of Tritheists, led by a Syrian philosopher named John Philoponus of Alexandria, and are sufficient to account for Muhammad's conception of the Blessed Trinity. The worship of the Virgin Mary had also given rise to a religious controversy between the Antiduo-Marionites and the Collyridians; the former holding that the Virgin was not immaculate, and the latter raising her to the position of a goddess. Under the circumstances it is not surprising to find that the mind of the Arabian reformer turned away from Christianity and endeavoured to construct a religion on the lines of Judaism. (Hughes' Dictionary of Islam, p. 53)

From the discussion above it is easy to see that at the birth and during the infancy of Islam, Christianity was present, but genuine Christian witness to the Saviour of mankind was missing from the scene. The religion of a typical Christian contemporary of the prophet of Islam consisted of a curious mixture of orthodoxy with heterodox ideas and cultic beliefs and practices. It is interesting that the teaching of the Koran about Christianity reflects this situation, for it, too, is a mixture of the orthodox with the legendry and the apocryphal. Jesus Christ is the very center of the Christian faith. The nature of His incarnation was the hot theological issue which absorbed the attention of ecumenical councils after Nicea until about the rise of Islam. Surprisingly enough, though, most of the teaching of the Koran about Christianity is Christological also. Therefore, a strategic point of contact between Islam and Christianity is Jesus Christ. About Him we can speak from our Scripture (Injil) to their scripture (the Koran) legitimately and fruitfully.

Chapter 2

The Bible and Early Islam

As noted in chapter one, Christology is the very essence of the Koran's teaching about Christianity. Moreover, it consists of a sort of two-nature delineation of the person and work of Jesus Christ. This approach to Christology is in line with the New Testament record of the Word of God "who became flesh and dwelt among us." At the same time it reflects the theological issue that occupied the attention of the Church when the founder of Islam appeared on the scene. From certain passages in the Koran it is easy to demonstrate the divine majesty of Jesus Christ as well as His unique life and miracles. Also, it is easy to show from other passages in the book that He was like other prophets and apostles of God.

In their dialogue with Christians, Muslims like to dwell only on those Koranic passages which speak of His servant form, endeavoring to rationalize and explain away other plain references to His divine glory. A proper and unbiased study of the Koranic witness to Jesus Christ calls for a balance between the two types of Christology it embodies. In a fair attempt to achieve this end, a student of the Koran is left perplexed as to who Christ really was. In the case of doubtful and obscure revelations in the Koran, the prophet (and Muslims) was advised by God to turn to those who had received revealed Scriptures before him. Thus it is written:

> And if thou [Muhammad] art in doubt concerning that which we reveal
> unto thee, then question those who read the Scripture [that was] before thee.
> (Sura 10:95, Pickethall)

It is quite evident from the verse that in the event of perplexity about revelations in the Koran, the prophet is directed by God to consult with Christians and Jews who possess revealed Scriptures. It is logical, therefore, to say that in issues pertaining to the Mosaic Law and old patriarchal history, the prophet was to consult the Jews. However, for the clarification of Christological points in the Koran, he was to seek advice from the Christians. If God so directed Muhammad, the prophet of Islam, how could Muslims afford to neglect the Bible as a source of enlightenment? But the sad fact remains that Muslims have chosen arbitrarily to refuse the light of the Bible upon themselves. Consequently in the case of doubts and perplexities raised by the teaching of the Koran, they resort to their traditions which are believed to be, at best, a revelation of the second rank as compared to the revealed Scriptures from God.

The result of this policy, especially in regard to the Koranic Christology, has often proved to be fruitless and even self-contradictory. Take, for example, the subject of the death of Jesus Christ. The Koran speaks of the day Christ was to die and of His mortal human nature. At the same time it teaches that He did not die upon the cross, but God raised Him up to himself. Here, there is a gap between the Koranic teaching about the birth and ascension of Christ. It concerns the time of His death. The Koran has nothing to say about that. This silence of the Koran is filled with traditions on the actual death of Christ which are not only varied but even contradictory. As a result, they leave the original gap in the Koranic revelation unresolved and further complicated with a confusion of divergent opinions.

In this situation the Muslims would have done well to give heed to the command of God to ask the Christians who read the Scripture before them. A reference to the Bible would have resolved the Koranic enigma about the death and ascension of Christ once and for all. Muslims have not only failed to obey a definite commandment of God in seeking enlightenment from the Bible, but they have also tried to explain away the very verse which embodies the divine guidance. W. Muir gives a good description of some of the attempts made by Muslim scholars to avoid the true implication of Sura 10:95.

> The learned doctors of Islam are sadly embarrassed by this verse, referring the prophet, as it does, to the people of the Book who would solve his doubts. They have striven to explain it in such a way as might maintain his dignity, and are thus driven to interpretations, the strangest one has ever heard, such as that it is addressed ostensibly to the prophet but really to such as question his claim—which is in the last degree opposed to the sense of the text. Others claim that it was Muhammad himself who is addressed, but, however much they change and turn the compass, it ever points to the same celestial pole—the purity and preservation of the Scriptures. If, again, we take the party addressed to be those who doubted the truth of Islam, this throws open the whole foundation of the prophet's mission; regarding which they are referred to the Jews [or Christians] for an answer to their doubts; which would only strengthen the argument for the authority of the Scripture—a result the Muslim critics would hardly be prepared for. (*The Beacon of Truth*, W. Muir. London: The Religious Tract Society, 1894, p. 100)

Since it was so important for the prophet Muhammad to consult with those who had the custody of the Bible (Sura. 21:7), it will be rewarding to study some further information about that Scripture as detailed in the Koran. The Judeo-Christian Scriptures are mentioned frequently in the Koran. They are regarded as plenary revelations just like the Koran. Thus it is written:

> Verily we have revealed our will unto thee, as we have revealed it unto Noah and the prophets who succeeded him; and as we revealed it unto Abraham, and Ishmael, and Isaac, and Jacob, and the tribes, and unto Jesus, and Job, and Jonas and Aaron, and Solomon; and we have given thee the Koran as we gave the Psalms unto David: some apostles have we sent whom we have formerly mentioned unto thee; and other apostles have we sent whom we have not mentioned unto thee; and God spoke unto Moses discoursing with him. (Sura 4:163 & 164, Sale)

The Biblical Scriptures are recognized as extant during the time of the prophet. They were in the custody of Jews and Christians who habitually read them (Sura 10:95), studied them diligently (Sura 2:113). Once, in order to settle a dispute, the prophet asked for a scroll of the Old Testament to be produced and read from:

> All food was lawful to the children of Israel, excepting that which Israel made unlawful to himself, before the Taurat [the Pentateuch] was revealed. Say, bring hither the Taurat and read it, if you be true. And whoever contriveth a lie concerning God after that, surely they are the transgressors. (Sura 3:93-94)

The statement here clearly implies the existence of copies of authentic Torah with the Jews of the prophet's time. The same must be conceded in regard to the Gospel (Injil) with the Christians. The Koran admonishes both Christians and Jews to abide by and judge according to the injunctions contained in their respective scriptures:

> And will we make thee their Judge since they have beside them the Taurat, in which is the command of God? Then will they turn their back after that, and these are not believers. Verily we have revealed the Taurat; therein is guidance and light. The prophets that submitted themselves to God judged thereby those that were Jews; and the doctors and the priest (did the same) in accordance with that which was confided to their charge of the Book of God, and they were witnesses thereof. Wherefore fear not man but fear me, and sell thou not the signs of God for a small price. And he that doth not judge by that which God hath sent down, they are transgressors. (Sura 5:43-44)

Advising the Christians specifically the Koran goes on to say:

> Let the people of the Gospel [Injil] judge by that which God hath revealed therein. Whoso judgeth not by that which God hath revealed; such are evil doers. (Sura 5:47, Pickethall)

The same warning is given to the Jews and Christians together:

> O ye people of the Book! Ye are not grounded upon anything until ye get up [or observe] the Taurat and the Injil, and that which hath been revealed unto you from your Lord. (Sura 5:68)

As a matter of fact, there is a telling analogy about those Jews who do not live up to the Torah:

> The likeness of those who are entrusted with the Law of Moses, yet apply it not, is as the likeness of the ass carrying books. Wretched is the likeness of folk who deny the revelations of God. And God guideth not wrongdoing folk. (Sura 62:5, Pickethall)

It is evident that if the Koran enjoins the Jews and the Christians to live up to their revealed Scriptures, these must be available with them and quite current. Surely God would not require His commandments to be obeyed unless He has made them accessible to His people. The fact that the Judeo-Christian Scriptures were current during the time of the prophet is further supported by God sending pagan Arabs to people of the Book in order to check the authenticity of the Koran itself:

> And we have sent before thee [as apostles] other men whom we inspired; ask, therefore, who are acquainted with the Book if ye know not. (Sura 21:7)

According to Jalaluddin "The people of the Book" in the verse above mean the learned men of Taurat (Torah) and Injil (the Gospel). Al-Baidhawi tells us regarding the verse:

> This is given as a reply to the speech of the Quresh—"what! Is this any other than a mortal like ourselves?" God directs them to ask the people of the Book regarding the character of the ancient prophets.

How could the pagan hearers of the claims of the prophet be expected to check up with the Jews and Christians if their Scriptures were not with them in an authentic form? The Koran considers the Bible—constituting the Judeo-Christian Scriptures—so important and indispensable for the welfare of mankind that even Muslims are categorically commanded to believe in it:

> We believe in God, and in what hath been revealed unto us, and in that which hath been revealed unto Abraham, and Ishmael, and Isaac, and Jacob, and the Tribes; and in what hath been given unto Moses and Jesus, and that which hath been given unto the prophets from their Lord. We make no distinction between any of them; and unto Him are we resigned. (Sura 2:136. Also, 2:1-5; 4:13)

Not only are Muslims required to believe in the Bible but also they are forbidden from making a distinction between these revelations and the Koran. Leaving out these revelations previous to the Koran would amount to making a serious distinction between them. Moreover, it will lead a Muslim to believing only a part of the total revelations from God. This will make a person not only a bad Muslim, but also will condemn him as an infidel:

> Verily they that reject God and His apostles and seek to make a distinction between God and His apostles; and say—"we believe in part and reject a part," and seek to take a [middle] path between the same, these are infidels in reality, and we have prepared for the infidels a ignominious punishment. But they that believe in God and in His apostle, and make no distinction between any of them, to these we shall give the reward, and God is forgiving and merciful. (Sura 4:150-152. Also, 2:89)

The awful consequence of rejecting God and His revealed Scriptures, believing only in part of them, are reiterated clearly:

> Those who rejected the Book, and that which we have sent our messengers with,—they shall know, when the collar shall be on their necks, and chains by which they shall be dragged into hell—then shall they be burned in fire. (Sura 40:70-72; 4:136)

To sum up the evidence presented above, the Koran clearly implies the existence and currency of the Judeo-Christian Scriptures in the time of the prophet of Islam. It attests their authenticity and inspired character. They are appealed to by the prophet and their observance inculcated. All Muslims are expected by God to believe in these Scriptures, and a rejection of them is fraught with dire consequences in the world to come. Despite this undeniable recognition of the Bible by the Koran, it appears from all available indications that both the prophet Muhammad and pagan Arabs had no direct access to it. They could learn about the Bible either from its custodians—Jews and Christians—or, as the prophet claimed, by a direct revelation from God. But, as the Koran testifies, many of the Jews and Christians themselves were ignorant of their Scriptures:

> And amongst them are ignorant persons, who know not the Book but only foolish stories; they follow naught but their imaginations. (2:78)

The Arabic word translated "ignorant" in the above-mentioned verse is "ummiun." It does not signify illiteracy in general. It implies ignorance and illiteracy in regard to revealed Scriptures of God. The Muslims use this verse as a proof text for their theory that "ummiun" means "unlettered," and since their prophet is called "ummi" in the Koran, he was totally illiterate. Hence, the Koran is considered a literary miracle from an illiterate prophet. However, the verse under discussion clearly shows that the term "ummiun" is a technical one related to the knowledge of revealed Scriptures. In this sense the prophet was an "ummi" (unlearned) as far as the Judeo-Christian Scriptures were concerned. But the question may be raised here as to why the prophet, pagan Arabs, and even many Jews and Christians were unlearned in the Bible. As to the scriptural ignorance of the Jews, it must be borne in mind that a majority of them in Arabia were proselytes rather than pure Hebrews. For example, speaking of the Jewish tribes of Kuraiza and Nadir in the city of Medina, the Muslim historian Yaqubi writes:

> They were not pure Jews but Judaized clans of the Arabic tribe of Djudham. (*Shorter Encyclopaedia of Islam*, p. 292)

It is also important to note that even real Jews had become Arabicized by the time Islam came on the scene. Wellhausen has aptly pointed out:

> The Arabian Jews by their language, their knowledge of the scripture, their manner of life, their fondness for malicious mockery, secret arts, poison, magic and cursing and their fear of death, make an unusual impression which cannot be explained simply by the Judaizing of pure Arabs. But on the other hand, it must not be forgotten that the Jews in Arabia were very much influenced by their surroundings and had assumed a character of their own. (*Shorter Encyclopaedia of Islam*, p. 292)

There was a widespread alienation from their scripture on the part of the Arabian Jews because they had succumbed to a degenerate type of belief and practice in religion. This spiritual corruption must have been aided by the great influx of proselytes from among pagan Arabs. The personal religion of a majority of the Jews consisted of crass superstition and heterodox beliefs and practices based on non-canonical, apocryphal and magical sources of information. Most of them could not even read their scripture in Hebrew. It had to be translated orally in free style Arabic during worship services in the synagogues. Hence the Koranic reference to their general ignorance of the Scripture is true to facts.

The Jews of Arabia had their Bible in Hebrew. It was a version prepared by the proselyte Aquila around the second century A.D. The Jews everywhere adheared to this post-Christian version in preference to the Septuagint—a Greek translation made in Alexandria around the second century B.C. One of the main reasons for the Jewish preference for Aquila's version was the Christians' use of the Septuagint to prove the messianic claims of Jesus Christ.

The roots of widespread ignorance among Jews of Arabia can easily be traced as far back in history as the time of Jesus Christ. In those days:

> The learned class or Scribes were busy on the twofold structure of Halaca, or legend, tradition and inference, supplementing and "hedging in" the Pentateuchal law and Haggada or fantastic exegesis, legendary, ethical or theosophic, under which the religious directness of the Old Testament almost wholly disappeared. The popular religious literature of the day seems again to have been mainly apocalyptic. The people never wearied of mysterious revelations couched in strange symbolic and enigmatic forms, and placed in the mouth of ancient patriarchs and worthies, which held forth golden visions of deliverance and vengeance in a shape which, because crasser and earthlier, was also more palpable than the spiritual hopes of the old prophets. Beyond the limits of Palestine thought took a wider range. In adopting the Greek language the Hellenistic Jews had also become open to the influences of foreign speculation and schools of Alexandria, whose greatest teacher, Philo, was a contemporary of the founder of Christianity, had in a great measure exchanged the faith of the Old Testament for a complicated system of metaphysical-theological speculations upon the Absolute Being, the Divine Wisdom, the Logos and the like, which by the aid of allegorical interpretation were made to appear as the true teaching of Hebrew antiquity. (*Encyclopaedia Britannica*, "Bible," Vol. III, p. 641)

The state of affairs described above appears to have been more true of the Jews in the city of Medina than elsewhere in Arabia. The Koran suggests that they were better acquainted with rabbinic writings than with their Scriptures. As to the Jewish use of the Scripture proper, Jeffery points out:

> The Jews of North Arabia and Syria read the Bible in synagogues in the Hebrew original, but for domestic study they probably used Aramaic translations as did the Christians. Many Biblical words that occur in the Quran have evidently gone through an Aramaic channel. (*The Foreign Vocabulary of the Quran*, p. 27, note 7)

The Aramaic translations of the Hebrew Bible were made orally in the synagogues by interpreters called the "Methurgemanim." These men used great freedom of embellishment and application in their readings. In due course of time these oral interpretations came to form written Targums or Aramaic paraphrases of the Hebrew Bible. The date of the earliest Targums is some centuries after Christ (*Encyclopaedia Britannica*, Vol. III, p. 641). The Targum of Pseudo-Jonathan on the Pentateuch is a good example of a typical Targum. It is a free Palestinian version full of legendary embellishments and additions to the original text. It is interesting to note that some Babylonian Targums have used a scriptural text that differs from the Massoretic text. The Jews of Arabia must have used these Aramaic Targums often in their synagogues and interpreted them in Arabic. Thus they further targummated the Targums which were handed down to them. At times some Jews wrote out the Arabic interpretations of the Aramaic Targums and tried to sell these as copies of the original Scripture. Apparently the Koran refers to a similar situation when it lays a curse upon certain scripturally ignorant Jews:

> Among them are unlettered folk who know not the Scripture except from heresay. They but guess. Therefore woe be unto those who write scripture with their hands and then say, "This is from God," that they may purchase a small gain therewith. Woe unto them for that their hands have written, and woe unto them for that they earn thereby. (Sura 2:78, 79, Pickethall)

These verses seek to criticize certain Jews who are called unlettered because they do not know their Scripture. Yet it is said about them that they transcribe with their hands something which they pass as Scripture from God. This was meant for sale—perhaps to be used for magical purposes such as amulets and charms. One might ask here how Jews who were ignorant of their Scripture could be expected to transcribe and sell it. Obviously, the Koran implies that what they were transcribing "with their hands" was not from the Scripture really. It is very plausible that such material was copied from Targums. In that case they could, in a way, claim that it was from God, for it consisted of embellished interpretations of the scriptural verses. But the legendary embellishments perhaps were so profuse that a given text of the Scripture was lost like a needle in a haystack. The haystack part certainly was not from God as was the Scripture hidden underneath!

The Old Testament remained inaccessible to the early Muslims and the prophet. It was in Hebrew and its Aramaic Targums. The Arabic Targums which were being sold as charms by certain ignorant Jews were interpretations from the Aramaic Targums. Hence they were thrice removed from the original Scripture and useless to pagan Arabs seeking spiritual enlightenment.

The next source of knowledge concerning the Bible was the Christians in Arabia. As to the Christian Scripture in and around Arabia we learn that:

> Around the end of the second century A.D. and beginning of the third, there appeared Latin, Syriac and Coptic translations of Christian Scripture. The origin and early history of these translations is obscure. The Septuagint formed the basis of the Old Testament in these translations—the Hebrew text was employed nowhere except Syria. (ERE, *The Bible in the Church*, Vol. 2, p. 584)

As far as the New Testament was concerned there were:

> Remarkable free texts differing from those otherwise known to us. It is possible that the different translations came into being independently of one another. (Ibid., p. 584)

There was a revision of the Syrian Bible by Rahulla about A.D. 410. During the fourth and fifth centuries, Armenian and Ethiopic translations appeared on the scene. It must be pointed out here that the Syriac Bible was used much more extensively than the other translations.

The Gospels were translated into Arabic from the original Greek as well as Coptic and Syrian versions. Barhebreus writes of an Arabic translation made by a monophysite named Johannes, by the order of an Arab prince in A.D. 640. Oldest extant fragments of Arabic translations from the Greek date from the early ninth century. The oldest extant translation in the Syriac also dates back to the same time. It is likely, however, that portions of the Gospels were rendered into Arabic at a much earlier date than that mentioned above. George, a bishop of the Arabs of Mesopotamia, wrote a Scholia on the Scripture around the sixth century. But it appears that Christian teaching and preaching in the sixth century (A.D.) Arabia was done mainly by quoting from the Syriac or Ethiopic scripture and then giving a free rendering of it in Arabic. According to Muslim authorities, Warqa used to copy or translate the Gospel. He had studied the Scriptures and was a Christian himself (Ibn Ishaq, op. cit., pp. 83, 107).

In addition to translations of the canonical Gospels, there were numerous Arabic translations of the New Testament apocrypha. Some of the better known of these like Protoevangelion of James, Gospel of the Infancy, Apocalypse of Paul and the Apocryphal Acts of the Apostles were available in Arabic translation before the Koran. Moreover, in those days the Christians, like the Jews, were given to a degenerate form of the religion which was based on a curious mixture of material from biographies of saints and martyrs as well as the apocrypha with targummated Arabic renderings (orally) from the Ethiopic or Syriac Gospels. This became a source of information for the prophet as it is reflected in the teaching of the Koran on Christianity and Jesus Christ.

According to Sura 16:103, the prophet was accused of receiving information from a man. Muslim tradition informs us that the person referred to in this verse was a Christian convert to Islam named Jabr. According to Hussain, Jabr was one of the people of the Book and well read in the Torah (Taurat) and the Gospel (Injil). The prophet used to hear him read these books as he passed by his house (Hughes' Dictionary of Islam, p. 223). It is very likely that not just one such convert from Christianity to Islam but many proselytes both from Judaism and Christianity shared their religious knowledge with him. Also, his close relatives and family members must also have been a further source of enlightenment about the two religions.

Briefly, in spite of the existence of various translations of the Bible in Arabia, there was no known translation in the Arabic language before Islam. Even if such a translation existed, it must have been quite inaccessible to pagan Arabs. They lacked a Scripture in their own language. In this regard they felt inferior to Jews and Christians who were proud of being people of the Book. A complaint to this effect has been discussed in the Koran:

> And this book we have sent down,—blessed; wherefore follow it and fear God that you may find mercy. Lest ye should say, "Verily the Scripture hath been revealed to two peoples before us, but we are unable to read it in their language." Or lest ye should say, "If the Scripture had been revealed to us,

we surely would have followed the direction better than they." And now verily hath clear exposition come unto you from your Lord,—a direction and mercy. (Sura 6:156-158)

The argument contained in the verse above is plain to see. The pagan Arabs excused themselves from submitting to God (Islam) because they had no Arabic translation of the revealed Scriptures. With the appearance of the Koran "in plain Arabic," this excuse was set at naught. If the hearers of the prophet had been aware of any Arabic version of the Bible, they would have been quick to oppose the whole argument in favor of the Koran by that fact. Hence it is evident that both the prophet and the pagan Arabs had no direct access to the Bible as it was available only in foreign languages. What they learned about the Bible must have been from Arabic Targums which the Jewish or Christian reporters culled from the sermons or popular discourses of their priests and rabbis.

Let us continue with the teaching of the Koran about the stature of the Bible and the prophet's attitude toward it. The prophet Muhammad often appealed to the Scriptures with his contemporary Jews and Christians for the authentication of the revelation he received. For example:

> Those unto whom we have given the Book rejoice for that which hath been revealed unto thee. (Sura 13:36)
>
> Verily this revelation from the Lord of creation, the faithful Spirit, hath descended upon thy heart, that thou mightest be a warner, in the tongue of simple Arabic. And verily it is borne witness to in the former scriptures. Was it not a sign unto them, that the wise men among the children of Israel knew it? (Sura 26:192-197)
>
> Say what think ye, if this revelation be from God, and you reject it, and a witness from among the children of Israel hath witnessed unto the like thereof [that is, to its conformity with the Old Testament], and hath believed therein, and ye turn away scornfully. (Sura 46:10)

The prophet became seriously concerned about an authentication of his call to prophethood by the Bible only after he came to dwell in the city of Medina. The Jews of Medina had a strained relationship with pagan Arabs of the city. They used to threaten them by saying that their expected Messiah was coming to destroy all paganism. Here was a favorable situation for a new religious leader. As we learn from an early Muslim source:

> God had prepared the way for Islam in that they lived side by side with the Jews who were people of the Scripture and knowledge, while they themselves were polytheists and idolators. They had often raided them in their district and whenever bad feelings arose the Jews used to say to them, "A prophet will be sent soon. His day is at hand. We shall follow him and kill you by his aid as Ad perished." So when they heard the apostle's message they said one to another, "This is the very prophet of whom the Jews warned us. Don't let them get to him before us." Thereupon they accepted his teaching and became Muslims. (Ibn Ishaq, op. cit., pp. 197, 198)

The Ansars—Helpers—of Medina were quick to accept the prophetic claims of Muhammad lest the Jews monopolize him as their expected deliverer. But on his arrival in Medina, he sought to appeal to the Jews and

Christians as well. He referred to the Bible for the authentication and support of the Koran. Soon he claimed that he was the prophet whom the Jews were waiting for. In the words of Ibn Ishaq:

> The apostle wrote to the Jews of Khybar, according to what a freedman of the family of Zaid b. Thabit told me from Ikrama or from Said b. Jubyr from Abbas: "In the name of God the Compassionate, the Merciful, from Muhammad the apostle of God, friend and brother of Moses, who confirms what Moses brought, God says to you, 'O, Scripture folk you will find in your Scripture, Muhammad is the apostle of God; and those with him are severe against the unbelievers, merciful among themselves. . . . That is their likeness in the Torah and in the Gospel, like a seed which sends forth its shoot and strengthens it and it becomes thick and rises straight upon its stalk delighting the sowers that He may anger the unbelievers with them' . . . I adjure you by God . . . that you tell me, do you find in what He has sent down to you that you should believe in Muhammad? If you do not find that in your Scripture then there is no compulsion upon you." (Ibid., p. 256)

A reference to the parable of the sower is interesting in the account quoted above. The prophet must have gathered it from the vague memory of a Christian who heard it in a targummated Arabic rendering of the Syriac New Testament. It is also interesting to note that the prophet asked the Jews to check if his name was mentioned in their Scripture. Here is another indication of the fact that he had no direct access to the Bible in Arabic. We learn that in answer to his inquiry the learned Jews in Medina were quick to say that he was not the prophet expected by them. Ibn Ishaq goes on to relate:

> Abu Saluba said to the Apostle, "O Muhammad, you have not brought us anything we recognize, and God has not sent down to you any sign that we should follow you." (Ibid., p. 256)

As the story goes on, when the pagans of Medina (who had accepted Islam) asked the Jews why they did not welcome the prophet they were looking for so eagerly, they received a curt reply:

> Salama b. Mishkam, one of Bani Nadir, said, "He has not brought us anything we recognize and he is not the one we spoke of to you." (Ibid., p. 257)

Or, again, we are informed:

> Malik b. Al-Sayf said, when the apostle had been sent and they were reminded of the condition that had been imposed on them and what God had covenanted with them concerning him, they said, "No covenant was ever made with us about Muhammad." (Ibid., p. 257)

It needs to be mentioned, in passing, that though some Jews accepted Islam, it failed to impress the learned rabbis and the majority of the community. To that effect Ibn Ishaq reports:

> When Abdullah b. Salam, Thalaba b. Saya and Usayad b. Saya and Asad b. Ubayd and other Jews became Muslims and believed and were earnest and firm in Islam, the rabbis who disbelieved said that it was only the bad Jews who believed in Muhammad and followed him. (Ibid., p. 262)

Moreover, we learn that:

> A number of them came in to the apostle and he said to them, "Surely you know that I am an apostle of God to you?" They replied, that they did not know it and would not bear witness to him. (Ibid., p. 265)

Such a strong resistance of the Arab Jews to the claims of the prophet finally disappointed him. He turned against them, and the Koran began to charge them with dishonesty in dealing with what they found in their Scripture in favor of the prophet. Those Jews who became Muslims were praised as righteous ones, but those who disbelieved were judged as misguided. Some of those thus condemned were even called Gentiles (Proselytes) and not genuine Jews because they did not know their Scripture firsthand but depended on the targummated renderings which were further targummated in Oral Arabic by their rabbis. The Koran also recognizes that there were some true Jews among the unbelievers who knew their Scripture. They were expected to follow the prophet Muhammad on the basis of what their Scripture contained about him. But they chose not to do so. Hence they mishandled prophecies about him. They did so in several ways, as detailed in the Koran.

First of all some Jews are accused of concealing the truth recorded in the Torah (from outsiders) regarding the prophet and the Koran:

> Those to whom we have given the Scripture recognize him [or it] as they recognize their own sons; but verily a portion of them hide the truth, although they know it. (2:146)

Al-Baidhawi interprets "him" in the verse as significant of the prophet Muhammad. If we read it "it" instead of "him," then Al-Baidhawi understands it as a reference to the Koran (Muir, *The Coran*. London: SPCK, 1875, p. 154). In other words, the Jews knowingly concealed what their Scripture had to say about the Koran or the prophet. There is another interesting verse in this connection:

> Verily they that conceal clear demonstration and guidance which we have sent down, after that we have manifested the same to mankind in the Scripture, God shall curse them, and the cursers shall curse them;—excepting such as repent and amend, and make manifest [the truth]; as to such I will forgive them, for I am forgiving and merciful. (Sura 2:159, 160)

Ibn Ishaq relates the following as to the occasion for the revelation of the verses quoted above:

> Concealment by the Jews of the truth contained in the Torah;—Muad, Sad and Kharija, inquired of a party of the Jewish doctors regarding some matters in the Pentateuch, and they concealed it from them, and refused to tell it unto them. Wherefore the great and glorious God revealed the verse,—verily they that conceal the clear demonstration and guidance, etc. (As cited by W. Muir, ibid., p. 155)

There is a repetition of the same idea in Sura 2:174:

> Verily they that conceal the Scripture which God hath revealed, and sell it for a small price—these shall eat naught but the fire in their bellies, and

God shall not speak to them on the day of Judgment. (Also 2:42)

One reason why the Jews concealed the truth in their Scripture was their fear that the Muslims might use the information in disputing with them:

> And when they [the Jews of Medina], meet the believers, they say, "We believe"; but when they retire privately one with the other, they say, "Why do you acquaint them with what God hath revealed to you, that they may therewith dispute with you before your Lord?" Why do ye not understand? Do they know that God knoweth what they conceal as well as that which they make public? (Sura 2:76, 77)

The expression "what God hath revealed to you" is understood by Al-Baidhawi and Jalaluddin as "made manifest to you in the Pentateuch regarding the description of Muhammad" (Quoted by Muir, ibid., p. 140). In the words of Al-Baidhawi, "Why do you acquaint them with many passages from the Old Testament which they may turn in their arguments for Islam" (Ibid., p. 140).

An example of another kind of concealment of their Scriptures that the Jews practiced in their dealings with Muslims is related in a tradition:

> A Jew came to the prophet and said, "A man and a woman of ours have committed adultery." And the prophet said, "What do you meet with in the book of Moses in the matter of stoning?" The Jew said, "We do not find stoning in the Bible, but we disgrace adulterers and whip them." Then Abdullah ibn Salam who was a learned man of the Jews, and had embraced Islam, said, "You lie, O Jewish tribe! Verily the order for stoning is in the book of Moses." Then the book of Moses was brought, and opened and the Jew put his hand upon the revelation for stoning, and read the one above and the one below it; and Abdullah said, "Lift up your hand." And he did so, and behold the revelation for stoning was produced in the book and the Jew said, "Abdullah spoke true O Muhammad! The stoning revelation is in the book of Moses." Then the prophet ordered both the man and woman to be stoned.
> (Mishkat, Book XV, Chapter I)

This story throws light on several things. First of all, it affirms the fact that the Jews of Medina had authentic Scripture with them. The prophet ordered it to be brought and read from the Pentateuch. The particular passage that was read is to be found in Deut. 22:20-27. The specific verse could have been v. 24 which speaks of the stoning of both the persons involved in adultery (comp. John 8:5). Secondly, the prophet could not read the Hebrew Scripture. It had to be read out and interpreted to him. In this way he was an "Ummi"—unlettered in the Bible, according to the technical use of the term in the Koran (62:2) and by the Jews (see *Shorter Encyclopaedia of Islam*, "Ummi," p. 604). Thirdly, it is significant that the prophet judged the Jewish couple according to the teaching of their scripture and not according to the Koran. This was in line with the admonition of the Koran for Christians and Jews to judge by their Scriptures and abide by them (5:68). Finally, it is clear that despite Jewish attempts to conceal their Scripture from Muslims, there is not the slightest doubt as to its authenticity. For example, the verse concerning the stoning of adulterers is to be found intact in the Bible today as it was during the time of the prophet. It is made eminently clear that when the Jews did hide or cloak their Scripture, they knew the truth all along, for it was always with them to read (Sura 3:69, 70).

Apart from the charge of hiding the Scripture, the Koran takes some Jews to task for twisting their tongues as they quoted from it:

> Of those who profess Judaism, there are those that dislocate words from their places and say, "We have heard—and have disobeyed," and "do hearken without hearing"; and "behold us"; twisting their tongues and reviling the faith. And if they had said, "We have heard and obeyed"; and, "hearken"; and "look upon us"; it had been better for them and more upright; but God hath cursed them for their unbelief, and they shall not believe excepting a few. . . . We deface your countenances, and turn them front backwards, or curse them as we cursed those who [broke] the Sabbath; and the command of the Lord was fulfilled. (Sura 4:46, 47)

Abd-Alqadir, an Urdu translator of the Koran, gives the following explanation of the instances of tongue-twisting on the part of the Jews that are detailed in the passage above:

> They used the word "Raina" as has been mentioned in Sura Bakr (2:104). Thus when the prophet addressed them they used to reply, "We have heard"—which meant, "We have accepted." But they would add, inaudibly, "We do not believe," that is, "We have only heard with the ear and not the heart." When they addressed the prophet they said, "May thou not hear." The ostensible significance of this expression is an invocation of good—be thou victorious so that thou may not hear an evil word from anyone. But in their heart they intended to say, "So thou become deaf." Such wickedness they used to perpetuate. (As cited by Muir, ibid., pp. 169, 170)

The text of the verse under consideration uses the significant expression "twisting with their tongues." Jalaluddin explains that this is identical with the word "dislocating" previously used. Hence, "twisting, i.e., dislocating [or perverting] with their tongues" (As quoted by Muir, ibid., p. 170). It is evident therefore, that the perversion of the Scripture by the Jews had to do only with their mischief in tongue-twisting as they quoted verses. It had nothing whatsoever to do with the corruption of the original text of the Bible with them.

The Koran also refers to some Jews who produced fictitious literature—most probably in Arabic, and sold it as portions of their Scripture:

> Wherefore woe unto those who write the book with their hands, and then say, "This is from God"; that they may sell it for a small price. Woe unto them for that which their hands have written, and woe unto them for that which they gain. (Sura 2:79)

This theme is also discussed in 2:174, as mentioned above. What these Jews passed out as portions from their Scripture was pure fiction. These must have come from the mass of targummated legendary and apocryphal material that was current among the Jewish laymen. Some smart Jews made money by writing out parts of this lore and selling it for a price to the many pagan Arabs who may have had a superstitious desire to possess revealed Scripture and to learn it in their native tongue. The Koran exposes the hoax. Abd-Alqadir makes the following comment on the Jews mentioned in the verse:

> These are they who after their own desire, put things together, and write them out for the common people, and then ascribe them to God or the prophet. (As quoted by Muir, ibid., p. 142)

Al-Baidhawi states the following in regard to the literary fiction the Jews sold to the ignorant people (according to the verse under consideration):

> And perhaps there is meant that which the Jews wrote out of commentaries or [interpretations] about punishment of the adulteress. (Ibid., p. 142)

Al-Baidhawi's allusion to the punishment for adultery has been dealt with in the discussion above. It is evident that the fictitious literary production of some Jews, meant for sale, had nothing to do with the soundness of the Hebrew Scripture. The spurious character of these writings was well known to the good Jews who knew their Scripture as well as to the Koran. This conclusion is further supported by a verse which speaks of Jews perverting the Scripture:

> Ah! do you indeed earnestly desire that they should believe in you, and verily a party among them hear the word of God; then they pervert it after they have understood it. (2:75)

Both Al-Baidhawi and Jalaluddin point out that the people addressed to here are the Jews, and their "hearing" concerns the Pentateuch. Al-Baidhawi goes on to elaborate upon the nature of the perversion the Jews are accused of:

> They hear the word of God, that is to say the Pentateuch. Then they pervert it, as the description of Muhammad; or the verse of stoning; or the explanation thereof, and they interpret the same accordingly as they desire. (Cited by Muir, ibid., p. 138)

In other words, some Jews are condemned for the reason that they, having heard from the Bible, deliberately pervert its meaning and application to suit their sinful convenience. Once again, this excludes the many good Jews who obeyed their Scripture and preserved them carefully as a heritage more precious to them than their own lives.

Chapter 3

Authenticity of the Bible

It is quite evident from the preceding discussion that the Koran accuses only some bad Jews of hiding as well as perverting the Scripture by twisting their tongues. Not all Jews are thus condemned. It is recognized by the Koran that there were some good Jews who had the authentic book of Moses (7:159). It is important to bear in mind that there is no such accusation against Christians. W. Muir sounds this word of caution:

> It is further to be well observed that the imputations contained in the Coran [whatever their nature] are from first to last confined to the Jews. There is not a passage in the whole Coran which could, by any possible construction, cast the slightest suspicion upon Christians tampering either with their Gospel or with their copies of the Jewish Scripture. The utmost charge brought against them is that they have "forgotten a part of that whereby they were admonished" i.e., fallen into erroneous doctrines and practices. (Ibid., pp. 231, 232)

Despite all evidence from the Koran to the contrary, Muslims developed a strange doctrine of the corruption of the Judeo-Christian Scripture during the centuries after their prophet. It is easy to see that such a fanciful theory not only goes against the Koran but also violates common sense.

It is alleged that both Jews and Christians have managed to corrupt their Scriptures. In accusing people of the Book for mishandling their scripture, the Koran speaks of the Jews only. But Muslims who believe in a corruption of the Bible include Christians also in the alleged conspiracy. In this, obviously, they claim to know what even the Koran did not know about Christians. However, in the name of common sense one might ask as to how the Jews and Christians, who were known to be irreconcilable enemies of each other (Sura 2:113), got together to corrupt the Bible. Both of them look upon the Old Testament as sacred Scripture. They could not be expected to have corrupted this part of the Bible separately. If we suppose that they did so and yet the result of their secret corruption of the sacred text tallied, it will amount to believing in a miracle of God. If, on the other hand, we suppose that they conspired together, then too it is hard to believe. According to the Koran the Jews alone are accused of misrepresenting their scripture, especially in regard to prophecies about Muhammad contained therein. That being the case the motive behind the alleged corruption of Jewish Scripture would be a concern to remove all prophecies about him.

Such a conspiracy could be expected, at best, of the Jews of Arabia who had some knowledge of the prophet of Islam and dealings with him. That would leave out millions of Jews around the world with their innumerable copies of the Scripture. If the Jews of Arabia, aided by their Christian opponents, managed to corrupt the Biblical manuscripts within their reach, how about the many beyond their reach, humanly speaking? If they did carry out this conspiracy against their own precious heritage, God and mankind, the news of it would certainly have leaked out in some corner of the globe! Moreover, wicked Jews and Christians of Arabia travelling all over the world to expunge all prophecies about the new prophet in Arabia from scriptural manuscripts everywhere would have published news about him and Islam far and wide. But this is not evident from the histories of the distant nations of the world in the first century of Islam.

Again, how could all available manuscripts of the Bible have been corrupted so completely and worldwide that not a single authentic copy survived? Such a preposterous vandalism could never have gone undetected in history recorded both by the friend and the foe.

Coming back to the Arabian scene, many Jews and Christians joined the ranks of Islam even during the lifetime of the prophet. Some of these proselytes were scholars and students of the Bible. They may have possessed copies of the Scripture. Earlier we mentioned Abdullah b. Salam who was a Jewish scholar of the Torah. Such Jews joining Islam should have been glad to preserve their original Hebrew Scripture which was supposed to contain an authentication of the Koran and the prophet. Something very much like this was done by those Hebrews who became Christians. They did not discard the Old Testament which prophesied about their Lord Jesus Christ. On the contrary they made it a part and parcel of the canon of their Scripture. Also, it is noteworthy that the Hebrews, who remained bitterly opposed to Christians and their interpretation of the Old Testament messianic prophecies, did not attempt to change or corrupt the text of their Scripture. If the Jews did not do it at that crucial juncture in their religious history, why and how could they be suspected of having done so when Islam appeared on the scene? The Christian and Jewish proselytes to Islam should have been only too glad to hold onto authentic copies of the Bible with them. In that case both the Old and New Testaments could have formed part of a comprehensive canon along with the Koran. Then it would have been easy for all concerned to see how the Koran authenticates and confirms the previous Scriptures and how they contain prophecies about the prophet of Islam!

It is significant that the Muslim theory of the corruption of the Biblical revelation goes contrary to the Koran as well as the early years of the Islamic movement. In this connection W. Muir points out cogently:

> Any imputation against the Jews and Christians of attempting to corrupt their scripture was not even thought of for many years afterwards;—not, indeed, until the Mohammedan doctors finding the Quran to differ from those Scriptures, betook themselves to this most groundless assumption as the simple mode of escaping the difficulty. (Ibid., p. 234)

The first Muslims could not read the Bible in the available Hebrew or

Syriac versions. Even if some knew these languages, they could not have had easy access to written manuscripts, especially that of the Torah—the Jews of Medina were reported to be reluctant to share their Scripture with pagan or Muslim Arabs. Whatever the Muslims learned about the Bible was based on heresay from Jewish and Christian laymen. These sources, in turn, depended usually on targummated interpretations of their Scripture picked up from worship services in the synagogues and the churches or from catechetical literature—which contained a lot of legendary and apocryphal elaboration of the scriptural texts. It is obvious that there was no exact correspondence between this material and the Bible. Since it found its way into the Koran, the same situation was reproduced.

The Koran contains a large body of material in common with the Bible. But often it does not tally in exact detail with its Biblical counterpart. So long as the Muslims did not have a firsthand knowledge of the Bible, they were not quite concerned about this issue. But when they began to learn from the Bible directly or through knowledgeable Jewish and Christian proselytes, they felt the need to account for its divergence from the Koran. Understandably, it was taken for granted that in each case of difference between the two Scriptures, the Koranic version was authentic. Hence the Biblical version was considered inauthentic. On the basis of the Koran itself, God never sent inauthentic Scripture. It was concluded, therefore, that the Jews and Christians are responsible for corrupting their Scriptures.

The technical term used by Muslim scholars to signify corruption of the Bible is "Tahrif." It is believed to be of two kinds; namely "Tahrif-I-Lafzi," a corruption of words, and "Tahrif-I-Manawi," corruption of the meaning only. The early commentators of the Koran and doctors of Islam who did not have a firsthand knowledge of the Bible believed in "Tharif-I-Manawi" only. In line with the teaching of the Koran, they refused to entertain the possibility of corruption in the Scriptures revealed by God and confirmed and guarded by the Koran. The prophet himself was cautioned not to doubt the books of Moses:

> And verily we gave Moses the book; wherefore be not in doubt as to the reception of it. (Sura 32:24)

If the prophet was forbidden from entertaining any doubt about the Bible, surely Muslims have no right or justification of doing so if they seek sincerely to obey the Koran and follow the Sunna—example of the prophet! As we have discussed earlier, the Koran commands Jews and Christians to abide by their Scriptures and the Muslims to believe on them. It would be strange if God commanded His people to believe in and abide by revealed Scriptures already corrupted. Therefore the Koran claims to be an attestation of the Bible:

> And when they refuse to be guided thereby, they say—this is an antiquated lie. Yet preceding it there is the book of Moses, a guide and mercy, and the Quran is a book attesting [previous revelations] in the Arabic tongue, to warn transgressors, and glad tidings to the righteous. (Sura 46:11-12. Also, 46:30; 2:89)

This attestation by the Koran covers not only the books of Moses but all revelations previous to it—now contained in the Bible:

> And that which we have revealed unto them is a truth attesting that which precedeth it. (Sura 35:31. Also, 6:93; 10:38)

Both Al-Baidhawi and Jalaluddin agree that the expression "that which precedeth it" means the sacred Scriptures revealed before the Koran. As to attestation of previous Scriptures, it is interesting to note that the Koran mentions Jesus Christ who came to authenticate the Old Testament revelation before Him:

> And [God] shall teach Him [Jesus] the Scripture, and wisdom, and the Torah, and the Gospel; and [shall send Him as] an apostle unto the children of Israel. [Jesus shall say] Verily I have come unto you . . . attesting the truth of that [Scripture revealed] before me in the Torah, and that I may make lawful unto you a part of that which is forbidden unto you. (Sura 3:48. Also, 5:48, Pickethall)

Since Jesus Christ attested the Old Testament Scripture, it constitutes a part of the Christian Bible and belief. As the Koran has attested the Bible, Muslims ought to believe and read it as Christians do the Old Testament. Along with attestation of the previous Scriptures, the Koran also claims to be a custodian of them and a watchman over them:

> And we have revealed unto thee the book in truth, attesting that [Scriptures] which precedeth it, and a custodian thereof. (Sura 5:48, Pickethall)

Al Baidhawi explains the important sentence "guardian or custodian over it," as follows:

> A keeper over the whole of the sacred books, such as shall preserve them from change, and witness to their truth and authority. (As quoted by W. Muir, CORAN, p. 205)

In view of clear teaching of the Koran about the authenticity of the Bible and its freedom from corruption, it is no wonder that not only the earliest doctors of Islam but also many other Muslim scholars after them have refused to entertain a belief contrary to that. Their position is further strengthened by a crucial verse in the Koran:

> The words of the Lord are perfect in truth and justice; there is none who can change His words. He both heareth and knoweth. (Sura 6:115. Also, 10:65, 6:34)

Later Muslim commentators who believed in the corruption of the Bible have sought to interpret this verse to suit them. They understand the changeless character of the words of God to mean certainty of His promises and threats. Some of them apply it to His particular promise to preserve the Koran from alterations, as are alleged to have happened to the Injil (Gospel) and Taurat (Torah). But it can easily be demonstrated from passages in the Koran that the Gospel and Torah are as much the Word of God as the Koran. If the revealed Scriptures of God could have suffered change and corruption once, what could stop it from happening in the case of the

Koran? Therefore, Imam Bukhari records the following considered judgment of Ibn Abbas in regard to "Tahrif":

> The word "Tahrif" [corruption] signifies to change a thing from its original nature; and there is no man who could corrupt a single word of what proceeds from God, so that the Jews and Christians could corrupt only by misrepresenting the meanings of the words of God. (Quoted in Hughes' Dictionary of Islam, p. 62)

This approach to the doctrine of "Tahrif" is based on the Koran and has been supported by other great Muslim commentators. Thus Shah Wali Allah in his famous commentary *Fauz al-Kabir* supports the same view. Ibn Mazar and Abi Hatim state in their commentary known as *Tafsir Durr-I-Mansur*:

> That they have it on the authority of Ibn Muniyah, that the Taurat [i.e. the books of Moses], and the Injil [i.e. the Gospels] are in the same state of purity in which they were sent down from heaven and no alteration had been made in them, but that the Jews were wont to deceive the people by unsound arguments, and by wresting the sense of the Scripture. (Hughes, ibid., p. 62).

Imam Fakhar al-Din Razi in his commentary on Sura 3:78 ("And lo there is a party of them distorting the Scripture with their tongues") speaks of Jews indulging in "Tahrif-I-Manawi" (corruption of the sense of the Scripture) only and goes on to maintain that it does not mean that they altered the text (Ibid., p. 62).

In the face of all the imposing evidence against a belief in actual corruption of the Bible, there are many Muslims who have chosen to allege "Tahrif-I-Lafzi" (corruption of the words of the Scriptures). This impossible position is not only an attempt to account for the divergence of the Koran from the Bible in material common to both of them, but is also a calculated explanation for the apparent lack of references which, according to the Koran, the Bible makes to Muhammad. Thus, for example, they allege that Christians have expunged the word "Ahamd" from the New Testament and inserted the expression "Son of God" in different places in their Scripture. The narrative of the crucifixion, death, and resurrection of Jesus Christ is also considered by these Muslims as an example of corruption of the Injil. It must be emphasized that the charges of corruption of the Christian Scripture are leveled against the Gospels only. They have no reference to the other books of the New Testament, strictly speaking. The term "Injil" (Evangel or the Gospel) is used in the Koran, the traditions and all Muslim theological works of the early centuries for a revelation of God to Jesus Christ. It is believed to be in the form of a book called the Gospel (Injil) (Sura 57:27). In this perspective all the books of the New Testament except the four Gospels fall outside the scope of discussion on the subject of corruption of the Christian Scripture.

As we have pointed out earlier, one of the main reasons for Muslim suspicion of Judeo-Christian Scripture is the existence of discrepancies between them and the Koran. Here it must be borne in mind that the presence of some discrepancies along with a large measure of agreement in material common to both the Scripture has discouraged Muslim belief in a total corruption of the Bible. But these small divergences can be accounted for easily without resorting to the drastic, unscriptural and impossible doctrine of "Tahrif." Most of this divergent material has parallels in the legendary, apocryphal and extra-canonical Judeo-Christian sources that were available in Arabia during the time of the prophet. C. Tisdall's book *The Sources of the Quran* and Arnold's *Islam and Christianity* deal with this important subject in considerable detail. Even if the majority of the differences between the Koranic and Biblical accounts could be traced to these sources, it should suffice to discourage any speculation about Christians and Jews corrupting their precious spiritual legacy—the Bible. In the area of the Old Testament, the following are a few examples of correspondence between the divergent Koranic details and the extra-canonical legend and apocrypha:

In Sura 5:27-32, we have the narrative as to how Cain murdered his brother Abel and then buried him. The argument between the two, prior to the first homicide in history, has an interesting similarity to the account contained in the Targum of Jonathan and Targum of Jerusalem. We are told that Cain said, "There is no punishment for sin, nor is there any reward for good conduct." In reply to this, Abel asserted that God rewards good and punishes evil. Cain became angry and smote his brother with a stone and killed him (Tisdall, *The Sources of the Quran*. London: SPCK, 1911, p. 63). The Koran relates how God sent a raven which scratched in the ground to show Cain how to hide his brother's corpse (5:31). This detail has a parallel in a Jewish legend related in Pirqey Rabbi Eliezer, chapter XXI, as follows:

> Adam and his help mate were sitting weeping and lamenting over him [Abel], and they did not know what to do with Abel, for they were not acquainted with burial. A raven, one of whose companions had died, came. He took him and dug in the earth and buried him before his eyes. Adam said, "I shall do as this raven." Immediately, he took Abel's corpse and dug in the earth and buried it.

There is a slight difference between the Jewish legend and the Koranic narrative. In the former the raven taught Adam how to bury the dead, whereas in the Koran he taught this to Cain. Sura 5:32 says that whosoever murders a man, it shall be as if he had murdered the whole mankind. This thought in connection with the murder committed by Cain has a parallel in Mishna Sanhedrin, chapter IV.5. The Hebrew commentator deals here with Gen. 4:10 where God said to Cain, "What hast thou done? The voice of thy brother's blood crieth unto me from the ground." Notice the word for blood, in the original, is in the plural—"bloods." The writer goes on to comment:

> Concerning Cain who slew his brother, we have found that it is said concerning him, "The voice of thy brother's *bloods* crieth." He saith not "Thy brother's blood" but "Thy brother's bloods"—his blood and the blood of his descendants. On this account was Adam created alone to teach thee that everyone who destroyeth one soul out of Israel, the Scripture reckoneth it unto him as if had destroyed the whole world, and everyone who preserveth alive one soul out of Israel, the Scripture reckoneth it unto him as if he had

preserved alive the whole world. (Ibid., p. 65)

The passage in the Koran (5:32) is almost an exact parallel of the quotation above.

Abraham is mentioned in different places in the Koran. Muslim writers have composed a full narrative out of these various references. Thus there is a version of it given by Abul Fida and another to be found in the book *Araish al-Majalis*. These narratives (based on Sura 21) are similar to the story in the Jewish Midrash Rabba, chapter XVII (in explanation of Gen. 15:7). The reference, in both sources, to Abraham's delivery from a fiery furnace is especially interesting. Tisdall points out that this detail, which is so divergent from the Biblical narrative, is due to a blunder made by an ancient Jewish commentator. The writer of the Targum of Jonathan ben Uzziel misunderstood the name of the city where Abraham came from (Gen. 11:28; 57:7). He imagined that the word "Ur" (city) meant the same as the Hebrew "Or" (light) which in the Aramaic means "fire." In this way he rendered Gen. 15:7 thus, "I am the Lord, who brought thee out of the furnace of fire of the Chaldees." He went on to say in fanciful elaboration of this strange translation, "When Nimrod cast Abraham into the furnace of fire because he would not worship idols, it came to pass that the fire was not given permission to injure him" (Ibid., p. 79. Compare Sura 21:69).

In Sura 7:171 it is written:

> And when We shook the Mount above them as it were a covering, and they supposed that it was going to fall upon them [and We said]: Hold fast that which We have given you, and remember that which is therein, that ye may ward off [evil]. (Sura 7:171, Pickethall)

Jalalain explains the above by informing us that God raised up Mount Sinai from its foundation and held it over the heads of the children of Israel, threatening to let it fall on them if they did not accept the commandments in the Law of Moses. Sura 2:63 (and 93) also contains the same story. It is very much similar to the account found in the Jewish tractate "Abodah Zarah," chapter II:2, "I covered you over with the mountain like a lid." Similarly, in "Sabbath" (Fol. 88:1) we read:

> These words teach us that the Holy One, blessed be He, inverted the mountain above them like a pot and said to them, "If ye receive the Law, well: but if not, there shall be your grave."

According to Sura 2:55-56 the Israelites told Moses that they would not believe him until they saw God for themselves. On this a thunderbolt struck them dead. But God raised them back to life. This story is to be found in Tract Sanhedrin 5. There we are told that the Israelites died on hearing the voice of God. But the Law made intercession for them so that they were restored to life (Tisdall, op. cit., p. 114).

It is the Muslim belief that the Koran is recorded on the "preserved tablet." This is in accordance with the teaching in the Koran itself:

> Nay, but it is a glorious Quran in a preserved tablet. (Sura 85:21.22)

The Jews speculated as to what the two tablets contained which Moses received from God. Tract Berakhoth has the following idea:

> Rabbi Simeon ben Laqish saith, "What is it that which is written, 'And I shall give thee tablets of stone, and the Law, and the commandment which I have written, that thou mayest teach them' (Ex. XXIV:12)?" *The tablets—* these are the ten commandments; *the Law*, that which is read; and *the Commandments*, this is the Mishnah, *which I have written*, these are the Prophets and the Hagiographa: *that thou mayest teach them*, this denotes the Gemara. This teaches that all of them were given to Moses from Sinai. (Fol. 5, Col. 1)

They also indulged in surmising the antiquity of these tablets. Thus in *Pirqey Aboth*, chapter V.6, we are informed that the two tablets of the Law were created, along with nine other things, at the time of the creation of the world, at sunset before the first Sabbath (Tisdall, ibid., p. 119). The tablet in heaven contains the original of which the Koran is believed, by Muslims, to be a copy. Moreover, it is also regarded as a record of the decisions of the divine will. As to the first idea, there is a parallel in the pseudepigraphical literature. In the Book of Jubilee (3:10) it is stated that the laws concerning purification of women after childbirth are written on tablets in heaven. Jubilee 12:8 sq says the same about laws regarding the "Feast of Booths" (Lev. 23:40-43). In Jubilee 5:13 it is stated that the divine judgment on all that exists on earth is written on tablets in heaven. Again, in the Book of Enoch, Enoch prophesies the future from the contents of these preserved tablets (xcii:2; cf. lxxxi; ciii:2; cvi:19. See *Shorter Encyclopaedia of Islam*, p. 288).

Sura 17:44 mentions seven heavens and 15:44 speaks of seven gates of hell. These are similar to the Jewish tradition in the Hagigah, chapter IX.2 and Zohar, chapter 2, p. 150. It is stated in the Koran that Satan and his fallen angels try to steal "a hearing" by listening to God's commandments given to angels in heaven (15:17-18. Also, 37:8). This belief is to be found in the Jewish Hagigah, chapter VI:1. It says that the demons "listen from behind a curtain" in order to obtain a knowledge of future events (Tisdall, op. cit., p. 124).

Describing the emptiness of hell on the Day of Judgment, the Koran represents God asking hell, "Art thou filled?" To this hell shall say, "Is there more?" (50:30). This idea is echoed in the Othioth of rabbi Aqiba viii:1:

> The Prince of Hell saith on a day and a day [i.e. day by day] "Give me food unto repletion."

This book refers to Isaiah 5:14 as a proof of the reported statement (Tisdall, ibid., p. 125).

Both the Talmud and the Koran mention that several members of the human body shall bear witness against the damned, and idols shall be punished along with their devotees (Chagiga, xxvi; Thaanith xi; Surahs xxiv:24; xxxvi:64; xli:19; Sukkah, xxix and Surah xxi:98). Islam believes the Talmudic idea that the dead will rise in the same garments in which they were buried (Sanhedrin xc:2; Khethuboth cxi.2).

The demonology of the Koran also is very much similar to that of the Talmud. Thus demons are believed to have three properties in common with angels, and three with humans. Like humans they eat, drink, and indulge in sex and die. Like the angels they have wings, can fly, and know things to come while listening to angelic conversations. They are driven away with stones (Chagiga xvi:1 and Sura xv:18, 26, 27; xxxvii:77; lxxxi:25: lxvii:5; lxxii:8, 9).

As to moral and ceremonial requirements, there are many injunctions in common between the Talmud and the Koran. For example, children can disobey their parents if they are required to do evil (Jebbamoth vi; and Sura xxix:8). Ablutions before prayers are required by both the books, and they allow the use of sand when water is not available (Berachoth xlvi and Sura 5:6). The Hebrew *Shema* prayer is to be made "when one is able to distinguish a blue from a white thread." The Koran uses the same test for the beginning of the fast during Ramazan (Mishna Berachoth i:2 and Sura ii:187).

In line with Talmudic embellishments of the Biblical narratives the Koran has parallels too (in the Mishana Sanhedrin, iv:5). The very words used about the murder of Abel by Cain are echoed in the Koran. Both the sources declare that the generation of Noah was punished with boiling water and report the same conversations between Noah and his contemporaries—who mocked him (Rosh Hashanah xvi:2; Sanhedrin cviii; and Sura xi:40; xxxiii:27). The Jewish doctors believe in common with the Koran that Abraham wrote books. Both Talmud and the Koran relate that the angels whom Abraham received appeared as ordinary Arabs, and Abraham was surprised when they declined to eat (Kiddushin lii). When some passages of the Scripture speak of eating by the angels, it was only in appearance that they ate.

In Sura 7:108, the Koran speaks of Moses using the sign of the leprous hand in the presence of Pharaoh. A Jewish tradition mentions exactly the same sign, though the Bible does not refer to it at all. According to this tradition:

> He put his hand into his bosom and withdrew it leprous, white as snow; they also put their hands into their bosoms and withdrew them leprous, white as snow. (Pirke Rabbi Elieser, xlviii)

The lowing of the golden calf made by Aaron is mentioned by the Koran as well as Jewish tradition but not in the Bible. The tradition states:

> The calf came forth roaring, and the Israelites saw it. Rabbi Jehuda says, Samuel entered the calf and roared to deceive the Israelites. (Pirke Rabbi Elieser, xlv; and Sura vii:159. Compare Ex. 32:26)

In regard to Solomon, the Koran tells us that he understood the language of birds. This was also the opinion of Jewish doctors. The winds or the demons obeyed Solomon and with birds and beasts formed part of his standing army (Sura xxi:81; xxvii:15; xxxiv:11; xxxviii:35). The Jewish sources also say that evil spirits of various categories were subject to Solomon (The Second Targum on Esther 1:2). The Koran mentions that Solomon got the help of demons in the building of the Temple. This is a belief in common with the Jewish sources (Gittin lxviii and Sura xxxiv).

Comparing the Koran with the Injil (Gospel) in material common to both of them, we come across a divergence of details—a situation similar to what has been discussed above relative to the Old Testament. Here too the Muslims do not need to resort to the unrealistic and unKoranic strategy of accusing Christians of corrupting the Injil. Most of the discrepancies between it and the Koran can be accounted for by material to be found in Christian apocrypha and extra-canonical literature. The Church fathers used the term apocrypha to describe spurious writings foisted as Gospels. Thus Iraneus speaks of a large number of such pseudo literature which heretics of the early centuries had forged to confuse the simple folk. Though these writings were patterned after the canonical Gospels, yet they remained poor imitations of the original. As to the existence of these apocryphal writings in the early Christian centuries, we have the report of Origen:

> The Church possesses four Gospels, heresy has a great many.
> (*Christianity Today*, Jan. 1978 issue, p. 19)

The production of spurious Gospels to be passed on to the ignorant masses as genuine Scripture was not a phenomenon of early Christianity alone. In the early days of Islam, too, we learn about some Arabian Jews who indulged in such a practice by producing imitations of the Torah and selling them as true Scripture. The Koran condemned all such fakery (Sura 2:79). But the Koran itself had to face the same problem very early in its history. Among pagan Arabs there were some contemporaries of the prophet of Islam who, too, felt the call to prophethood. One of them was a well-known man called Musailma. He declared himself a prophet of God and produced a Koran of his own. Some of his prophetic utterances have been preserved by historians. They are very much like the earliest suras of the Muslim Koran with their short rhyming sentences and curious oaths. He had a large following, especially from among his own tribe of Hanifa. In the hotly contested battle of Yamama (12 A.H.), the Muslims destroyed him and his followers. They also burned his literary production which sought to rival the Koran. Had this composition of Musailma and other known attempts at imitation of the Koran been allowed to survive, they would have made quite a collection of apocryphal Korans! But unlike the Church, Islam destroyed all such literature.

The Koran is believed by Muslims to be the *read revelation* from God, whereas the traditions are considered the *unread revelation*—a revelation of the second rank. Among the host of traditions that appeared within Islam, a large number has been recognized by Muslim scholars as apocryphal and spurious. The orthodox Muslims (Sunnis) accept six collections of authentic traditions. These collections were made out of a bewildering mass of traditions that were in free circulation. As to the abundance of apocryphal traditions, we learn that the famous authority Al-Bukhari chose only 7,000 out of a host of 600,000 traditions that were current in his own time. Unlike apocryphal Korans, apocryphal traditions were allowed to exist and multiply during the early days of Islam. The Shia have their own collections of authentic traditions.

But all these attempts to sift the authentic from the unauthentic traditions remain inadequate as is demonstrated by the very existence of so many collections that claim to be authentic. The main standards used by these collectors to distinguish an authentic tradition from the apocryphal are easy to imitate. Therefore, it is extremely difficult to distinguish between a carefully fabricated tradition and an authentic one. Yet Muslims believe that they have thousands of authentic traditions to enable them to model their lives after the pattern of their prophet. Compared to the situation that prevails in the area of Muslim traditions, the distinction between the canonical Gospels and their apocryphal imitations is quite easy to make.

Let us next consider some examples of parallels between the Koran, apocryphal Gospels, and some Christian legends. An entire sura in the Koran is named after the Virgin Mary. She is referred to in glowing terms both in the early and late suras. One of the puzzles in the Koran concerns the designation of Mary as "sister of Aaron":

> O Mary truly thou has done a strange thing. O Sister of Aaron, thy father was not man of wickedness and thy mother was not rebellious. (Sura 19:28, 29)

Both the Muslim and Christian students of the Koran have wondered how Mary, the mother of Jesus Christ, came to be identified with Mary the sister of Aaron and Moses. This puzzle deepens further when in Sura 3:35 Mary is mentioned as offspring of Imran. Sura 66:12 plainly calls her "daughter of Imran." Imran is the Arabic form of the Hebrew *Imram* mentioned in Numbers (26:59) as the father of "Aaron, Moses and Miriam." The title "sister of Aaron" is given to Miriam in Ex. 15:20. Tisdall points out that the reason for the identification of the mother of Christ with another Hebrew woman who lived about one thousand five hundred and seventy years before His birth is evidently the fact that in Arabic both names, Mary and Miriam, are one and the same in form, "Maryam" (op. cit., p. 150). This explanation takes into consideration the fact that a lot of information about the Bible was available to the prophet only in a second-hand heresay form from his friends and relatives. It consisted of a mixture of a small core of Biblical material with a lot of apocryphal and legendary stories. With this picture in mind, rabbi Abraham Geiger has suggested another explanation of the Koranic identification of the two Marys. He quotes a Jewish tradition according to which the angel of death did not have power over Miriam (sister of Aaron and Moses). She died only with a divine kiss, and worms did not corrupt her body. Tisdall objects to this theory:

> But even so, the Jews never ventured to assert that Miriam remained until the time of Christ, nor to identify her with the Virgin Mary. (Ibid., p. 152)

Though we may have no evidence of Jewish tradition identifying the two Marys, Sale does mention some Muslim writers who have done so. According to them, "Mary the sister of Moses was miraculously preserved alive from his time till that of Jesus Christ, purposely to become the mother of Jesus" (*Koran*, p. 34, note x on "Imran").

Some Muslim commentators have attempted other interesting explanations of the mystery. For example, Al-Baidhawi says that the Virgin Mary is called the sister of Aaron because she was of the Levitical race. On the contrary Husain maintains that Aaron in Sura 19:28 is not the same person as the brother of Moses (Hughes' Dictionary, p. 328). In the Sahih of Muslim under the chapter Kitab al-Adab, we are informed that the Christians of Najran pointed out to Al-Mughairah this case of a mistaken identity in the Koran. He, in turn, consulted the prophet but received no satisfactory explanation.

The following references in the Koran dwell upon certain details of the life of the Virgin Mary which are not found in the Gospels. But they do occur in apocryphal literature. About the birth of Mary we read:

> When Imran's wife said, "My Lord, verily I have dedicated to thee what is in my womb, as consecrated: receive it therefore from me; verily thou art the hearer and knower." When, therefore she bore her, she said, "My Lord, verily I have borne her, a female,"—and God was well-aware of what she had borne, and the male is not as female, "And verily I have named her Mary, and verily I commit her and her seed unto thee from Satan, the stoned." (Sura 3:35, 36)

In explanation of the passage, Al-Baidhawi adds that Imran's wife was barren and advanced in age. One day she saw a bird feeding her young and so she herself longed for an offspring. She prayed to God for a child and promised to present it to the Temple in Jerusalem. God heard her prayer and she gave birth to Mary. The apocryphal Protoevangelium of James the Less mentions the following details about Mary, which are remarkably similar to what we have in the Koran and traditions:

> And having gazed fixedly into the sky Anna saw a nest of sparrows in the bay tree, and she made lamentation in herself saying, "Woe is me! to what am I likened? I am not likened to the birds of the air, for even the birds are productive in the sight of the Lord!" . . . And lo! an angel of the Lord stood by saying unto her, "Anna! Anna! the Lord God hath hearkened unto thy petition, thou shalt conceive and shall bear, and thy seed shall be spoken of in all the world." But Anna said, "As the Lord my God liveth, if I bear either male or female, I shall offer it as a gift unto the Lord my God, and it shall continue to do Him service all the days of its life." . . . Anna brought forth . . . And she gave breast to the child and called her Mary. (Quoted by Tisdall, op. cit., pp. 156-157)

The 32nd verse of Sura III tells us that Mary was brought up in the Temple and Zacharias was her guardian. Often she was provided with food miraculously while living in the Temple. This legend of Mary being reared up in the Temple is to be found in many apocryphal works. Protoevangelium of James the Less quoted above goes on to say:

> But Mary was like a dove reared in the Lord's shrine and she was wont to receive food from angel's hand. But when she became twelve years of age, there was held a council of priests who said, "Lo! Mary has become twelve years old in the shrine of the Lord, what therefore are we to do with her?" . . . And lo an angel of the Lord stood by him saying, "Zacharias! Zacharias, go forth and call together widowers of the people, and let them bring each a rod, and whosoever the Lord God shall show a sign, his wife shall she

be. . . . " And the priest took the rods of all and prayed. . . . (Ibid., pp. 157, 158)

Sura 3:37-42 speaks of men "throwing their reeds" to see who of them should marry Mary. Al-Baidhawi and Jalaluddin say in reference to these "reeds" or pens that Zacharias and twenty-six other priests were rivals to one another for the guardianship of Mary. They went to the river Jordan and threw their reeds into the water. But all reeds sank except that of Zacharias on account of which he was appointed guardian over Mary (see G. Sale, *The Koran*. London: Fredrick Warne & Co., p. 36, note 1). It is obvious that both the Koran and some of its outstanding commentators have a common ground with the Christian apocrypha. The Koran speaks of an accusation against Mary in Sura 19:28, 29. In the same strain Protevangelium Jacobi says:

> And the priest said, "Mary why hast thou done this and hast humbled thy soul. . . . " But she wept bitterly, saying "As the Lord God liveth, I am pure in His sight and I know not a man." (Ibid., p. 160)

Sura 19:23-26 records an incident about Mary and the palm tree. This is to be found in the apocryphal History of the Nativity of Mary (Ibid., pp. 162, 163).

The apocryphal Arabic "Gospel of Infancy" or *Injil Al-Tufuliyyah* is another parallel source of information on what the Koran says about the childhood of Jesus Christ. It relates:

> We have found it recorded in the book of Josephus the Chief Priest, who was in the time of Christ (and men say that he was Caiaphas) that this man said that Jesus spoke when he was in the cradle and said, "I am Jesus, the Son of God, the Word which thou hast borne, according as the angel Gabriel gave thee the good news; and my Father hath sent me for the salvation of the world." (Ibid., pp. 169, 170)

The above agrees with Sura 3:46, where Gabriel gave the news to Mary, "And He will speak unto mankind in his cradle." Furthermore, since the prophet could not agree to calling Christ the "Son of God," instead of using this expression the Koran calls the Messiah "the Word of God conveyed into Mary" (Sura 4:169). Tisdall points out that the style of the Arabic translation of the apocryphal Gospel is bad, and it does not appear to date back from the time of the prophet of Islam. He says that it is evident from a study of the Gospel that it has been translated into Arabic from the Coptic, in which language it may have been written originally. According to him the prophet may have heard the legend contained in the book from his concubine Maria, the Copt (Ibid., p. 170). Some of the miracles of Jesus Christ in the Koran are not found in the Gospels, but they are reported by the apocrypha. We shall deal with them in the sequel.

In regard to extra-canonical sources of the Koranic use of John 16:7 (Sura 61:6), we have the case of Mani, the Iranian prophet. He used the text to support the claim that his coming was promised by Jesus Christ. But unlike Muslims, he did not accuse Christians of corrupting the scriptural text. Hence he read Paraklitos (Comforter) rather than "Periklutos" (the praised one, or Ahmad). He claimed to be the "Comforter" promised by Christ. Several centuries before the rise of Islam, Mani, too, confirmed the purity and authenticity of the Gospels and especially that of the crucial verse in John which Muslims today like to use to support the case for their prophet.

Chapter 4

Authenticity of the Bible (continued)

We have given two main reasons for Muslims' suspicion of the authenticity of the Bible. One of them has been dealt with in the preceding pages. The second reason is based upon teaching of the Koran to the effect that the Judeo-Christian Scripture contain references to the prophet Muhammad:

> Those who follow the messenger, the prophet who can neither read nor write, whom they will find described in the Torah and the Gospel [which are] with them. (Sura 7:157, Pickethall)

In this passage it is important to note that the Koran encourages belief in the authenticity of the Judeo-Christian Scriptures of its own time. It goes on to maintain that there were prophecies concerning Muhammad to be found in them. In accordance with this hint from the Koran, early Muslim scholars searched for such prophecies in the Bible. The most important prophecy they claimed to have found in the Old Testament is in Deut. 18:15:

> The Lord thy God will raise up unto thee a prophet from the midst of thee, of thy brethren, like unto me; unto him ye shall hearken.

They argue that Muhammad was a prophet like Moses. He too brought a law like Moses. He was a brother to Moses, being of the Semitic race. We will consider this topic briefly in the sequel.

Some other Old Testament passages claimed by Muslims as prophecies about their prophet are as follows: Since according to Gen. 21:21, Paran was the abode of Ishmael, and according to Sura 2:125 he stayed in Mecca, Paran is identified with Mecca. On the same basis Deut. 33:2 is referred to the prophet of Islam. In Deut. 33:12 they find a reference to the seal of prophecy (Khatim al-Nubuwwa). This seal is understood by the Muslims to be a mole of an unusual size on the prophet's back. In the New Testament they use John 16:7 as a major prophecy about their prophet. It is written in the Koran:

> And remember when Jesus the son of Mary said, "O children of Israel! of a truth I am an apostle to you to confirm the Law which was given before me, and to announce the apostle that shall come after me, whose name is Ahmad. (Sura 61:6)

This interesting verse has a variant reading according to the testimony of one of the secretaries of the prophet, Ubayy b. Kab. It reads:

O children of Israel, I am God's messenger to you, and I announce to you a prophet whose community will be the last community and by which God will put the seal on the prophets and messengers.

In this version there is no reference to "Ahmad." This omission is to be found in Ibn Ishaq and Ibn Hisham's account of the verse too. In his life of the prophet Ibn Ishaq writes:

> Among things which have reached me about what Jesus of Mary stated in the Gospel which he received from God for the followers of the Gospel, in applying a term to describe the apostle of God, is the following. It is extracted from what John the apostle set down for them when he wrote the Gospel for them from the Testament of Jesus son of Mary: "He that hateth me hateth the Lord. And if I had not done in their presence works which none other before me did, they had not sin: but from now they are puffed up with pride and think that they will overcome me and also the Lord. But the word that is in the Law must be fulfilled, 'They hateth me without a cause' [i.e. without reason]. But when the Comforter has come whom God will send to you from the Lord's presence, and the spirit of truth which will have gone forth from the Lord's presence he [shall bear] witness of me and ye also, because ye have been with me from the beginning. I have spoken unto you about this that you should not be in doubt." The Munahhemna [God bless and preserve him] in Syriac is Muhammad, in Greek his is the Paraclete. (Op. cit., pp. 103, 104)

In his footnote to the above, Guillaume points out that the quotation from John 14:23 does not come from the ordinary Bible of the Syriac-speaking churches but from the Palestinian Lectionary. He goes on to say that:

> The most interesting word is that rendered "Comforter" which we find in Palestinian Lectionary, but all other Syriac versions render it "Paraclete" following the Greek. . . . " Munahhemna in Syriac means the life-giver and specially the one who raises from the dead." (Ibid.)

Ibn Ishaq identifies Munahhemna with the prophet Muhammad. But neither he nor Ibn Hisham make any mention of the name "Ahmad" from Sura 61:6. These men knew their Koran well. Why did they not use it in the relevent context? Some Western scholars have even suggested that the name "Ahmad" (Ismu-hu Ahmadu) in the Koranic passage is an interpolation (G. Parrinder, *Jesus in the Koran*. London: Sheldon Press, p. 98). This appears plausible in view of Ubayy b. Kab's different version of 61:6 and the silence of Ibn Ishaq and Ibn Hisham as to the word "Ahmad." Add to that what W. M. Watts has researched about the currency of the name "Ahmad" during the time of the prophet and subsequently:

> Muslim children are never called Ahmad before the year 125 A.H. But there are many instances prior to this date of boys called "Muhammad." Very rarely is the name "Ahmad" met with in pre-Islamic time of ignorance (Jahiliya), though the name Muhammad was in common use. Later traditions that the prophet's name was Ahmad show that this had not always been obvious, though commentators assume it after about 22 (A.H.). (As quoted by Parrinder, ibid., pp. 98, 99)

If we assume that "Ahmad" in Sura 61:6 is not an interpolation, then the silence of Ibn Ishaq and Ibn Hisham can be explained another way. They probably understood the word "Ahmad" not as a proper name but as an adjective. In this sense the sentence reads, "Announcing the tidings of a messenger who will come after me, whose name is worthy of praise." This position is maintained by J. Schacht who says:

> It has been concluded that the word Ahmad in Quran 61:6 is to be taken not as a proper name but as an adjective . . . and that it was understood as a proper name only after Muhammad had been identified with the Paraclete. (*Encyclopaedia of Islam*, Vol. I, 1960, p. 267)

There is evidence to the effect that before the middle of the second century A.H. the Muslims did apply to their prophet the prediction of the Paraclete in John 16:17. But the terms they used were either the Greek "Parakletos" or its correct Aramaic translation "Menahhemana" (The New Encyclopedia of Islam, Vol. I, 1960, p. 267). This was the practice of Ibn Ishaq as is clear in the long quotation above. It appears that in the course of years after the middle of the second century A.H., some Christian proselyte to Islam who knew Greek may have come up with the exciting suggestion that the very name used for the Comforter in John 16:17 is the name mentioned in Sura 61:16. This idea could only have arisen out of a naive confusion on his part between two different Greek words. The word used for the Comforter in the Gospel is "Parakletos." However, if we read it "Periklutos," it means "celebrated" or "praised one," which in Arabic is "Ahmad." This was a better approach to John 16:17 for Muslim scholars. They understandably preferred a reference to their prophet by a name used by the Koran as well. A direct reference was much better than reference by implication or interpretation. But this approach missed the fact that the Greek for the Comforter was different from the Greek word for Ahmad. However, such a fine linguistic distinction was not known to all scholars. The Arabic word for the Paraclete was "Faraqlit." It was not a direct translation from the Greek. Rather it was taken from the Syriac. In the Gospel in Syriac it is rendered as "Paraqlet." The Arabic "Faraqlit" is a further distortion of it—being once removed from the Greek original. "Faraqlit" is as vague and deceptive as the Greek "Periclutos" when compared to the original in John 16:17—"Parakletos."

To sum up the discussion, it is for sure that the name of the prophet as used in Sura 61:6 does not occur in the Gospels, because "Parakletos" is manifestly different from "Periklutos." If the position of Ibn Ishaq be maintained and the reference to the Comforter be applied to the prophet then, we must learn more as to the nature and function of Him from the Gospel. That should settle the issue whether or not the Comforter could be the prophet of Islam. The first promise of the Comforter is given by Jesus Christ as follows:

> And I will pray the Father, and he shall give you another Comforter, that he may abide with you forever. (John 14:16)

If this be applied to the prophet of Islam, one may ask as to how he can abide with the disciples of Jesus and his own followers, forever? The Koran says, "Every soul must taste death" (26:63), and the prophet speaks of his death and mortality (6:163). Another reference to the Comforter is found in John 14:26:

> But the Comforter, which is the Holy Ghost, whom the Father will send in my name, he shall teach you all things, and bring to your remembrance, whatsoever I have said unto you.

In this passage a clear statement is made by Jesus Christ as to the identity of the Comforter promised by Him. He is the Holy Ghost. The Muslims might accept it as a description for the angel Gabriel but hardly that of their prophet. Again, the Holy Spirit is sent by the Father in the name of Jesus Christ. This too Muslims cannot accept. Their prophet did not come in the name of Jesus Christ. In John 15:26, we read again:

> But when the Comforter is come, whom I will send unto you from the Father, even the Spirit of truth, which proceedeth from the Father, he will testify of me.

In the earlier reference Jesus said that the Father was going to send the Comforter "in my name." But in the passage under review, He goes on to say, "Whom I will send unto you." The Muslims would not agree to the possibility of Jesus Christ being the one who sent their prophet into the world. Moreover, the nature of the Comforter is also made plain. He is the Spirit of truth proceeding out of God the Father. In other words, He is divine in essence. This certainly is not applicable to the prophet of Islam. Finally we come to John 16:7:

> Nevertheless I tell you the truth; It is expedient for you that I go away: for if I go not away, the Comforter will not come unto you; but if I depart, I will send him unto you.

Here, once again, Jesus Christ is the one who sends the Comforter to His disciples after His death and resurrection. Muslims would hardly agree to this proposition in regard to their prophet. In three references to the Comforter Jesus Christ talks about God, His heavenly Father. In all of these references the Comforter proceeds from the Father—it does not say God. In other words, the Holy Trinity is implied in all the references to the Comforter promised by Jesus Christ. This too would not suit the Muslim frame of reference.

The Christians did not change or corrupt their Scripture. It was authentic during the rise of Islam. It has remained so unto this day. Even if some Christian contemporaries of the prophet of Islam desired to corrupt their Bible, they could not possibly have changed all the copies and manuscripts of it all over Christendom and in many languages of the world! The Koran bears clear testimony, time and again, to the authenticity of the Bible and admonishes Christians and Jews to live by its commandments. If the Bible was free from corruption at that time, it remains so today. As a matter of fact, the manuscriptural authentication of the present Christian Scripture goes back centuries before the rise of Islam!

We have several manuscripts of the Bible and the Gospels which go way back to the earliest centuries of the Christian era. Today there are more than 70 papyri, over 230 unicals MSS, and nearly 200 minuscules and about 250 lectionaries. The oldest of these is the Chester Beatty papyri of the Gospels, Acts and of Paul. It belongs to the third century A.D. The oldest unical codices belong to the fourth century. One of the reasons why many thousands of these earliest manuscripts of the New Testament did not survive was persecution of Christians. The persecuting pagans forced Christians to surrender manuscripts of their Scripture and then destroyed them. However, persecution ceased in the fourth century and official copies of the Scripture had a better chance of survival. The acceptance of Christianity by the Roman Empire gave an impetus to the circulation of the Christian Scripture and its translation into different languages. Therefore, from the fourth century onward it became possible for Christians to freely possess complete copies of the New Testament or even the entire Bible. The earliest extant MSS of any considerable size belong (apart from the Chester Beatty papyri) to the fourth century. It must be borne in mind that despite a favorable atmosphere created under the Christian Rome, persecutions of Christians and destruction of their Scripture went on during different periods of history and in those parts of the world which did not recognize Rome. The fact remains, however, that we have manuscripts of part and whole of the New and Old Testaments dating from centuries before the rise of Islam. Some of these extant MSS are detailed below:

Codex Vaticanus. It is to be found in the Vatican library. It is numbered 1209 and has been in the library since about 1481.

Codex Sinaiticus. Another codex that belongs to the fourth century. It was given by monks of Sinai to the Czar of Russia in 1862. In 1933 it was bought from Russia for the British Museum for £ 100,000.

The Washington Codex. It consists of the four Gospels. It belongs to the fourth or fifth centuries of the Christian era.

Codex Alexandrinus. It was written in Alexandria around the fifth century. It is to be found in the British Museum. It contains the whole Greek Bible with the exception of forty lost leaves.

Codex Bezae. This Codex was obtained from the monastery of St. Irenaeus at Lyons in 1562. It was presented to the Cambridge University library in 1881. It dates back to the fifth or early sixth century.

Codex Claromontanus. This too dates from the sixth century. It is preserved in the Biblotheque Nationale at Paris.

Codex Petropolitanus. Contains the Gospels written on purple vellum. It dates back to the sixth century. One hundred eighty-two of its leaves, out of a total of two hundred and twenty-eight, are to be found in Russia.

Codex Rossanesis. Consists of Matthew and Mark written in silver letters on purple vellum. It dates from the sixth century.

Codex Beratinus at Berat, Albania. It is a sixth-century production consisting of Matthew and Mark written in silver letters on vellum.

Codex Ephraemi. To be found in Biblotheque Nationale of Paris. It is a palimpsest manuscript of which the original writing has been partially washed or scraped off the vellum in order to reuse it for another writing. It belongs to the fifth century. The original of this palimpsest was the text of the Greek Bible. It was washed off in the twelfth century to reuse the vellum to inscribe some treatises by St. Ephraem of Syria. It is often difficult to decifer the original writing consisting of the Bible. A number of fragments from Egypt also deserve mention here. They are bilingual—Greek and Coptic. The most important of these is T or T^a, in the library of the Propaganda at Rome. It consists of 17 leaves from Luke and John. It belongs to the fifth century.

Codex P^5. It was perhaps a lectionary originally. It contains fragments of the Gospel of John. It belongs to the third century. We have other codices of this nature dating from the third century, like P^{20}, P^{37}, P^{45} (a third century Codex of the four Gospels and the Book of Acts), P^{46}, P^{47}, P^{48}, P^{49}, P^{52}, P^{53}, P^{64}, P^{66}, P^{67}, and P^{72}.

It is important to mention next the Lectionaries. These were books used in worship services and instruction in which the Gospels, Acts, and Epistles were divided into portions to be read each day in the course of a year. They were divided into two major categories: (1) Evangeliaria or Evangelia—lessons from the Gospels; (2) Prarapostoli—lessons from the Acts and Epistles. There are over two hundred manuscripts of the former type and 100 of the latter. These MSS are, however, of a comparatively late date—around the ninth century or later. But they represent a type of literature going back to years before Islam.

There are several versions of the Christian Scripture that existed long before the rise of Islam. These are translations of the Scriptures in languages other than Greek. The early versions may be divided into the Eastern (Syriac, Coptic, Armenian, Ethiopic, Arabic, etc.) and the Western—Latin and Gothic.

The Eastern Versions:

The Syriac versions: The Diatessaron had a wide circulation in Syria. In this area it was the only form of the Gospels available and in use until the fifth century. It was compiled by Tatian, a disciple of Justin Martyr and a Syrian Christian himself, around A.D. 170. It is a harmony of the four Gospels. Two copies of an Arabic version of it were published by Ciasca in 1887. Many early manuscripts of the Diatessaron were destroyed during the fifth century.

Old Syriac versions: An imperfect text of the Gospels in Syriac was published by Cureton in 1858. It is older than the well-known Peshitta. It was brought from the convent of S. Maria Deipara in Egypt to the British Museum. Another manuscript of the like nature was discovered in the monastery of St. Catherine at Sinai. It is a palimpsest containing a Gospel text closely akin to the Curetonian manuscript. It contains a large part of the four Gospels. Both the manuscripts described here belong to the fifth century. However, they are copies of an earlier version which dates back to the second or early third century.

The Peshitta: Before the discovery of the above mentioned manuscripts, it was believed to be the older Syriac version. It is dated anywhere from the second to the fourth century. It was current both in the Nestorian and Monophysite churches whose Christological disputes date back to A.D.

431. There are over 180 Gospel manuscripts in this Peshitta version and over 150 such manuscripts of the Catholic epistles and Paul. One of these Gospel manuscripts can be dated A.D. 463-464. The British Museum has another such manuscript from the same period of time.

The Philoxenian Syriac: In A.D. 508 a Jacobite bishop named Philoxenus from Matrig in eastern Syria ordered a new translation of the New Testament in the Syriac. This was done by Polycarp. Only a small part of this translation has survived the ravages of time.

The Harklean Syriac version: A complete revision of the Philoxenian version was made by Thomas of Harkel in A.D. 616. About 35 manuscripts of Harkel are known, dating from the seventh and eighth centuries onward.

There was an early translation of the New Testament in Armenian that was made from the Syriac text in A.D. 400.

In the West the Vulgate is famous. This became the Bible of the West. Jerome undertook the compilation of this Latin version at the request of Pope Damascus (A.D. 366-384). He began with the Gospels in the year A.D. 382.

A Coptic version of the New Testament was current toward the end of the third century (see Dictionary of the Bible article, "Text of the New Testament," p. 987). The Gospels were translated into Arabic from the Greek, Syriac, and Coptic versions. Barhebraeus speaks of such a translation made between A.D. 631-640. George, bishop of Arab tribes of Mesopotamia, a friend of James of Edessa (d. A.D. 578) wrote a Scholia on the Scriptures. According to Al-Baidhawi and other Muslim commentators, their prophet received instruction from learned Christians like Warqa b. Naufal, Jubra and Yasara (Baidhawi on Sura 16:105). Also, traditions relate how the prophet used to stop and listen to these two men as they read aloud the Books of Moses (Torah) and the Gospels (Injil). Apparently there was a translation of portions of the New Testament that was extant in Mecca during the rise of Islam. Such a translation must have existed along with full versions of the New Testament in Syriac and Syriac Lectionaries.

Chapter 5

The Evangel Incarnate and the Evangelical Record

The Muslim scholars call the highest form of inspiration "Wahi." They distinguish it from another type called "Ilham." Al-Ghazali explains the two usages as follows:

> The recipient knows the medium, i.e., the angel by whom he received the information. This is "Wahi," the inspiration of prophets, the inspiration of the Quran. The recipient receives information from an unknown source and in an unknown way. This is the inspiration of saints and mystics. It is called "Ilham." The difference between "Wahi" and "Ilham" is that in the former an angel is the medium of communication, and in the latter he is not. It comes direct to the mind of the prophet. (*Encyclopaedia of Religion and Ethics*, Vol. 7, p. 354)

The Muslims look upon the Koran as "Wahi" or verbal inspiration delivered to their prophet through the agency of the angel Gabriel. Ibn Khalkan goes to the extent of claiming this to be a unique feature true only of the Koran and no other revealed Scripture (Ibid., p. 355). There is a definite reason why an angelic medium was used in the delivery of the Koran to the prophet:

> It befitteth not a man that God should address him except by "Whai" or from behind a veil, or should send a messenger who would reveal [awha] what he will. Thus we revealed to you [Muhammad] a spirit from our affairs. (Sura 42:51, 52)

Despite this expressed unsuitability of God speaking directly to man, the Koran makes an exception in the case of Moses. It is written:

> And when Moses came at our appointed time, and his Lord spoke unto him (Sura 7:143). And God spoke directly unto Moses. (Sura 4:164)

In regard to 7:143, Al-Baidhawi says that God spoke to Moses, "without mediation of any other, and face to face, as He speaks to angels" (Quoted by Sale, op. cit., p. 118, note e). In other words, it is recognized that for some reason God does not speak to humans directly, but He does so with His angels. The Koran made an exception of Moses to this rule, and the traditions add the name of Muhammad to it. Tradition says that during his "Miraj" (ascent to heaven), he talked to God directly. As Al-Ghazzali explains it:

> He speaks, but not with tongue as men do. He speaks to some of His ser-

vants without intervention of another, even as He spoke to Moses, and to Muhammad on the night of ascension to heaven. He speaks to others by instrumentality of Gabriel, and this is the usual way in which He communicates His will to the prophets. (Al-Ghazzali, quoted in Hughes' Dictionary, p. 147)

Though the Muslim tradition has elevated Muhammad to the status of a "speaker with God" (Kalim-Allah)—a title otherwise reserved for Moses only, yet it has no significance for the Koranic revelation. Some of the traditions dealing with the prophet's ascent to heaven tell us that his dialogue with God concerned only fixing times of prayers a day for Muslims—a subject that is not dealt with in the Koran. On the contrary, Moses' tryst with God dealt with the revelation granted to him. He received directly from God the tablets of the Law written by His finger (Ex. 24:12; 31:18). The Koran also supports this position:

> And we wrote for him upon tablets, the lesson to be drawn from all things, and the explanation of all things, then [bade him], "Hold it fast: and command the people [saying] 'Take the better [course made clear] therein.' " (Sura 7:145, Pickethall)

The general rule governing prophetic revelations is believed to be the agency of the angel Gabriel. The Koran is considered to be the most perfect example of this. According to the orthodox connotation of the term "Wahi," as quoted above from Al-Ghazzali, the books of Moses do not belong to the category of revelation true of the Koran. Moses received the tablets of the Law directly from God without the aid of Gabriel. Is it a superior manner of revelation than the one where God speaks through His angels? Muslims do not believe so. They consider the Koranic revelation to be the best delivered. Ibn Khalkan states:

> Of all the divine books the Koran is the only one of which the text, words and phrases have been communicated to the prophet by an audible voice. (Quoted in *Encyclopaedia of Religion and Ethics*, Vol. 7, p. 335)

The audible voice Khalkan has in mind was that of the angel Gabriel. Keeping in mind what is said in Sura 42:51, God is too transcendent and holy to be addressing human beings directly. Therefore, He used the agency of His holy angels to communicate His message to the prophets. However, the Tablets of Moses are a daring exception to this rule, for he received them directly from God. There is another noteworthy exception of this type that is mentioned in the Koran. It is the revelation granted by God to Jesus Christ:

> We caused Jesus son of Mary, to follow in their footsteps, confirming that which was [revealed] before him, and we bestowed on him the Gospel wherein is guidance and a light, confirming that which was [revealed] before it in Torah—a guidance and an admonition to those who ward off [evil]. (Sura 5:46, Pickethall)

The Gospel was bestowed upon Jesus Christ directly by God himself. There was no angelic agency involved in the process as is believed to have happened in the case of the Koran. If someone objected to this apparent sense of the verse quoted above and others like it, we may point out that the angel Gabriel is not mentioned anywhere in the Koran in the context of the revelation of the Gospel. In the case of Jesus Christ he is referred to only as a messenger of the great news of a miraculous birth to Mary—"Glad tidings of the Word from Him" (Sura 3:45). As Gabriel is believed to be the agent of revelation, Mary herself became a prophet the moment she received the news about the birth of the child of promise to her. The revelation she was granted thus was not a book or something to be read—as it was true in the case of Muhammad. It was a revelation about the Word of God to be born of her. Hence it was a revelation from God about the revelation of Him.

Some Muslims may reason that if Jesus Christ did not receive the Gospel through the agency of Gabriel, He was at least aided by the Holy Spirit. As it is written:

> We formerly delivered the book [of the Law] unto Moses, and caused messengers to succeed him, and gave evident miracles to Jesus the Son of Mary, and strengthened him with the Holy Spirit. (Sura 2:87. Also, 253; 5:110)

The Holy Spirit in the quotation is identified by Al-Baidhawi and other Muslim commentators as the angel Gabriel. Even if this interpretation be allowed, Gabriel is not mentioned as an agent of revelations to Jesus Christ. He only strengthened Him (provided the name "Holy Spirit" implies Him). As to this function of strengthening Jesus Christ, Hughes observes:

> The Jalalan, Al-Baidhawi and the Muslim commentators in general, say this Holy Spirit was the angel Gabriel who sanctified Jesus and constantly aided Him, and who also brought the Koran down from heaven and revealed it to Muhammad. (Dictionary of Islam, p. 177)

Apparently Gabriel is believed to have a twofold ministry as a messenger of God to the prophets. He brings revelations down to them, but in the singular case of Jesus Christ he only strengthened Him. Such a ministry on the part of the angels of God, in connection with Christ, is also recognized by the New Testament. We read of an angel who strengthened Him in the Garden of Gethsemane as He agonized in prayer to the Father (Luke 22:43):

> And there appeared an angel unto him from heaven strengthening him.

This angel might have been Gabriel, but the Scripture is silent at this point. We also read of angels ministering to Jesus Christ in the wilderness as He faced Satan (Mark 1:13). We will return to the subject of the Holy Spirit, in the Koranic passages dealing with Jesus Christ, in the sequel. Let us now consider briefly the nature of the Gospel of Jesus Christ according to the Koran and the Bible.

It is significant that the Koran uses the term "Injil" (the Gospel) in two different connotations. First, it is used to designate the revelation granted to Jesus directly by God:

> . . . And we caused Jesus, son of Mary to follow, and gave him the Gospel. (Sura 57:27, Pickethall)

Secondly, the designation "Injil" is used for the Scripture that was in the possession of the Christian contemporaries of the prophet and read by them. The Koran addresses these Christians, saying:

> Let the People of the Gospel judge by that which God hath revealed therein. Whoso judgeth not by that which God hath revealed; such are evil-livers. (Sura 5:47, Pickethall. Also Sura 7:157)

As it has been mentioned earlier, the Gospels by which the Koran required its Christian contemporaries to abide are all with us today. Their manuscripts dating from long before the rise of Islam can be seen in the libraries and museums of the world. The Christian Scripture consists of not one Gospel but four of them plus other books which together constitute the New Testament canon. Evidently, these books do not satisfy the Koranic description of the one Gospel given to Jesus Christ by God. Some Muslim polemical writers love to ask Christians the seemingly embarrassing question. "What happened to the Gospel (Injil) given to Jesus Christ?" They clearly perceive that the Gospels in the possession of Christians are four in number, not one. Here is a puzzle which cannot be solved on the grounds of the Koran alone. In this case the Muslims need to consult with the Christians "who read the revealed Scripture before them"—a salutary practice advised by the Koran itself (Sura 10:95).

The word "Injil" passed on to the Arabic language from its Greek original via Syriac's (Jeffery, op. cit., pp. 71, 72). In Greek the word has a technical scriptural connotation. Its use in a peculiarly Christian sense can be traced back to Jesus Christ himself. He launched His public ministry by the first proclamation about himself from a synagogue in Nazareth. He read from Isaiah:

> The Spirit of the Lord is upon me, because he hath anointed me to preach the gospel [Injil] to the poor; he hath sent me to heal the brokenhearted, to preach deliverance to the captives, and recovering of sight to the blind, to set at liberty them that are bruised. To preach the acceptable year of the Lord. (Luke 4:18-19)

Having concluded reading of the Isaiahic prophecy, He made the world-shaking declaration: "This day is this scripture fulfilled in your ears" (v. 21).

The Gospel (Injil) consists in the long-awaited appearance of Jesus Christ on the scene of history to release captives under sin and powers of darkness and to bring spiritual, mental, and physical healing to humanity. This "Injil" or Good News is meant for the entire race because all are subject to the besetting predicaments outlined in the prophecy from Isaiah. The positive aspect of this Gospel consists of man's reconciliation with God and participation in His Life.

The fundamental source of all spiritual, mental, and physical woes of man lies in his alienation from God due to personal and racial sin. This gulf could not be bridged by anything within the power of man or angels. The revealed Law of God was mediated to mankind by angels (Acts 7:38, 53; Ps. 68:17; Gal. 3:19; Heb. 2:2). The natural laws were discovered by man through reason and conscience in dealing with creation and society (Rom. 1:20; 2:14-15).

Law, whether natural or revealed, only gives us knowledge of sin and our own sinfulness. In this way it shows us the immense distance between us and our Maker (Rom. 3:20; 7:7). Hence the Law, as such, cannot be good news—Gospel. It only shows those under the Law their dire need for a Saviour who might redeem them from their sin, and consequent separation from God. That is why the Law of Moses as well as prophets of the Old Testament looked forward to the appearance of a great Saviour—the Messiah of God. Jesus Christ came preaching the Good News because He himself was the promised author and finisher of human redemption. Hence His preaching, which opened with the announcement of the acceptable year of the Lord and advent of the kingdom of God, came to rest squarely upon His own person and work. Thus the messenger himself became the message—the Gospel. As it is written: "Behold the Lamb of God, which taketh away the sin of the world" (John 1:29); "For God so loved the world, that he gave his only begotten Son, that whosoever believeth in him should not perish, but have everlasting life" (John 3:16).

This advent of the Messiah of God itself is the "Injil"—the Good News of the incarnation of the Word of God. Upon this both the Bible and the Koran agree. Interestingly enough, both the scriptures concur that it was the angel Gabriel who came to the Virgin Mary with the Good News that the Word of God was to be born of her (Sura 3:45; Luke 1:26-33). This "Injil"—the Word of God Incarnate—came to reconcile man with God. In order to accomplish this mission He went to the cross to offer himself for the atonement of the sins of the world. Rising again from the dead on the third day, He ascended to His heavenly glory at the right hand of God the Father. Now He is a Mediator forever between man, God, and the rest of His creation.

In short, Jesus Christ, the son of Mary, was sent by God to publish the Good News of salvation to all mankind which was made available in history by Him and in Him. In this remarkable way He was given the Gospel to proclaim which Gospel He himself was. God who does not hesitate to use weak and inadequate human languages like Arabic or Hebrew in order to establish contact with the fallen man, did not abhor a virgin's womb to accomplish the redemption of mankind. This is the one Injil (the Gospel) of our Lord Jesus Christ, the Word of God (John 1:4; Sura 4:171), who came from God the Father (John 3:16, 17; Sura 57:27) and was strengthened by God the Holy Spirit (John 1:32-34; Sura 2:87, 253).

The Koran tells us about a heavenly Book which is the source of all revealed Scriptures including the Koran itself:

Every age hath its book of revelation: God shall abolish and shall confirm what He pleaseth. With Him is the Mother of the Book. (Sura 13:39)

And if they treat thee as a liar so did those who were before them treat their apostles who came to them with the proofs of their mission, and with the Scriptures and with the clear Book. (Sura 35:25)

Verily it is We who will quicken the dead, and write down the works which they have sent on before them, and the traces which they shall have left behind them; and everything We have set down in a Clear Book of our decrees. (Sura 36:12)

Muslims of the first century of the Islamic era did not bother to indulge in a theological examination of the nature of "the Clear Book" or "Mother of the Book" in heaven and its relation to the Koran with them. After about a century and a half of its inception, Islam came into contact with the full stream of religious and intellectual activity outside its comparatively isolated place of birth. Around A.D. 800, Christian thought about the Logos (the Word of God) and nature of the Godhead began to influence Muslim inquiry into the Koran as the Word of God and its relationship with the mysterious Mother of the Book. Also, they became increasingly concerned about the defense of Islamic Monotheism in view of the Koranic teaching about a Book with God before creation. These were the days of heated controversy between the Liberals (Mutazila) and the orthodox parties in the history of Muslim theology.

It is significant to note that the Muslim orthodoxy, despite strong protests from the Liberals, managed to transfer to the heavenly Mother of the Book the Biblical concept of the uncreated Word of God (Logos) which they learned from Christians. As a result, the Koran was declared to be the uncreated Word of God. (Some orthodox scholars went so far as to look upon the written Koran in their hands—recognized to be a copy, as well as its original Mother of the Book—as eternal and uncreated.) The great "Imam" of the Sunnis, Abu Hanifa, expressed the orthodox point of view as follows:

> The Quran is the word of God, and is His inspired word and revelation. It is a necessary attribute of God. It is not God, but still is inseparable from God. It is written in a volume, it is read in a language, it is remembered in the heart, and its letters and its vowel points, and its writing are all created, for they are the works of men, but God's word is uncreated. Its words, its writing, its letters, and its verses are for the necessities of man, for its meaning is arrived at by their use, but the word of God is fixed in the essence of God, and he who says that the word of God is created is an infidel. (Kitab al-Wasiyah, p. 77)

According to Abu-Hanifa, the Koran has two aspects—creaturely and divine. On its divine side it is the word of God in the very essence of God. It is obvious from the quotation above that Abu-Hanifa has identified the Mother of the Book mentioned in the Koran with the Logos who is of one nature with God. This Muslim belief came to be applied not only to the Koran but also to other revealed scriptures, chief among whom are the Torah and Injil. In this connection Al-Ghazzali explains:

> The Quran, the Law, the Gospel and the Psalter are books sent down by Him to his apostles, and the Quran indeed is read with tongues, written in books, and kept in hearts: yet as subsisting in the essence of God, it doth not become liable to separation and division whilst it is transferred into hearts and papers. (Al-Ghazzali: quoted from Al-Maqsud al-Asna, Hughes' Dictionary, p. 146)

It is no exaggeration to say that Muslims claim for the Koran what Christians have always testified about the Lord Jesus Christ. Duncan B.

MacDonald, discussing the Muslim doctrine of the uncreated Koran, makes a sound observation:

> Whatever proofs of the doctrine may have been brought forward later from the Quran itself, we can have no difficulty in recognizing that it is plainly derived from the Christian Logos and that the Greek Church, perhaps through John of Damascus, has again played a formative part. So in correspondence with the heavenly and uncreated Logos in the bosom of the Father, there stands the uncreated and eternal word of God; to the earthly manifestation in Jesus corresponds the Quran, the Word of God which we read and recite. (Muslim Theology and Jurisprudence and Constitutional Theory, pp. 146, 147)

The teaching of the Koran about the heavenly Mother of the Book as the only source and original of all scriptures revealed from God poses a real problem for Islamic monotheism. In view of this, Muslim theologians developed a doctrine of revelation which is barely distinguishable from the Johanine doctrine of the Logos. The Bible teaches us that the true source of all revelations from the living God is in His very nature. This source in God is His eternal Word (Logos) and not a creature as it is written:

> In the beginning was the Word, and the Word was with God, and the Word was God. (John 1:1)

The same Word of God through whom all things were created is also the source of revelation and redemption of lost humanity and creation. In redemptive history God who spoke to His prophets and seers through His (Logos) Word in sundry times (Heb. 1:1; John 1:9), finally and decisively addressed the human race through the same Logos Incarnate (Heb. 1:2; John 1:14). Several centuries before Islam, Justin Martyr explained this scriptural perspective on the revelation of God in his own words:

> Whenever God says . . . "The Lord spoke to Moses . . . " You must not imagine that the unbegotten God Himself came down or went up to any place. For the ineffable Father and the Lord neither has come to any place, nor walks, nor sleeps, nor rises up, but remains in His own place wherever that is, quick to behold, quick to hear, having neither eyes nor ears, but being of indescribable might He sees all things, and none of us escapes His observation, and He is not moved or confined to a spot, or in the whole world, for He existed before the world was made. How then could He talk with anyone, or be seen by anyone, or appear in the smallest portion of the earth, when the people of Sinai were unable to even look on the glory of Him who was sent from Him? . . . Therefore neither Abraham, nor Isaac, nor Jacob, nor any other man ever saw the Father and ineffable Lord of all . . . but [saw] Him who was according to His will His Son Being God and the angel . . . because He ministered to His will . . . who also was the fire when He conversed with Moses from the bush. (Justin: *Dialogue with Trypho*)

At the right moment in the redemptive plan of God, His Word, who conversed with Moses in the wilderness, led Israel as the Angel of His presence, inspired His prophets directly or indirectly through angelic beings, became flesh and dwelt among us (John 1:14). His appearance in the Holy Land some two thousand years ago was the culmination of a long process of preparation through the Law of Moses and the prophets of the Old Testament. John the Baptizer who heralded the arrival of the Messiah was the last link in the chain (Matt. 11:13).

According to the Koranic perspective, angels have a direct access to the Mother of the Book. Thus the angel Gabriel is considered the chief agent of inspiration for the Koran and other revealed scriptures. If human beings had a direct access to the divine source of inspiration, then no angelic agency would have been required. The Koran does not say why the source of divine revelations is inaccessible to man. It could not be due to the sinfulness or mortality of man because the prophet Moses was granted the privilege of speaking with God and receiving the Torah from Him. It also indicates that there is no absolute hindrance on the part of God Most High to establish a redemptive contact with man without the mediation of angels. The Bible explains the existing separation between God and natural man by the Fall and continued sinfulness of humanity. This tragic gulf of alienation between sinners and God could never have been bridged except by the atonement provided by "the Lamb of God, which taketh away the sin of the world" (John 1:29).

The "Injil" (Gospel) consists in the news that the very Word of God manifested himself some two thousand years ago, according to the Old Testament prophecy, to bring God and man together through His atoning death, resurrection, and ascension to the right hand of God the Father. To put this "Injil" in the vocabulary of the Koran, "the Mother of the Book" himself became flesh, as Gabriel the angelic medium of revelation had informed the Virgin Mary (Luke 1:26-35; Sura 3:42-46). In brief, "God was in Christ, reconciling the world unto himself, not imputing their trespasses unto them" (2 Cor. 5:19).

The apostles and first disciples of Jesus Christ were in intimate, personal contact and continued communion with this Incarnate Word (Book) of God. They were, thus, more privileged than the angel Gabriel who, according to Muslim belief, had an occasional access to the Mother of the Book by the command of God. One of the apostles expresses this supreme honor graphically as he wrote:

That which was from the beginning, which we have heard, which we have seen with our eyes, which we have looked upon, and our hands have handled, of the Word of Life. . . . That which we have seen and heard declare we unto you. (1 John 1:1, 3)

Out of this, their unique intimate communion with the Incarnate Book of God "in whom are hid all the treasures of wisdom and knowledge" (Col. 2:3), the apostles and first disciples bore a testimony for the salvation of the whole world. There are four written records of this testimony going back to the apostles. These are the four Gospels that form part of the New Testament. To put it in a way that would be meaningful to a Muslim, there is the one and self-same Gospel (Injil) of the Lord Jesus Christ reported by eyewitnesses in the Gospels according to Matthew, Mark, Luke, and John. The Muslims find it easy to believe that the one heavenly Mother of the Book has been reproduced in the Torah, Psalter, the Gospel, the Koran and some other revealed scriptures.

As far as the New Testament is concerned, the same Gospel of the Incarnate Book of God is reproduced not only in the four written Gospels but also in the remaining books of the Canon. The four evangelists may vary in reporting minor details of the life, teaching, and ministry of the Word of God in flesh, but they represent the same person who himself is the Gospel. As a matter of fact, a lack of a perfect harmony among them as to minute details and perspective is a clear and sure indication of the firsthand nature of the narratives. Though Christians have attempted to produce works on the harmony of the four Gospels in order to get a full view of the Incarnate Gospel of God, yet they never dreamed of doing away with the Gospels in the interest of an artificial harmony in the Scripture.

Here is a situation which can be compared to the story of the Koran. The Koran was reportedly revealed in seven recensions. All of these versions except two are lost (*A Shorter Encyclopaedia of Islam*, p. 283). Apart from the seven recensions, once there were four different collections of the Koran that were current before the present collection became the one and only official collection under the Caliph Uthman. These four unofficial collections belonged to Abd Allah b. Masud, Abu Musa, Abd Allah al Ashari and Mikdad b. Amr. As to some differences between these collections, including the official collection, the reader may refer to Itiqan and Fihrist (see: Ibid., p. 277). If, as the Muslims must allow, the same Koran (from the Mother of the Book) can be recorded in seven recensions and five different collections and yet convey essentially the same message, why should it be hard to understand that the selfsame living Gospel of Jesus Christ was reported in four written Gospels and elaborated upon in the remaining books of the New Testament under the inspiration of the Holy Spirit of God?

According to the orthodox Muslim view, the Koran is the "recited revelation," while the traditions are "the unrecited (read) revelation." The traditions are regarded as a sort of second-class revelation as compared to the primary revelation in the Koran. There is a traditional authority behind this position. The prophet is reported to have said:

> My sayings do not abrogate the word of God, but the Word of God can abrogate my sayings. (Mishkat Book I, Chapter 6)

Muslim traditions are a record of what the prophet did (Sunnat al-fail), what he enjoined (Sunnat al-qual), and what was done in his presence which he did not forbid. They include also the authoritative sayings and doings of the companions of the prophet.

According to the Christian perspective, all canonical revelation is primary in nature. It alone constitutes the source for Christian doctrine and life because it is centered in the Book (Word) of God who became flesh and dwelt amongst us. He came as a personal revelation of God who is Love. He taught us the supreme ideal involved in human life in the light of this, His revelation (Matt. 5:48). Moreover, He himself lived in perfect accord with what He taught so much so that He never made a mistake or committed a sin despite the fact that He was tempted and tried like us (Heb. 4:15). Thus in a remarkable and unique way the supreme revelation of God and the ultimate tradition for the ordering of our lives in the paths of His righteousness coincided in the Jesus Christ. The Gospels are four eye-witness accounts of the same revelation—tradition, the Gospel of Jesus Christ the Son of God (Mark 1:1). It is interesting to note that the famous Muslim Chronicler Al-Bairuni came close to this conclusion in regard to the Gospel witnessed by the four Gospels:

> The four Evangelists to him are four recensions which he compares with the three copies of the Bible, the Jewish, the Christians and the Samaritan. (*Shorter Encyclopaedia of Islam*, p. 169)

The New Testament contains twenty-seven books. After the four Gospels come twenty-three books. They contain an account of the impact of the Gospel of Jesus Christ upon His companions and the world around them. They also record apostolic elucidations of facets and mysteries of this very Gospel dealing with Christian life and history. These illuminations were granted to the apostles by the Holy Spirit of God who came upon the Church in a unique experience of divine presence for the first time at Pentecost. During their sojourn with the Gospel-Incarnate, they were spiritually unprepared to take in all that they needed to know. Therefore, He told them, "I have many things to say unto you, but you cannot bear them now" (John 16:12). However, He promised to send them His Holy Spirit as a guide at all truth after His death, resurrection and ascension to the right hand of God the Father:

> Howbeit when he, the Spirit of truth, is come, he will guide you into all truth: for he shall not speak of himself; but whatsoever he shall hear, that shall he speak: and he will shew you things to come. He shall glorify me: for he shall receive of mine, and shall shew it to you. All things that the Father hath are mine: therefore said I, that he shall take of mine, and shall shew it unto you. (John 16:13-15)

After the Pentecost, instead of an angel bringing revelations from the unseen God to a prophet, the Holy Spirit himself began to reveal those details of the Gospel to the apostles which their Lord and Master could not share with them at one time due to their spiritual immaturity (Eph. 3:5). Here is an interesting contrast between the angel Gabriel reading from the Mother of the Book bits and pieces of revelation to bring it to a prophet and an apostle receiving a deeper comprehension of the Gospel of Jesus Christ by revelations from the Holy Spirit who in turn hears it from the Word of God himself (John 16:13). The revealed sayings and teaching of the apostles as contained in the New Testament are as authentic and primary as the teaching of Jesus Christ when He was in flesh. In other words, the written record of the four Gospels is of the same caliber as the rest of the books of the New Testament. All contain the one Gospel of Jesus Christ received either directly in His presence in flesh or indirectly from His presence in and through the Holy Spirit (1 Cor. 15:45; 2 Cor. 3:18; Gal. 24:6). The Holy Spirit is also known in the Scripture as the "Spirit of Jesus Christ" (Phil. 1:19)—just as the news of salvation provided by Him is called "the Gospel of Jesus Christ."

Chapter 6

Jesus Christ, the Word of God

The Koran confirms the Injil in the declaration that Jesus Christ was the Word of God who became flesh and dwelt amongst us. We read in Sura 3:45:

> When the angel said, "O Mary verily God gives you good tidings of the Word from Himself; His name is Jesus Son of Mary exalted both in this world and world to come and one of those near the throne."

Muslim commentators have endeavored to minimize the full impact of the plain declaration of the Koran that Jesus Christ was the Word of God Incarnate. For example, Fakhar al-Din Razi explains the passage thus:

> "The Word from Him" i.e., the essence of the word, as one would say of a brave man, "the essence of bravery or generosity itself". The following traditions on the Messiah; so called because kept clear from the taint of sin, or anointed with oil like other prophets or at his birth, or touched by the wing of Gabriel when born, to avert tact of Satan. "Exalted in the world" by the rank and wonderful miracles and vindication from the accusation of the Jews, and "in the world to come", in virtue of his exalted place with God, intercession of his people and heavenly graces. "The Word from Him," the pronoun (Him) refers back to the "Word", just as the same pronoun "in his name" refers to the Messiah. Why then the pronoun is not of the same gender as "the Word"? Because the person referred to is masculine. (Razi, as quoted by W. Muir, *Beacon of Truth*, p. 122)

It is obvious that Razi has a great difficulty in explaining away the simple connotation of the Koranic expression used for Jesus Christ—"the Word from Him." In order to achieve his purpose he goes easy with the grammar and literal sense of the expression. Thus he refers the pronoun (Him—masculine in form) to "Word" (Kalima—feminine in form). It amounts to saying that the "Word was from the Word." To put it in other words, "Jesus, as it were, is the father of Jesus (Ibid., p. 123).

As opposed to the exegesis of Razi, another great commentator, Ibn Hazam, recognizes the evident meaning of the expression under review. He grants that Jesus Christ is the Word (Kalima) from God. But he goes on to say that this Word is a created being, not divine—a position similar to the Arians (Hirschfield, *New Researches into the Composition and Exegesis of the Quran*, London, 1902, p. 16). The difference of opinion between Razi, who says Jesus Christ is not the Word of God, and Ibn Hazam, who says He is, illustrates the perplexity of Muslim commentators in dealing fairly with Christological passages in the Koran. In order to shed more light on the crucial expression "the Word from Him," it is wise to seek first the meaning of the Koran from the Koran itself.

The Koran describes John the Baptist (Yahya) as the one who came proclaiming "the Word" (Kalima) from God (Sura 3:39). Here is an echo of the Gospel narrative according to which John was sent by God to be a herald of Jesus Christ (Matt. 2:11, 12; John 1:23-27). There is no doubt as to the identity of the Word from God whom John came to announce to Israel. In the expression "Word from Him," the participle (from) "min" signifies a generic relationship between the noun and pronoun linked together by it. Therefore, it means that "the Word" is of the same divine essence as Him (hu)—God. To further support the authenticity of this connotation, we have the interesting passage quoted earlier:

> Verily Jesus Christ Son of Mary is the apostle of God and His Word which He conveyed into Mary and a Spirit from Him. (Sura 4:171, Sale)

In the light of this verse, the expression "Word from Him" is equal to "His Word." It should be plain for any reasonable person to see that the Word of God must be of the same nature as God. But Muslim commentators have sought to avoid this conclusion in regard to Jesus Christ. However, when it comes to dealing with the Koran as the word of God, they hasten to acknowledge the validity of the argument. The father of the Rationalist movement in Islam (Mutazila), Jahm, used to refer to the verse quoted above in order to prove that the Koran was created. His line of reasoning is worthy of note in the present context. He said:

> I have found a verse in God's book to prove that the Quran is created. . . . It is God's word: "The Messiah, Jesus, Son of Mary, is only an apostle of God and His Word." Now Jesus (the Word) is created, (so why cannot the Quran be created). (As quoted by M. S. Seale, *Muslim Theology*, Luzac & Co., p. 110)

To this trenchant argument we have a feeble reply from Imam Ibn Hanbal in his treatise Al-Radd:

> God has deprived you of reason: the things said concerning Jesus in the Quran cannot be said of the Quran. Jesus is called offspring, infant, child and youth; he used to eat and drink, he was commanded and restrained with promise and threat, he was, moreover descended from Noah and Abraham. We cannot say about the Quran what we can say about Jesus. Did you ever hear God do so? But what God means when He says, "The Messiah, Jesus, Son of Mary, is only an apostle of God and His Word which He conveyed into Mary", is that the Word which God cast into Mary was His saying "Be" [Kun]. Jesus was, therefore, brought into being by "Be" but not himself that "Be". "Be" is God's Word and is uncreated. (As quoted, ibid., p. 110)

According to Ibn Hanbal "the Word of God" is divine when used of the Koran; but when the expression is used in the case of Jesus Christ, it must be understood as divine "fiat" creating Him. In other words, he still understands that the Word of God is divine but maintains that Jesus Christ was not the Word of God. This position, however, goes flatly against his argument which precedes it, for there it is presupposed that Jesus Christ is the

Incarnate Word of God. On that basis Ibn Hanbal goes on to argue against Jahm that we cannot say about Jesus Christ what we can say about the Koran. As to this argument itself, it is quite obvious that we cannot say about a book all that can be said about a living person. But it has nothing to do with the question of the eternity of the Word of God Incarnate in Christ.

Using Hanbal's approach, therefore, we can say that things said about God in the Koran cannot be said about the Koran itself. For example, God sees. He is omnipresent and omniscient. He created all things. Using Ibn Hanbal's reasoning, are we to say God is not divine or eternal since these statements cannot be affirmed of the Koran? Moreover, in this, his argument, he mentions the created (human) nature of Jesus Christ in comparison to the eternal nature of the Koran according to his belief. In all fairness he should have compared the creaturely aspect of the Koran with the humanity of Jesus Christ. Not many Muslims will be willing to grant that the binding, paper, and ink used in the makeup of a copy of the Koran is eternal. They do have to make an allowance for this contingent and creaturely aspect of the written Koran; otherwise they will imply a belief in the eternity of matter—thus setting up another god besides God! The humanity of Jesus Christ belonged to the realm of creation as much as the material on which the Koran is written. But as we shall see in the sequel, His humanity was created in a unique way, both according to the Koran and the New Testament. Nevertheless, for the sake of argument, if Jesus Christ "is called offspring, infant, child, youth and he used to eat and drink" (Ibn Hanbal), then the Koran also is a book, written down in ink by human hands.

Let us, for a moment, return to Ibn Hanbal's denial of the Koranic statement that Jesus Christ was the Word of God conveyed into Mary. He maintains that it means only that Jesus Christ came into being by divine fiat. It does not mean that He was the incarnation of the Word of God. We remember that the same angel Gabriel who spoke to the Virgin Mary is believed to have conveyed to the prophet of Islam the word of God from the preserved Tablet. Using the logic of Ibn Hanbal in the case of the Word conveyed to Mary, we should be able to say that the word conveyed to the prophet did not mean that the very Word of God was embodied in the Koran. It only meant that by divine fiat the Koran was created, which is rated as the miracle of the prophet. Both Ibn Hanbal and orthodox Muslims will strongly object to this application of a line of reasoning which they feel free to use about the Word of God and Mary.

We have said in the earlier chapter that the orthodox doctrine of the uncreated Koran is a later development in Muslim thought under the influence of the Christian doctrine of the Logos. Seale reminds us:

> The Quran was more than a book: it was a faithful reproduction of the original scripture in heaven. To this heavenly copy, it is not implausible to hold, was transferred the Christian conception of the uncreated Word of God, the Logos, which Muslims had come to know from Christian polemics. It was this conception which was later applied by the orthodox to the Arabic copies of the Quran which was so vehemently opposed by Jahm and Mutazila. (Ibid., p. 66)

Whatever arguments the Muslims use to prove the eternity of the Word of God embodied in the Koran will apply, by and large, to the divinity of the Word of God incarnate through the Virgin Mary. The humanity of Jesus Christ was not divine by nature just as the Arabic language and material used in the production of copies of the Koran cannot easily be called divine even by Muslim orthodoxy. The Muslims hold a sort of two-nature theory about the Koran as do Christians about Jesus Christ. It may be asked, is the Koran read in material books of the same nature as its heavenly original—Mother of the Book? If so then this position is akin to the Monophysitic theory that the divine and human nature (created) of Jesus Christ fused into one. On the other hand, if they say that the material books of the Arabic Koran are different in nature from what they contain, then they come close to the Nestorian position on the Incarnation. Let us recapitulate here what has been said about the two-nature controversy among the Christians before and during the appearance of Islam.

The early Chruch made tremendous strides of progress in a world teeming with pagan missionary cults, ideologies, and philosophies. In those days of expansion she soon faced the urgency of articulating the Gospel in such theological terms and creeds as may guard against infiltration by hostile and foreign ideas. Thence the Church felt called to express as precisely as feasible the divine majesty of the Saviour of mankind and His relationship to the Father and the Holy Spirit. It was not an angel or one of the pagan gods who appeared in Christ. Rather, "God was in Christ, reconciling the world unto himself, not imputing their trespasses unto them" (2 Cor. 5:19). After a hard battle with the heresy of Arianism, the Church was able finally to express the scriptural testimony to the divinity of Jesus Christ in the famous Nicene Creed. It settled the dogma of the Holy Trinity for centuries to come. The task that began to occupy the center of attention of the Church soon after Nicea was a theological delineation of relationship between the divine and human natures of Jesus Christ. This issue was intimately related to the cult of the Virgin Mary and her place in the divine plan of salvation. Hence it was vigorously contested by various denominational leaders of those days. It led to a lot of mutual recriminations and physical violence on rare occasions. As to the Incarnation it was asked, did the human and divine natures of Jesus Christ remain distinct even after the Incarnation or did they merge into one nature? If they did fuse into one nature (the position of Cyril of Alexandria and all devotees of the cult of the Virgin Mary), then the humanity of Jesus Christ could be called "Son of God" in the same sense as His divinity. That would justify the title of "Theotokos"—"bearer of Christ" for the Virgin Mary, and she may even be called Mother of God. Hence the crucial question was, in what sense was He the Son of God as far as His human nature was concerned?

The Koranic passage quoted earlier (3:45) maintains a position very much similar to the Nestorian Church. Nestorius, who was bitterly opposed by Cyril, maintained that Jesus:

Consubstantial with the Father is Christ: This is true, for in the divinity He is eternal. Consubstantial with us [is He] naturally: This is true, for He too was a man as we also are. (*The Bazaar of Heraclides*, Clarenden Press, 1925, p. 196)

Having recognized the divinity of Jesus Christ in full accord with the Nicene Creed, Nestorius goes on to make statements about His humanity which appear to be echoed in several Christological passages from the Koran (cf. 5:75). Thus, for example, Nestorius says that He who was born of Mary was "a man who is truly our Saviour" (Ibid., p. 201).

In order to show further an affinity between the Koran and Nestorianism on the two natures of Jesus Christ, we may quote from an official creedal statement of the Nestorian Church in Iran. This statement belongs to a period of time close to the rise of Islam:

> Whenever we speak of Jesus Christ as God, it is in His divine nature—the eternal immutable, etc.; and whenever we speak of Him as the Being who took on a servant's form, we see in Him His human nature, and these two natures should not be mixed. God is the Word—and the Word became flesh and dwelt among us—a perfect Being of human nature.
>
> Jesus Christ was born a human Being—His mother was the Virgin, the holy Mary. He had His divine nature from eternity—His human nature He got at birth. His divine nature cannot change—in His human nature He was circumcised, and grew up among men like other children, gained knowledge and increased in wisdom and stature and favour with God and men. He kept the Law and was baptized by John the Baptist in the river Jordan. Then He began to preach the New Testament. In His divine nature He performed miracles. He healed the leper, made the blind to see, devils were cast out, the dead arose and the sick were restored to health. . . . He himself felt not need. In His human nature He felt hunger, thirst, became sleepy and tired like other human beings. (G. D. Malech, *History of the Syrian Nation and the Old Evangelical Apostolic Church in the East*, Minneapolis, 1910, pp. 209-211)

It must be pointed out that in the verse quoted earlier (3:45), the Koran mentions the divine and the human natures of the Jesus Christ together without any logical or theological uneasiness about it. This attitude is maintained even in those passages that are manifestly intended to deny a false deification of the human nature of the Incarnate Word. Thus we read:

> O people of the scripture! Do not exaggerate in your religion nor utter aught concerning God save truth. The Messiah, Jesus Son of Mary, was only a messenger of God and His Word which He conveyed into Mary and a Spirit from Him. So believe in God and His messengers and say not three—Cease! [It is] better for you. (Sura 4:171, Pickethall)

These remarks could easily have been made by a Nestorian contemporary of the prophet of Islam to a Monophysite except the expression, "say not three." The interesting posture of the Koran as to the then current two-nature Christology is further supported by an incident involving the prophet and a delegation of Christians from Najran. According to Ibn Ishaq, these Christians belonged to the Byzantine rite. In other words, they adored the Virgin Mary as the Mother of God and tended to believe that Christ in His humanity was the Son of God the same way as He was in His pre-incarnate nature because after the Incarnation His divine and human natures fused into one reality. Ibn Ishaq quotes from the Koran to say that the Christian sects in those days differed in regard to the nature of Christ, a statement true to the history of the Church. Again, we learn that the prophet chided these Najrani Christians for rebellion against God. They had not submitted to Him:

> He said you lie. Your assertion that God has a son, your worship of the cross, and your eating pork hold you back from submission. (*Life of Muhammad*, p. 272)

The Najranis strove to explain themselves when charged that they believed God had a son. They asked the prophet who was the father of Jesus Christ. The prophet became silent (ibid.). Apparently the discussion here devolved around the sonship of Christ due to His birth of the Virgin Mother. This had nothing to do with His divine nature and eternal sonship. The prophet broke his uneasy silence when a revelation came to him in reply from God. This consisted, reportedly, of more than eight verses from the Sura of the Family of Imran. All these verses dwell upon the humanity of Jesus Christ and thereby prove that He could not be the immutable God. Ibn Ishaq adds other verses to the eight, all implying the creaturely aspect of the Messiah. His lengthy discourse, in terms of recitation of several Christological verses and those dealing with the transcendence and unity of God, ends with the intriguing suggestion (Ibid., p. 276):

> The likeness of Jesus with God is as the likeness of Adam whom God created of earth and then said to him: Be, and he was. (3:59)

The rejection of the idea that Jesus Son of Mary was the son of God is in line with the Nestorian position. It is opposed to calling Mary the Mother of God and Jesus the Son of Mary, the son of God. Again, it is enlightening to note that Nestorius himself regarded the sonship of Christ due to the virgin birth as a creative reality similar to Adam. Referring to the Nativity narratives in the Synoptics, Nestorius explains that the Holy Spirit of God acted creatively in the virgin birth. In this way Christ was born of Mary as a new creation—the type-man for a redeemed humanity, Adam (*The Bazaar*, pp. 196, 311, 62). On first impression one wonders why the Koran and the prophet himself in his discourse with Najranites did not simply leave out all reference to the Messiah being the Word of God and the Spirit from Him. A plain statement that He was the Son of Mary born miraculously would have saved a lot of confusion of thought. But the prophet, while objecting to the Najranites calling Messiah the Son of God, did not hesitate to share the Koranic revelation:

> Then the angels said: "O Mary God giveth thee good tidings of Word from Him whose name is the Messiah, Jesus Son of Mary." (*Life of Muhammad*, p. 275)

These considerations suggest that the prophet and the Koran did not want to deny the Nestorian confession as to Messiah's divine nature—"Word of God" and "Word from Him." At the same time they had the typical Nestorian aversion to any suggestion that the humanity of Christ—His sonship to Mary—was divine by nature. Also, there appears to be an apprehension implied in calling Mary "Theotokos"—bearer of God or even Mother of God, after the Byzantines and Monophysites ("Say not three," 4:169ff.).

After the death of the prophet, the Islamic movement quickly overflowed Arabia and began to take over the neighboring countries. In the process it came into contact with the mainstream of Christian theology and Greek philosophy. During the active period of conquest of non-Muslim lands, conditions were not suitable for dialogues between Christians and Muslims. In conquered lands Christians were even forbidden by law to try to persuade Muslims to change their religion. Gradually, peaceful conditions prevailed and mutual sharing of religious ideas between Christians, Muslims and philosophers began. One such period was the rule of the Umayyads. In this new, comparatively free, intellectual and religious ethos, Muslims began to take a second look at some of the Christological passages in the Koran in the light of the New Testament and Christian theology. Some of the theological expressions regarding the pre-incarnate nature of Christ that were retained both by the Koran and the prophet in the hey-days of the two-nature Christology, became a source of perplexity for Muslim commentators and theologians. Hence they endeavored to tone down their plain implications or even explain them away. The two expressions "Word from Him" and "Spirit from Him" as used in the Koran in regard to the Messiah became a source of endless difficulty for them.

The Injil declares that the Word of God in creation and in final perfect revelation is the same Divine Agency:

> In the beginning was the Word, and the Word was with God, and the Word was God. . . .
> . . . All things were made by him, and without him was not anything made that was made.
> And the Word was made flesh and dwelt amongst us. (John 1:1, 3, 14)

The Koran makes a distinction between the Word in creation and the Word in revelation which is recorded in the preserved Book in heaven. According to the Koran, Jesus Christ is the Word of God belonging to the essence of God—"His Word." The Koran is the word of God insofar as it is a true copy of the heavenly book which is an entity existing along with God. Muslim theologians have tried to relocate the Mother of the Book in the very essence of God after what they learned about the Christian doctrine of the Logos. But if we stay strictly with the Koran, it claims to be a book—a true copy of the heavenly original. Jesus Christ as the Word of God is a personal revelation of God in flesh, while the Koran (granting the orthodox Muslim belief) is only a read or recited revelation of the will of God preserved in material books and human memories. The first is a revelation of the very nature of Godhead to the extent of human capacity for God. The second is believed to be a revelation of His will for the submission of man to God who otherwise remains transcendent and hidden. In other words, one is a self-revelation of God, while the other constitutes a revelation, at best, of His imperial will for the control of an otherwise rebellious race.

Chapter 7

The Son of Mary

Knowing or unknowingly the natural, unregenerate man lives in rebellion against God, his Maker and source of all sweetness and life. In the pursuit of sinful pleasures and lusts of the flesh, he subjects himself to an ever-increasing alienation from God and moral and spiritual disintegration. As a result, he loses his native freedom and spontaneity to demonic powers and influences who become his tyrant lords. Thus begins for him an experience of hell here and now which stretches beyond the grave to a truly horrible hereafter. There is no way out for such a person caught in the spider-web of Satan. He cannot shake himself free from it, for salvation is beyond all his natural means. Neither an angel from heaven nor any other creature could help him out of such a predicament. *It is possible only with God truly to save sinners.*

On the positive side this salvation connotes a return of the Prodigal Son from a far-off famine-stricken land to the open arms of his loving father (Luke 15:11-32). On the negative side it calls for an atonement for his sins and consequent forgiveness and removal of all guilt by God who mediates His mercy and love in holiness and righteousness. In order to accomplish this great salvation, God took the initiative in the redemptive history of mankind. He chose a man called Abraham in fulfillment of His gracious promise given originally to Adam and Eve soon after their fall (Gen. 3:15). Through him He entered into a covenant relationship with a particular section of humanity. This was done with a view to preparation for the supreme manifestation of His salvation for the whole world.

During the period of preparation under the Old Covenant, God did not hesitate to use inadequate means of communication like the Hebrew prophets and language. He gave Israel the Law embodying His gracious will for them and meant to be a schoolteacher to the final manifestation of His Word in flesh (Gal. 3:24). A long line of His prophets was sent successively through the centuries of sacred history in order to reveal progressively essential details pertaining to the Incarnation. The longed-for vision of the prophets and the Law was finally brought to fruition when the Word of God himself became flesh and tabernacled with mankind. As it is written:

> God, who at sundry times and in diverse manners, spake in times past to the fathers by the prophets, has in these last days spoken unto us by his Son, whom he appointed heir of all things, by whom also he made the worlds. (Hebrews 1:1, 2)

In the former days, the eternal Son of God used the weak instrumentality of the Hebrew language to deliver His will to the prophets who, in turn, communicated it to the covenant people. In the last days—a period in sacred history which began about 2000 years ago, the same Only-Begotten Son of the Father (His Word) did not abhor a virgin's womb. Through a creative incursion in history, He became the Son of Man in order to establish a direct redemptive contact with sinners to be saved. This supreme salvation began with a unique miracle. The Word of God became flesh by being born of the Virgin Mary, without a human father. This miraculous inauguration of the redemptive outreach of God is freely testified to by the Koran:

> The angel said, "O Mary! Verily God announceth to thee the Word from Him: His name shall be Christ Jesus the Son of Mary, honourable in this world and the world to come, and one of those who approach near the presence of God. He will speak to mankind in his cradle and in manhood, and he is of the righteous." She said: "My Lord! How can I have a child when no man hath touched me?" The angel said, "So God createth what He pleaseth; when He decreeth a thing, He only saith unto it 'Be' and it is." (Sura 3:45-47. Also, 19:16-21)

It is evident from the Koran that the incarnation of the Word of God took place through a unique creative miracle rather than by way of natural procreation. This insight is in line with the birth narratives in the Gospel according to Matthew and Luke. We learn that the angel Gabriel was sent to the Virgin Mary in the city of Nazareth with the following message:

> And, behold, thou shalt conceive in thy womb, and bring forth a son, and shalt call his name Jesus. (Luke 1:31)

When the perplexed lady wondered how it could be, "seeing I know not a man" (v. 34), Gabriel replied in words that have echoed across the centuries:

> The Holy Ghost shall come upon thee, and the power of the Highest shall overshadow thee: therefore also, that holy thing which shall be born of thee shall be called the Son of God. (Luke 1:35)

Here a combination of the Spirit of God and His power is reminiscent of the story of creation in Genesis. It signifies the manifestation of a creation of God in conjunction with the old. The Virgin Mary became a receptacle of the Word of God. Thus came about the new creation—the humanity of Jesus Christ. The Koran agrees with this insight as it says, "So God createth what He pleaseth, when He decreeth a thing, He only saith to it 'Be' and it is."

It may be asked, why did God create a new reality with the virgin birth and what was the nature of this new creation? The Koran is almost silent here except a solitary reference to the similarity of Jesus Christ with Adam:

> Lo, the likeness of Jesus with God is as the likeness of Adam. He created him out of dust, then He said unto Him "Be" and he was. (Sura 3:59)

The point of similarity between Adam and Jesus consisted in their being direct creations of God as archetypes. They were not born of procreation. As Adam had no physical father, Jesus Christ too had no human father. The body of Adam was formed out of "potter's clay of black mud altered" (Sura 15:28). The body of Jesus was formed in the womb of Mary out of her flesh and bones under the creative power of the Holy Spirit of God (Sura 4:171). Since Adam had no human father but the Spirit of God was breathed into him (Sura 15:29; Gen. 2:7), in a very real sense he can be called the son of God. In the same way Jesus Christ, born of Mary under the power of the Spirit of God, was the Son of God. This is exactly what the Gospel according to Luke bears testimony to. Speaking of the creative movement of the Holy Spirit upon the Virgin Mary (Luke 1:35), the angel Gabriel went on to say, "Therefore also that holy thing which shall be born of thee shall be called the Son of God." This dimension of the sonship of Jesus Christ is further elucidated in His genealogy. Having affirmed the Adam-like creation of the humanity of Jesus Christ, Luke traces His lineage back all the way to Adam. He concludes it with the highly significant statement: "Seth, which was the son of Adam, which was the son of God" (3:38).

To express it clearly in the perspective of the New Testament, Jesus Christ had two kinds of sonship. First of all, He was the eternal Son of God begotten but not created. Again, He became the Son of God having been born miraculously of the Virgin Mary. In this capacity He was created but not begotten. Adam was the son of God on God's side. On the side of creation below him, he could justifiably be called "the son of dust" (or "potter's clay of black mud altered," Sura 15:28) as it is written, "For dust thou art" (Gen. 3:19). Similarly, Jesus Christ, being born under the Holy Spirit and power of God, was the Son of God. But on the side of creation below Him He was the Son of Mary. It is interesting that the Koran too prefers to call Him "Son of Mary." It does not mention Joseph, His legal father.

The Koran leaves us alone after having touched briefly on the case for an analogy between the creation of Adam and Jesus Christ. It gives us no enlightenment as to the divine purpose in creating another like Adam. Here Muslims may ask "those who read the Scripture before them." According to the Bible, God performs miracles publicly to confirm and prove His message as well as messengers. He also manifests His miraculous power not in public but in comparative secrecy to further plans of His salvation and new creation. The creation of Adam was such a miracle. So also the creation of "Jesus, the Son of Mary." The birth of Jesus Christ was not a sporadic manifestation of God's creative power as it might appear from the passing reference, in the Koran, to His likeness to Adam. It was the very heart of God's plan to redeem fallen humanity and a creation subjected to vanity (Rom. 8:20). Adam, who was created in the image of God (Gen. 1:26), fell from his destiny due to sin. This disease of sin which first infected Adam and Eve did not terminate with them. On the contrary, it became a hereditary moral epidemic. As a result, not only the first parents of humanity sinned, but "all have sinned and come short of the glory of God!" (Rom. 3:23). This pernicious corruption of human nature is known to everyone who takes time to look dispassionately into his own moral life and relationship with God. The truth about it all is described by Saint Paul out of his own life:

> For I know that in me (that is, in my flesh,) dwelleth no good thing: for to will is present with me; but how to perform that which is good I find not. For the good that I would I do not: but the evil which I would not, that I do. (Rom. 7:18, 19)

In order to break the vicious circle of human sinfulness, God did something literally out of this world. It confounded human wisdom and took the inimical powers of darkness completely by surprise. Once, speaking before a Jewish audience about Jesus Christ, Saviour of the World, Saint Paul quoted from Habakkuk:

> Behold, ye despisers, and wonder, and perish: for I work a work in your days, a work which ye shall in no wise believe, though a man declare it unto you. (Acts 13:41)

This astounding work of God, that Paul was referring to, was accomplished by the incarnation of the Son of God himself. As He became flesh to dwell among us, He also became the beginning of God's new creation. The old creation began with creatures below Adam and culminated in the creation of Adam. The new creation of God was inaugurated about two thousand years ago. It began in the One created like Adam, directly by God, but superior to him in stature. Adam was created out of dust and became a living soul when the breath of life was infused into him by God. Jesus' body—His humanity—was created out of Mary by the creative power and Spirit of God, and the Word of God came to tabernacle in it. In other words, if we define the first Adam "a rational animal," the last Adam should be defined as "divine-human." In the last Adam, the vicious circle of sin since first Adam was broken. Also, a decisive victory over the arch enemy, Satan and his hosts, was won for the redemption of man and renewal of the whole creation:

> For as by one man's disobedience many were made sinners, so by the obedience of one shall many be made righteous. (Rom. 5:19)

The superiority of the last Adam over the first appears to have been recognized by the Koran, though indirectly and in a rather difficult passage:

> And [remember] when thy Lord said unto the angels: "Lo! I am creating a mortal out of potter's clay of black mud altered, so when I have made him and have breathed into him of my spirit, do ye all fall down, prostrating yourselves unto him." So the angels fell prostrate, all of them together, save "Iblis" [Satan]. He refused to be among the prostrate. He said, "O Iblis, what aileth thee that thou art not among the prostrate?" He said, "Why should I prostrate myself unto a mortal whom thou hast created out of potter's clay of black mud altered?" He said, "Then go thou forth from hence, for verily thou art an outcast." And lo! the curse shall be upon thee till the day of Judgment. (Sura 15:28-35, Pickethall)

Here is an interesting story regarding the fall of Satan and his expulsion from paradise. The occasion was the creation of Adam. God gave a rather unusual command to all His angels to fall prostrate before Adam as soon as He breathed His spirit into the body made of "potter's clay of black mud altered." Satan refused to obey God, pleading the impropriety of such a command. He did not relish the idea of having to fall prostrate before a being made of clay. It is interesting to note that, according to the story, Adam was created a mortal despite the breath of the Spirit of God. However, Satan's refusal to do homage to Adam was not just due to this factor of mortality. According to Sura 7:12 (Pickethall):

> He said, "What hindered thee that thou didst not fall prostrate when I bade thee?" [Iblis] said, "I am better than him. Thou created me out of fire while he thou didst create of mud."

The story, as a whole, involves a difficult issue. Why did God order all His angels to fall prostrate before a being inferior to them in nature? This manner of prostration is reserved for the worship of God. It was not proper, therefore, to employ it in showing respect to creatures, including Adam. Realizing the problem involved in the use of the term "Sajda" (prostration) in the passage under discussion, Jalal al-Din made the following observation:

> The original word signifies properly, to prostrate one self till the forehead touches the ground, which is the humblest posture of adoration and strictly due to God only; but it is sometimes used to express civil worship or homage which may be paid to creatures. (W. T. Wherry, *A Comprehensive Commentary on the Quran*, Vol. I, p. 301)

Despite Jalal al-Din's apology, strictly speaking, "Sajda" (prostration) is due only to God. That is why the commentator did not support adequately the exception he has made to the rule, from the Koran. The "Wahhabis," who consider themselves strict Muslims and true Monotheists, forbid worship of any creature. God alone deserves to be worshipped, according to them. They would not allow "Sajda" to a civil authority—the kind of prostration which is meant to be used in prayers to God. Even if we allow prostration before high civil authorities, with Jalal al-Din, the objection of Satan before God was still valid. He was created out of fire. Hence he was superior to Adam. Adam should have prostrated himself before God's angels rather than the other way about. Moreover, it is true that strictly speaking prostration before any being other than God is a practice against monotheism and spirit of the Koran, as Wahhabis would say.

There are two alternatives involved in the Koranic story that God required His angels to fall prostrate in homage to an inferior being, Adam. Either it means that adoration and homage by prostration by a superior being to an inferior creature is justifiable—a position strongly resented by Satan. Or, one may hold that the being to be adored by all the angels of God was not a mere creature. The first position is hard to maintain. God would not allow even a hint of idolatry by commanding His angels to adore a mere creature in a way meant for His worship. The second possibility has a lot in its favor from the Koran, Patristic tradition, and the Bible.

As it has been mentioned already, the Koran affirms that Jesus, in the eyes of God, is like Adam. In regard to some early church fathers, Sale writes:

> The occasion of the devil's fall has some affinity with an opinion which has been pretty much entertained among Christians viz., that the angels be-

ing informed of God's intentions to create man after His own image, and to dignify human nature by Christ assuming it, some of them thinking their glory to be eclipsed thereby, envied man's happiness and so revolted. (Sale, *Koran*, p. 5., note b)

These early Christians did not allow the possibility of God asking His angels to do homage in prostration before Adam. But they did believe in a plausible reason for the downfall of Satan—envy not only of the initial status of Adam, but of the assumption of the human nature by the Son of God. The Gnostic Ebionites, before Islam, had a version of the story very much similar to the early Christian version. According to it, the pre-existent Christ-Spirit descended on the first Adam. It successively manifested itself through the patriarchs and finally came to be clothed in the body of the last Adam (Epiphanius Haer XIX). Here Jesus is regarded like Adam on whom Christ-Spirit came to dwell. Mani believed that the primeval man was the prototype not only of mankind, but also of celestial Jesus. He made a distinction between the primeval man and the first man—Adam (A.V.W. Jackson: *Researches in Manichianism*. Cambridge University Press, p. 304). According to Mandaen theology, the fire-angels came and made a submission to Adam and Eve, but the devil departed from the word of his Lord and was imprisoned for that reason. The Mandaeans are known as "Sabians" in the Koran (cf. J. B. Lightfoot, *Dissertations on the Apostolic Age*, p. 390, n. 3.).

The Injil mentions adoration of the last Adam by angels. An angel announced the good news of His advent to shepherds in the field:

> For unto you is born this day in the city of David, a Saviour which is Christ the Lord. (Luke 2:11)

He called the child "Saviour" and "the Lord." He is the Lord of mankind and angels alike, worthy of their worship and adoration. That is why as soon as the angel delivered his message, a multitude of the heavenly host, accompanying him, fell spontaneously into a hymn of praise to God saying, "Glory to God in the highest and on earth peace and goodwill toward men" (v. 14). Angels ministered to Jesus Christ as He faced the archenemy of mankind, Satan, in the wilderness (Mark 1:13). He told a bewildered Nathaniel, "Verily, verily, I say unto you, Hereafter ye shall see the heaven open, and the angels of God ascending and descending upon the Son of man" (John 1:51). This promise of Jesus Christ belongs, possibly, to His Second Advent. In connection with that great event in sacred history, we read of angels worshipping the last Adam in words very much similar to those used in Sura 15:29 of the Koran. It is written:

> And again, when he bringeth in the first begotten into the world, he saith,
> And let all the angels of God worship him. (Hebrews 1:6)

The One who is to be worshipped by angels at the express command of God is not a mere creature. Only God must be worshipped, as Scripture makes it plain time and again. This person who deserves worship is the Incarnate Son of God. Having been born of the Virgin Mary, in the likeness of Adam, He has become the first-born of many brethren (Rom. 8:29)—the

Archetype of a divine humanity called the "Children of God." As to the term "first-born," as it is used in the scriptural reference under review, C. Bernhard Moll comments:

> The term "prototokos" is not identical in meaning with "monogenes." The latter epithet represents this as an exclusive relation which no being sustains to God, except the Messiah. The former especially signalizes His preeminence in the relations belonging to the Messiah whether to the creation (Col. 1:5) or to the theocratic children of God (Rom. 8:29; Col. 1:18; Heb. 2:10; Rev. 1:5) partly in respect to the mode and time of His entrance on the stage of being, partly in respect to position, dignity and power. As the word stands here with no limiting epithet, it is to be taken without any special reference as a *terminus technicus*, founded on Psalm LXXXIX:28. To this Messianic King and Son of God the angels, by divine command, are to render adoring homage. (*Epistle to the Hebrews*, "A Commentary on the Holy Scriptures," p. 37)

The terms "last Adam" and the "First-born," as used in Scripture, are indicative of the same truth. They speak of the creative incursion of the eternal Word of God into human history in order to inaugurate a new creation. In brief, the eternal Son of God came down to tabernacle with us. Having become the Son of Mary through a creative miracle of the virgin birth, He became the Son of God in the sense Adam was the son of God. Thus He inaugurated a process of new creation which is meant to transform ultimately not only all those who believe on Him, but also the entire old order of things.

The title "Son of Mary" is used only once in the Injil (Mark 6:3). It has been surmised that the title passed on to the Koran through Ethiopic channels. Its use in the Koran belongs to a period when the second group of emigrants from Abyssinia returned. T. Parrinder points out:

> The Abyssinians were divided in their interpretation of the nature of Jesus, some maintaining that He was human only, though divinity was later infused into Him. The normal Monophysite view which dominates the Ethiopian and Coptic churches, allows Jesus even less humanity. It does not appear from Christological controversies that the title "Son of Mary" was used in story or liturgy of Abyssinia. (Parrinder, *Jesus in the Quran*, p. 25)

It is plausible that the adoptionists in Abyssinia called Jesus "the Son of Mary," who was infused with divinity at a given time in His life. This point of view, being heretical, is not expected to find its way into the church liturgy or folklore. The use of the title by the prophet could also be accounted for by Nestorian influence on him, which is detectable in other parts of the Koran too. The title may also have found favor with the prophet on account of its use in the Arabic and Syriac (apocryphal) Gospels of Infancy. To the Nestorians, the One born of the virgin was the Son of Mary because she was "anthropotokos" (bearer of the humanity of Christ) and not "Theotokos" (bearer of God).

This important insight is preserved even in a famous messianic prophecy first given through the prophet Isaiah (9:6) and then echoed at the time of its fulfillment in the Gospels:

For unto us a child is born, unto us a Son is given: and the government shall be upon his shoulder and his name shall be called Wonderful, Counsellor, The mighty God, The everlasting Father, The Prince of Peace.

Here a distinction is maintained between child who is "born" and a Son who is "given." As to the given Son, the description that follows clearly shows that He is God. "The child born" indicates the human nature of Jesus Christ. In that capacity He can be called "Son of Mary" or "Son of God" in the sense Adam was the son of God.

Chapter 8

The Messiah and the Prophet

The word "Al-Masih" (the Messiah) was well known in Arabia before Islam. The Koran uses it several times. In two places it occurs by itself (4:172; 9:30). Elsewhere, it is used with the expression "Son of Mary" (5:17, 72, 75; 9:31), or with "Jesus Son of Mary" (3:45; 4:157). It appears that the designation ("Al-Masih") is used as a proper name only in 3:45. In this connection it has been suggested that the definite article "Al" (the) is not used in the Koran with non-Arabic names. But we must note that the designation had been arabacized long before its use in the Koran. Hence, it is reasonable to maintain that "Al-Masih" has been used as the proper name of Jesus in the Koran.

Taking the name to be of Arabic origin, Muslim scholars have suggested interesting derivations. Some say it is derived from "Saha"—to travel. Jesus is believed to have travelled much. Others have derived the word from "Masah"—to smear. There are authorities like Al-Baidhawi and Zamakshari who reject all attempts to derive it from an Arabic root. They acknowledge it to be a foreign vocabulary in the Koran (Jeffery, op. cit., p. 265). Horovitz entertains the hypothesis that the word as used in the Koran was derived immediately from Ethiopic. It is important to mention that the title "Al-Masih" occurs only in the late chapters of the Koran at a time when the prophet's knowledge about the people of the Book was much advanced. In brief, it is reasonable to maintain that the word "Al-Masih" had become a part and parcel of the Arabic language before Islam. Also, that it came to Arabic through the Ethiopic or the Syriac language. But it originated as a technical term of religious import only with the Bible.

According to the Bible the title "Messiah" means "the anointed one." Holy things were dedicated to God by anointing. When Jacob anointed the stones at Bethel, God recognized this consecration (Gen. 28:18; 35:14). The Tabernacle and its furniture were anointed to set them apart for divine services (Ex. 30:26; 40:10; Lev. 2:1). It is significant that no oil was to be poured on sin offering (Lev. 5:11; Num. 5:15). During the days of the first Temple we learn of the holy oil in custody of the priests. It was compounded of olive oil, cinnamon, cassia, flowing myrrh, and root of the cane. It was used only for special anointings prescribed by the Law and its unauthorized preparation was strictly forbidden (Ex. 30:33). We hear of several things missing from the second Temple—the Temple where Jesus Christ taught and worshipped. Among them was the very formula of mixing the sacred oil. The high priest could no more be anointed with oil prepared in the traditional way prescribed by the Law.

Temple priests were set apart for God by anointing. Aaron was anointed twice. It was true of other high priests also. The first time oil was poured on his head after he was robed before the sacrifice of consecration (Lev. 8:12; Ps. 133:2). He was anointed a second time by sprinkling after the sacrifice. Ordinary priests were sprinkled with oil once only after the application of the blood of sacrifice. Hence the high priest came to be called the anointed priest (Lev. 4:3, 5; 6:22). In other words, the fully anointed priest was twice anointed and that was true of the high priest only (Edersheim, *The Temple*. Eerdman Co., pp. 61, 62).

An appointment to kingship in Israel was secured by anointing. Saul and David were anointed and set apart for God (1 Sam. 10:1; 16:13). It is noteworthy that this act of anointing on behalf of God was accompanied by the gift of the Spirit of God in both cases. When David was anointed to replace Saul, the Spirit descended on him but departed from Saul. David became a thrice-anointed king. He was anointed once when he was chosen to be the king of Israel. He was anointed again when he became the king of Judah and a third time when he came to be the ruler of United Israel (2 Sam. 2:4; 5:3).

At God's command, individuals were set apart for the prophetic office by anointing. Thus Elijah was commanded to anoint Elisha. In Ps. 105:15, the words "anointed" and "prophet" are used synonymously. In short, anointing was used in the Old Testament times to set apart things and people for God. High priests, priests, kings, and prophets were consecrated this way. Anointing, as sanctioned by God, was the human counterpart of divine approval often revealed by a special enduement by the Holy Spirit.

According to the record in the New Testament, when Jesus Christ began His ministry, He was anointed by the Holy Spirit. This consecration came over and above His unique anointing in terms of the way the Virgin Mary conceived Him (Luke 1:35). At the outset of His ministry He was baptized by John the Baptist in the river Jordan. God confirmed this anointing with water by pouring out the oil of His gladness upon Him: The Holy Spirit descended upon Jesus Christ in the form of a dove. The physical symbol was indicative of the sinlessness of God's Messiah. Also it enabled John to identify the Promised One, for he testified:

> And I knew him not: but he that sent me to baptize with water, the same said unto me, Upon whom thou shalt see the Spirit descending, and remaining on him, the same is he which baptizeth with the Holy Ghost. And I saw, and bear record that this is the Son of God. (John 1:33, 34)

What John the Baptist actually saw with his own eyes, as he baptized Jesus Christ, is detailed in the synoptics. We read in Mark:

> And it came to pass in those days, that Jesus came from Nazareth of Galilee, and was baptized of John in Jordan. And straightway coming up out of water, he saw the heavens opened, and the Spirit like a dove descending upon him. (1:9-11)

Along with the visible symbol used by the Holy Spirit to indicate the sinlessness of the Messiah of God, there was an audible testimony from God the Father:

> And lo a voice from heaven saying, This is my beloved Son, in whom I am well pleased. (Matt. 3:17)

Experiencing the unusual phenomenon following upon the baptism of Jesus Christ, John was thrilled to declare to his hearers that not only the long-awaited Messiah of God was come but the wonder of wonders, He was the very Son of God. Moreover, in a flash of astounding revelation, he realized that this sinless Son of God who had assumed human form was going to be the fulfillment of the Hebrew sacrificial system, nay, that of the whole mankind, as the Lamb of God:

> And looking upon Jesus as he walked, he saith, Behold the Lamb of God. (John 1:36)

The Koran acknowledges that the mission of John the Baptist was to bear witness to Jesus Christ, "the Word from God":

> There Zecharias called on his Lord and said, "Lord give me from thee a good offspring, for thou art the hearer of prayer." And the angels called him, while he stood praying in the chamber, saying, "Verily God promiseth thee a son named John who shall bear witness to the Word from God." (Sura 3:38, 39)

Though the word for "angels" in the passage above is in the plural form, yet several Muslim scholars believe that it was the angel Gabriel who spoke to Zecharias. The expression "Word from God" occurs also in the birth narratives of Jesus Christ. It plainly reaffirms His divinity, in the context of His messianic call. This evident sense of the statement under consideration does not suit the bias of Muslim commentators against the divinity of Christ. Hence they have sought to explain it away one way or the other.

Al Baidhawi says that the expression "Word from God" refers to Jesus Christ who is so called because He was conceived by the word of the command of God, without a father (Sale, *Koran*, p. 48, n. 4). Using this interesting logic, Adam too should be called "the Word from God" because he also was created out of dust by a word of the command of God (see Sura 3:59). But nowhere does the Koran mention him by that designation. It is an expression uniquely used of Jesus Christ. The Koran confirms what is recorded as to the witness of John the Baptist about Jesus Christ in the New Testament. He testified, "This is the Son of God!" (John 1:35). The expressions "the Son of God" and "the Word from God" indicate the self-same truth about Jesus Christ—His divinity. In other words, according to both the New Testament and the Koran, Jesus the Messiah was Emmanuel— "God with us" in human form.

The Koran refers to the anointing of Jesus for His messianic ministry in its own way: "We strengthened Him [Jesus] by the Holy Spirit" (Sura 2:87; also, 253). The Holy Spirit in this above reference and its like is taken by Muslim scholars to mean the angel Gabriel. This interpretation is given in line with their general belief as to the way God sends revelations to His prophets. But there is no mention in the Koran of Gabriel bringing revelations to Moses or Jesus Christ. In the case of the latter, Gabriel is mentioned only in the birth narratives—something in accord with the Gospel record. However, in the entire ministry of Jesus Christ, as recorded in the Koran, Gabriel plays no part. The Evangel (Gospel) which was given Him was reportedly a direct revelation from God (Sura 5:46), without any angelic mediation. It is arbitrary to interpret the "Holy Spirit" as angel Gabriel in the context of the messianic ministry of Jesus Christ. An examination of the various references to the "Spirit" in the Koran will shown the variety of connotations involved in it.

1. "We strengthened Him (Jesus) by the Holy Spirit (Ruh al-Qudus)" (Sura 2:87).
2. "We strengthened Him (Jesus) by the Holy Spirit (Ruh al-Qudus)" (Sura 2:253).
3. "The Messiah Jesus Son of Mary is only an apostle of God, and His Word which He conveyed into Mary and a Spirit (proceeding) from Him (Ruhun min hu)" (4:171).
4. "When I strengthened thee (Jesus) with the Holy Spirit (Ruh al-Qudus)" (5:110).
5. "He will cause the angels to descend with the Spirit (Ruh) on whom He pleaseth among His servants, bidding them warn that there be no God but me" (16:2).
6. "The Holy Spirit (Ruh al-Qudus) hath brought it down with truth from thy Lord" (16:102).
7. "They will ask thee of the spirit (Al-Ruh). Say the Spirit proceedeth at my Lord's command but of knowledge only a little to you is given" (17:85).
8. "The faithful Spirit (Al-Ruh al-Amin) hath come down with it (the Koran)" (26:193).
9. "He sendeth forth the spirit (Al-Ruh) at His own behest on whomsoever of His servants He pleaseth" (40:15).
10. "On the hearts of these (the faithful) hath God graven the faith, and with a spirit proceeding from Him (Rhuhun Min hu) hath strengthened them" (8:23).
11. "The angels and the spirit (Al-Ruh) ascend to him in a day whose length is fifty-two thousand years" (70:4).
12. "Therein descend the angels and the spirit (Al-Ruh) by permission of their Lord for every matter" (97:4).
13. "Thus we have sent the spirit (Al-Ruh) to thee with a revelation by our command" (42:52).
14. "And we sent our spirit (Ruhi-na) to her (Mary) and he took before her the form of a perfect man" (19:17).
15. "Into whom (Mary) we breathed of our spirit (Ruhi-na)" (21:91).
16. "Into whose womb (i.e., Mary's) we breathed of our spirit (Min Ruhina)" (66:12).
17. "And breathed of His Spirit (min Ru-hi) into him (Adam)" (32:8).
18. "And when I shall have finished him (Adam) and breathed of my spirit (Min Ruhi) into him" (15:29).
19. "And when I have formed him (Adam) and breathed of my spirit (Min

Ruhi) into him" (38:72).

Hughes says that all Muslim commentators agree that quotations nos. 1, 2, 4, 5, 6, 8, 11, 12 and 14 refer to the angel Gabriel. Nos. 3, 15 and 16 are references to Jesus the Spirit of God (Ruh Allah). Nos. 17, 18 and 19 imply the life (Ruh) breathed into Adam, while Nos. 9 and 13 speak of "the spirit of prophecy." No. 10 is supposed to refer to God's grace and strength. In regard to No. 7 there is some difference of opinion. For example, Ibn Abbas held that it referred to Gabriel while Mujahid felt that it means "beings of another world" (Dict. p. 605). It is plain from the exhaustive references from the Koran that the word "Spirit" by no means refers to Gabriel alone. In the case of Jesus Christ, even in the virgin birth narratives, only one reference to the Spirit is supposed by Muslim scholars to imply Gabriel. In other references (Nos. 15, 16 above) the spirit breathed into the womb of Mary is not (for obvious reasons) understood, by the commentators, to mean Gabriel. It is something similar to God breathing His breath of life into Adam (see above 17, 18, 19).

The case for Jesus Christ being strengthened by the Holy Spirit—equal to being aided by Gabriel, stands on a particular theory of revelation popular among Muslims. However, since their prophet received revelations of the Koran through Gabriel, it should not make it an inviolable rule for others. As a matter of fact, on the basis of the Koran itself, there were three prophets who were unaided by the angel Gabriel or any other angel. These were Adam, Moses and Jesus. They received revelations directly from God. The Koran testifies to an intelligence in Adam superior even to the angels of God. When God was creating Adam His angels protested due to envy. God having created him taught him names of all animals and plants. Then He called upon angels to compete with Adam in naming those names. They could not do so and acknowledged their inferiority at this point (Sura 2:30-34). Obviously, the names and classification of animals and plants were revealed to Adam directly by God. If Gabriel had been a messenger of this revelation, he should have been able to compete with Adam and establish angelic superiority over him. Again, as mentioned earlier, God spoke directly with Moses (7:143) and gave him tablets "with lessons to be drawn from all things and explanation of all things" (7:145). Similarly, Jesus Christ received the Evangel directly from God (5:46).

In order to shed more light on the Koranic reference to a person being strengthened by the spirit, we may refer to a crucial passage:

> On the hearts of these [the faithful] hath God given faith and with a spir-
> it proceeding from Him [Ruhun Minhu] hath strengthened them. (58:22)

Here, the strengthening of believers by the spirit proceeding from God could not possibly mean that they are aided by the angel Gabriel. How could one angel attend to the needs of millions of people? This would give ordinary believers a privilege equal to choice men of God and keep Gabriel busy to the end of time! (Moreover, only prophets are believed to be the ones who had visitations from Gabriel to receive revelations from God.) It is manifest that in the passage under review believers are to be aided by the Spirit of God who is not an angel. To put such an exciting possibility in its proper perspective, let us refer to the New Testament teaching on the Holy Spirit and His dealings with true believers. Jesus Christ taught that one of the functions of the Holy Spirit is to strengthen and aid them in their spiritual lives. We have it in His own words:

> And I will pray the Father, and he will give you another ["Paraklitos"] that he may abide with you for ever. . . . But the ["Paraklitos"], which is the Holy Ghost, whom the Father will send in my name, he shall teach you all things, and bring all things to your remembrance, whatsoever I have said unto you. (John 14:16, 26)

The Holy Spirit of God is called "Paraklitos." It is translated "Comforter" in John 14:16, 26; 15:26; 16:7. It is rendered "Advocate" in 1 John 2:1. It means one called to the side of another to help or counsel. As we have observed earlier, the Holy Spirit aids the believers in their spiritual life and warfare against satanic powers of darkness. As an example, the Scripture speaks of the positive aid of the Holy Spirit for believers in prayer:

> Likewise the Spirit also helpeth our infirmities: for we know not what we should pray for as we ought; but the Spirit [himself] maketh intercession for us with groanings which cannot be uttered. (Romans 8:26)

The Holy Spirit is also indispensable for believers as they labor for the extension of the Kingdom of God. After the first disciples of Jesus Christ had seen Him risen and fellowshiped with Him for forty days, they were set on fire to go out into the world proclaiming His Gospel everywhere. But Jesus Christ advised them not to venture abroad in their own power and zeal alone. They were to tarry in Jerusalem and wait for the day when the Holy Spirit was to be poured out upon them to enable them to be truly powerful witnesses of the risen Saviour all over the world (Acts 1:3, 8). This is another dimension of the "aiding" and "strengthening" ministry of the Holy Spirit.

It is clear now that Jesus Christ was strengthened by the Holy Spirit in the sense of the anointing He received at the very outset of His messianic ministry. As the Bible tells us, this experience at His baptism testified to His absolute sinlessness and divinity. The "We" of the Koran in connection with Jesus' anointing of the Holy Spirit is the Father in heaven (Sura 2:87), who according to the Biblical record, declared His pleasure with His Son (Matt. 3:17).

To place the work of Jesus Christ in its proper perspective let us briefly recapture some of the messianic ideas current in His time. The Hebrews of those days were alive with earnest messianic expectations. These, their dreams and visions, consisted of a variety of ideas which often were loosely related to each other both in popular and official thinking. Some of these lines of thinking came remarkably close to what Jesus Christ taught and demonstrated through His unique life and work. However, such rare intuitions and insights, based on the Old Testament Scripture, were usually confined to a few who were spiritually mature. They never found currency among the Hebrew populace.

As we have observed, these interesting speculations about the Messiah were not left to imagination run riot. Rather, they were anchored in the Law, prophets, Psalms and extra-canonical literature of the intertestamental period when the voice of prophecy was silent. It is also significant that by the time Jesus Christ appeared on the scene, the messianic excitement of the Hebrew nation was running high and desperate. There were people who even took to predicting the exact time of the advent of the Messiah. According to one speculation preserved in the Talmud, the Messiah was to appear 4,000 years after the creation. Curiously enough, this reckoning would fix the date during the time of Jesus Christ. Along with an attempt at predicting the time of the appearance of the Messiah, the Talmud expressly taught that the Messiah's coming did not depend on repentance, nor any other condition that may be fulfilled by Israel. It depended on the free grace and sheer mercy of God (see Edersheim, *The Life and Times of Jesus the Messiah*, Vol. I, p. 170).

The ancient synagogues found many references to the Messiah in the Old Testament. According to Edersheim, the number of such references runs as high as 456. Of these, 75 were found in the Pentateuch (Torah of Islam), 243 in the Prophets, and 138 in the Hegiographs. The messianic application of these passages is supported by more than 558 references to the most ancient writings (Edersheim, ibid., p. 163). The rabbinic comments on messianic times frequently state that all the miracles and deliverance of Israel's past will be re-enacted in the days of the Messiah. Summarizing the situation Edersheim writes:

> Accordingly, a careful perusal of their scripture quotations shows, that the main postulates of the New Testament concerning the Messiah are fully supported by Rabbinic statements. Thus, such doctrines as the premundane existence of the Messiah, His elevation above Moses, and even above angels; His representative character; His cruel sufferings and derision; His violent death; and that for His people; His work on behalf of the living and of the dead; His redemption and restoration of Israel; the opposition of the Gentiles; their Judgment and conversion; the prevalence of His law; the Universal blessings of the latter days, and His kingdom—can be clearly deduced from unquestioned passages in ancient Rabbinic writings. Only, as we might expect, all is there indistinct, incoherent, unexplained, and from a much lower standpoint. At best, it is the lower stage of yet unfulfilled prophecy—the haze when the sun is about to rise, not the blaze when it has risen. Most painfully is this felt in connection with one element on which the New Testament most insists. There is, indeed, in Rabbinic writings frequent reference to the sufferings, and even death of the Messiah, and these are brought into connection with our sins—as how it could be otherwise in view of Isaiah Liii and other passages—and in one most remarkable comment the Messiah is represented as willingly taking upon Himself all these sufferings, on condition that all Israel—the living, the dead, and those yet unborn—should be saved, and that, in consequence of His work, God and Israel should be reconciled, and Satan cast into hell. But there is only the most indistinct reference to the removal of sin by the Messiah, in the sense of vicarious sufferings. (Edersheim, ibid., pp. 164, 165)

It needs to be mentioned that there were also solitary protests against the messianic excitement of those days. It is well known that the famous rabbi Hilliel asserted that all messianic prophecies were fulfilled in King Hezekiah of old. However, despite such a negative pronouncement from a leading authority, the people's longing for the day of the Messiah kept gaining momentum. Due to the predisposition of the common man to materialistic thinking and stress of adverse political circumstances, the popular dreams about the Messiah and His kingdom tended toward the mundane and the gross. They talked about an earthly messianic kingdom, sovereign over other nations, that would mean the golden age of peace, prosperity and longevity for the people of Israel. It was expected to be ushered in by supernatural means, yet it was surmised that the people could lend a hand to God to hasten its advent. Scattered among the masses there were those called Zealots. They were always ready to join any revolution that was calculated to hasten the messianic age. There was also a small but powerful party of the Jews called the Sadducees who avoided all messianic speculations and even disregarded prophetic utterances supporting them in favor of their own traditions.

When Jesus Christ launched His ministry, the national ethos was rife with quasi spiritual and nationalistic expectations from the Messiah and His kingdom. It was something poles apart from what the Scriptures had to say. Jesus Christ sought carefully to avoid any hint of identification with the current popular misconceptions as He manifested the fulfillment of the Law and the prophets in His own person and work (Luke 16:16). He made an unmistakably clear distinction between the Kingdom of God, which He came to establish in love and righteousness, and the kingdom of the world which is built upon lust, hatred and bloodshed.

The Temptation narrative depicts one of the crucial achievements of Jesus Christ (Matt. 4:5; Luke 4:5). After His baptism in the river Jordan, He received His messianic anointing and commission from the Father. Immediately He was led to the wilderness for His first order of business in the world He came to save. It was a single-combat confrontation with Satan, the tyrant god of the Godless world. Man was created to be a free member of the Kingdom of God. But through the deception of sin, he chose to rebel against God and become a bondsman of Satan. As sin continues to abound, Satan goes on ruling over individuals and kingdoms of the world in opposition to God. Having vanquished the archenemy of the human race in a direct encounter, Jesus Christ inaugurated His great messianic ministry of redemption. He described the import of this, His victory, thus:

> How can a man enter into a strong man's house, and spoil his goods, except he first bind the strong man? and then he will spoil his house. (Matthew 12:29)

All through His days in flesh, Jesus Christ continued the work of "spoiling the goods" of the slave driver of sinners, freeing prisoners from spiritual darkness into His marvelous light and peace with God. His unique mission has been summarized in the words of the apostle Peter, an eye-witness:

> The word which God sent unto the children of Israel, preaching peace by Jesus Christ (he is the Lord of all:) That word, I say, ye know, which was published throughout all Judaea, and began from Galilee, after the baptism

which John preached; how God anointed Jesus of Nazareth with the Holy Ghost and with power: who went about doing good and healing all that were oppressed of the devil; for God was with him. And we were witnesses of all things which he did both in the land of the Jews, and in Jerusalem; whom they slew and hanged on the tree: him God raised up the third day, and showed him openly; not to all the people, but unto witnesses chosen before of God, even to us, who did eat and drink with him after he rose from the dead. (Acts 10:36-41)

The people who were waiting for the advent of the Messiah did not appreciate the profound difference between the Kingdom of God and kingdoms of the world. Jesus Christ came to establish His kingdom upon the earth, yet He declared before Pilate:

My kingdom is not of this world: if my kingdom were of this world then would my servants fight, that I should not be delivered to the Jews: but now is my kingdom not from hence. (John 18:36)

To avoid all misconceptions and even a hint of encouragement of pseudo messianic expectations, Jesus Christ chose the self-designation, "Son of Man." But He acknowledged indirectly the homage of others as they called Him the Messiah. He also quoted numerous Old Testament messianic passages in the course of His teaching and discussed them with His disciples, Jewish rabbis and people at large. He left the profound impression on all those who were drawn to Him that He was truly the Messiah but not after the popular expectations. In His personal life, teaching, and public ministry He combined the various current messianic hopes into a creative whole which no mortal could have imagined or dreamed about. This, His divine fulfillment of the Law and the prophets, encompassed all the former fragmentary revelations in such a unique way that the whole was infinitely more than the parts—spanning time and eternity!

He chose the self-designation "Son of Man" as an apocalyptic and comprehensive representation of His person and mission. When His disciples or other people called Him "the Son of David" or "the Son of God," He accepted these designations, often by implication and a reticence calculated to arouse faith of the hearers in himself and a sense of expectancy as to His further self-revelation.

The name "Son of Man" has a twofold significance: It is employed when Christ's claim to power and authority are stated both during His lifetime and in His future kingdom of glory (Mark 2:10; Matt. 12:8). It is also used in immediate connection with His human nature, lowliness, poverty, suffering and death (Matt. 14:21; 10:45; 8:31). Thus the title involves a combination of the two contrasted ideas of the Old Testament scripture—the transcendent conception of the apocalyptic and the Isaiahic ideal of the suffering servant. It is to be noted that, according to Isaiah, the Suffering Servant of the Lord is also "the Prophet" who is the anointed revealer of truth. Jehovah makes His mouth like a sharp sword (Isa. 49:2) and puts His Spirit upon Him so that He shall bring forth judgment to the Gentiles (Isa. 42:1; 59:21; 61:1).

Jesus the Messsiah as the Prophet

Many of the contemporaries of Jesus may have experienced difficulty in recognizing His messiahship. But they appear to have no difficulty in acknowledging Him as a mighty prophet (Luke 7:16; Matt. 21:11; Mark 6:15; Matt. 21:26; Luke 24:19; John 4:19; 6:14; 7:40; 9:17). According to a report from His disciples, some of the Jews surmised that He was Jeremiah or like one of the other prophets of old. There were others who thought He was John the Baptist who came back to life. Still others were of the opinion that He was Elijah whose return before the advent of the Messiah was expected by them (Matt. 16:13, 14). Jesus Christ, too, claimed the title of prophet for himself. When He opened His ministry in Nazareth, He read from Isaiah 61:1:

> The Spirit of the Lord is upon me, because he hath anointed me to preach good tidings to the poor. (See also Mark 6:4; Luke 13:33.)

He started His discourse in a manner typical of a prophet by declaring, "This day is this scripture fulfilled in your ears" (Luke 4:18, 21). Toward the conclusion of His ministry in referring to the immanence of His violent death, He placed himself in line with the former Old Testament prophets, foretelling that like them He could not perish out of Jerusalem (Matt. 23:29 ff.; Luke 13:33). It is also significant that in the parable of the Vineyard, the familiar Old Testament figure for the Kingdom of God, He deliberately made himself the last of the long line of the martyrs and messengers of God. Only He was the very heir of the kingdom, while other prophets of Israel were sent as mere servants. He was sent as God's final gesture of love and reconciliation calling Israel to repentance (Luke 20:9-18).

The Koran has no hesitation at all in declaring the prophetic dignity of Jesus Christ:

> Whereupon the child said, "Verily I am the servant of God, He hath given me the book of the Gospel, and hath appointed me a prophet." (The Koran, 19:30)

Going by the Koranic narrative, Jesus Christ, unlike other prophets, was a born-prophet. He began to exercise His prophetic call while He was still a babe in the cradle. (See also Sura 19:29.) But this, His prophetic mission, was a part of His messianic call. That is why in the Koran He is called both a prophet and the Messiah. He was like other prophets as He demonstrated some characteristics typical of a prophet. The Old Testament prophets like Moses, Isaiah, Jeremiah, and Ezekiel were introduced to their prophetic career by a voice (Isa. 6:1-8; Jer. 1:4-10; Ezek. 3:10-14, etc.).

Jesus Christ, too, began His ministry by receiving a vision from heaven after His baptism and hearing the voice of His heavenly Father (Mark 1:10, 11). He was anointed of the Spirit of God from the very conception (Luke 1:35). In agreement with this unique anointing, the Koran calls Jesus Christ, "A Spirit from God" (4:169). Al-Baidhawi states that this title, "a spirit proceeding from God," is special to Jesus Christ only (Hughes' Dictionary, p. 229).

No other prophet mentioned in the Koran was the embodiment of the

Spirit of prophecy from the very conception. This alone makes Jesus Christ a unique prophet above others. He came not to destroy but to fulfill the Law and the prophets (Matt. 5:17). That, too, makes Him superior to all prophets. However, in the humility of His spirit He decided to fulfill the prophetic tradition by observing it and then transcending it. In Him dwelt the fullness of the Godhead bodily (Col. 2:9). Therefore, His life and work soon overwhelmed the old prophetic patterns like a deluge overflowing a riverbed. In other words, He was not just a prophet but a perfect prophet because He really was more than a prophet. When He offered himself to be baptized, John the Baptist hesitated to oblige Him saying, "I have need to be baptized of thee, and comest thou to me?" (Matt. 3:14). But Jesus Christ constrained John by telling him: "Suffer it to be so now; for thus it becometh us to fulfil all righteousness. Then he suffered him" (John 3:15). John the Baptist knew Jesus Christ to be far superior to him not in the ordinary sense of the word but in an extraordinary connotation. He testified that Jesus Christ was the Son of God, while he himself was only a servant of God (John 1:34). He did not consider himself worthy even to unloose the latchet of the shoes of Jesus (Mark 1:7). The superiority of Jesus consisted in the fact that He came from above as the prince of God, while John belonged to the creaturely realm below (John 1:15; 3:31). We need to hear the testimony of Jesus Christ about the position of John the Baptist himself. He too was no ordinary prophet. Jesus Christ said:

> For I say unto you, Among those that are born of women there is not a greater prophet than John the Baptist: but he that is least in the kingdom of God is greater than he. (Luke 7:28)

Among the natural born John was the greatest prophet ever—even greater than Moses! There were two reasons for his great stature. First of all he was the last of the Hebrew prophets foretelling advent of the Messiah. As Jesus put it: "For all prophets and the Law prophesied until John" (Matt. 11:13). Secondly, John was the herald of the Messiah of God. One who came in the spirit of Elijah preparing Israel for the coming King (Matt. 11:14). Such a person of Highest prophetic stature testified to the qualitative superiority of Jesus Christ—who in His role as a prophet proved always far more than a prophet.

The baptism of Jesus Christ was a human counterpart of God the Father pouring out the Holy Spirit upon Him. It was like a prophet or king of old who received the gift of the Spirit as he was anointed with the oil of consecration. The Holy Spirit came upon Jesus in the meaningful symbol of a dove. It indicated the absolute sinlessness of the recipient. John the Baptist was enlightened by a revelation that on whomsoever he saw the Spirit descend in the form of a dove was the anointed—Messiah—of God (John 2:33). He came baptizing with water so that he might prepare the way for the long-awaited advent of the Messiah and to identify Him to the people (John 2:31). Jesus Christ was born sinless, unlike the prophet David who lamented his sinfulness saying, "In sin did my mother conceive me" (Ps. 51:5). What was true in the case of David has been true of every single prophet except Jesus Christ. His miraculous conception took place as the

Holy Spirit came upon the Virgin Mary and the creative power of God Most High overshadowed her (Luke 1:35).

As we have mentioned it already, the Koran too testifies to this in its own words. In another passage an angel from God announced to Mary that she was to receive a "holy son" (19:19). The Koran goes on to relate an interesting story about the birth of the Virgin Mary. Her mother placed her newborn daughter and her future issue under a special protection of God saying: "Lord, verily I have brought forth a female [and God well knew what she had brought forth], and a male is not like a female; I have called her Mary; and I commend her to thy protection and also her issue, against Satan driven away with stones" (3:36). In this vein there is a suggestive tradition about Mary and her child:

> Every child that is born, is touched [or stung] by Satan, and his touch makes it cry, except Mary and her Son. (Bukhari-Anbiya, Bab44, tafsir sura3, b.2. Muslim-Fadail, tradition 146, 147. Ahmad b. Hanbal. Musnad II: 233, 247 sq, 288, 292, 319, 523)

The sinlessness of Jesus Christ at birth and during His childhood was not inherently inviolable. He was subject to temptation as much as any other human being (Heb. 2:14, 17). His freedom from sin was manifested and demonstrated in the teeth of the worst temptations that the archtempter himself could devise. To meet this challenge Jesus Christ was in the wilderness. For forty days He fasted, tempted of the devil (Luke 1:2). At the end of this period of sore trial and privation, He faced the Enemy of the human race in a decisive combat. This situation was quite a contrast to the first temptation in history. At that time Adam and Eve lived in the luxury of the Garden of Eden and were well fed and cared for. They succumbed to the very first onslaught of the tempter despite serious warnings from God.

The Bible classifies all the arsenal of weapons that Satan can use against people into three categories: lust of the eye, lust of the flesh, and pride of life (1 John 1:16). All these he let loose upon the Anointed of God. But he was defeated on his own ground. Having suffered this ignominious defeat, the Devil departed from the champion of God for a season (Luke 4:13). Having lost the battle He dared not meet Jesus Christ face to face again. Now he had to resort to his usual strategy of using the demoniac hosts and human beings under his sway. The Devil could not tempt or accuse Jesus Christ of committing a single sin—neither on the Mount of Temptation nor all through His matchless life.

As we read about the life of Jesus Christ, His ministry, and His teaching recorded in the New Testament, we cannot help being moved profoundly by, among other things, His unique sinless life. This is the same impression He made upon His contemporaries, both friend and foe.

Simon Peter, having witnessed the miracle of a netful of fish, was so overwhelmed by Jesus' holiness that he cried out spontaneously, "Depart from me; for I am a sinful man, O Lord!" (Luke 5:8). Peter's reaction reminds us of Isaiah's experience when he saw the glory of God in the Temple (Isa 6:1-7).

As an example of the impact the character of Jesus Christ had on the foes, we remember the Roman centurion at the foot of the cross. When he witnessed the way Christ died, praying for His enemies, forgiving those who rejected Him, he exclaimed, "Truly this man was the Son of God" (Mark 15:39). The wife of Pilate, the governor who judged Jesus Christ, sent word to her husband, "Have thou nothing to do with this just man." He was so moved by the innocence of Christ that he went to the unusual length of washing his hands in public. Before pronouncing sentence upon Jesus under the pressure of the Jews' leaders and their mob, he announced, as he washed his hands:

> "I am innocent of the blood of this Just person: see ye to it." (Matthew 27:24. Also, John 19:6)

Judas who finally betrayed Jesus Christ was nevertheless deeply impressed by His moral purity and innocence. When he saw that Jesus was condemned, he suffered an awful remorse. He groaned, "I have sinned in that I have betrayed the innocent blood." He could not live with his guilt. He went out and hanged himself (Matt. 27:3-5).

There are noteworthy statements in the New Testament as to the unique sinlessness of Jesus Christ, based on a personal fellowship with Him. John the beloved apostle testified, "Ye know that he was manifested to take away our sins; and in him is no sin" (1 John 3:5). Peter summed up his impressions in a sermon on the day of Pentecost when he called Jesus "The Holy and Righteous One" (Acts 3:14). Again, in one of his epistles he wrote, "Christ also hath once suffered for our sins, the just for the unjust" (1 Pet. 3:18). The testimony of Paul, who met the risen Christ first on the road to Damascus, was in harmony with the testimony of those who knew Him in flesh. He says that Jesus Christ knew no sin (2 Cor. 5:21). Again, the Epistle to the Hebrews says that He was "holy, guileless, undefiled, separated from sinners" (Heb. 7:26).

Jesus Christ himself told of His total victory over sin and Satan. On one occasion He challenged His opponents, "Which of you convinceth me of sin?" (John 8:46). This challenge covered His whole life and conduct. All through His life in the flesh He was not conscious of ever violating the will of His Father in heaven (John 4:34). He always did perfectly the will of Him who sent Him (John 5:29). The Devil had no part in His life at all, as He told His disciples at the Last Supper (John 14:30). He never made a confession of personal sin. On the other hand, He forgave sinners their sins and changed their lives (Matt. 9:1-8; John 8:4-11). He claimed that He had power on earth to forgive sins (Matt. 9:6). He proved it then and continues to make good His claim in the lives of all those who come to Him by faith.

In contrast to the spotless life and sinless character of Jesus Christ, the Bible mentions sins and trespasses of saints and prophets, both great and small. God is no respecter of persons, says the Scripture (Acts 10:34). Therefore, one of the proofs of the Bible being the book of God is to be found in the way it deals with the lives of great heroes of the faith and of small. It narrates their laudable qualities as well as making mention of their sins. Jesus Christ is the only person in the Bible about whom sin is not mentioned at all, either in prophecies concerning Him or the actual account of His matchless life!

The Koran refers to sins of various prophets from Adam to Muhammad. Adam and Eve, on being convicted of sin, said:

> "O our Lord, with ourselves we have dealt unjustly: if thou forgive us not and have not pity on us, we shall surely be of those who perish." (Sura 7:23)
> Noah said: "Unless thou forgive me and be merciful to me, I shall be one of the lost." (Sura 11:47)
> Abraham said: "When I am sick, He healeth me, and who will cause me to die, and quicken me, and who, I hope, will forgive me my sins in the day of reckoning." (Sura 26:80-82)

Moses murdered a man. This was brought about by the devil (Sura 28:15). He repented of this, his sin, and prayed: "O my Lord, I have sinned to my own heart, forgive me. Then He forgave him, Lo! He is the forgiving and merciful" (Sura 28:16).

Like the above-mentioned prophets, the prophet Muhammad also is advised to seek forgiveness for his sins:

> Then have patience (O Muhammad). Lo! the promise of God is true. And ask forgiveness of thy sin, and hymn the praise of thy Lord at fall of night and early hours. (Sura 40:55, Pickethall)

The orthodox Muslims believe that prophets are either free from all sins or free at least from major sins. The Asharites hold that even the power of sinning does not exist in them. Some Shia Muslims believe that the prophets can sin but Imams are pure. Among those who maintain that the prophets can commit only lesser sins, some say that they commit these sins before inspiration (Wahi) comes to them; others, that they may do so even after inspiration has come, but that such small sins being mere frailties and slight imperfections do not really amount to sin, properly so called: All these theological positions come into clash with the teaching of the Koran, some instances of which have been quoted above. However, the Muslim commentators explain these and other similar passages from the Koran in such a way as to suit a doctrine of innocence of the prophets. Thus in dealing with the reference as to their prophet's need for forgiveness (40:55), they give various explanations:

> Some say that it refers to remission in the propagation of Islam; others to neglect in rendering thanks to God; but one popular explanation is that the Prophet was to seek pardon for sin merely as an act of worship and as an example of that confession of sin which was to be a portion of the worship rendered by his followers. If this explanation is not enough, then it is said that the word (dhanb) is used. It conveys the idea of a fault-only, or what is technically called a "little sin". The objection is that this word (dhanb) is used to describe the sin of ordinary people (9:103; 28:78; 12:29). It is quite clear, in general, that the word used to describe the sin of Muhammad does not denote a mere trivial offense, but a great sin. Again, "Ask pardon for thy sins and for believers both men and women" (48:21), is similarly explained. (Edward Sell, *Sin, Muslim ERE*, Vol. 11, p. 568)

There is another passage which deserves mention:

Verily, we have won for thee a undoubted victory, in order that God might forgive thee that which went before of thy fault and what followed after. (Sura 48:1, 2)

The commentators have sought to explain the above-mentioned reference to the prophet's sin by saying that the "former fault" refers to the sin of Adam when Muhammad was yet in the loins of his great ancestor. The "later fault" is understood as sin of the followers of Muhammad (see Sell, ibid., p. 568).

There are traditions which record the prophet praying for the forgiveness of his sins: On the authority of Aisha it is reported that the prophet used often to say:

By the praise of God, pardon me: "O God, I ask pardon of thee for my offence, and I ask of thee thy mercy."

On the authority of Abu Huraira it is recorded that Muhammad said:

I ask pardon of God and repent [return] towards Him more than seventy times a day. (Mishkat al-Masabih. Quoted by Sell, ibid., pp. 568, 569)

In the same vein there is another tradition which deserves mention here:

The prophet of God said, "In the Day of Resurrection Muslims will not be able to move and they will be greatly distressed, and will say, 'Would to God that we had asked Him to create someone to intercede for us, that we might be taken from this place, and be delivered from tribulation and sorrow?' Then these men will go to Adam, and will say: 'Thou art the father of all men, God created thee with His hand, and made thee a dweller in Paradise, and ordered His angels to prostrate themselves before thee, and taught thee the name of all things. Ask grace for us we pray thee!' And Adam will say, 'I am not of that degree of eminance as you suppose, for I committed a sin in eating of the grain which was forbidden. Go to Noah, the prophet, he was the first who was sent by God to the unbelievers on the face of the earth.' Then they will go to Noah and ask for intercession, and he will say, 'I am not of that degree which ye suppose.' And he will remember the sin which he committed in asking the Lord for the deliverance of his Son Hud, not knowing whether it was a right request or not; And he will say, 'Go to Abraham, who is the Friend of God.' Then they will go to Abraham and he will say, 'I am not of that degree which ye suppose.' And he will remember the three occasions upon which he told lies in the world; and he will say, 'Go to Moses, who is the servant, to whom God gave His law and whom He allowed to converse with Him.' And they will go to Moses and Moses will say, 'I am not that degree which ye suppose.' And he will remember the sin which he committed in slaying a man, and he will say, 'Go to Jesus, he is the servant of God, the apostle of God, the Spirit of God and the Word of God.' Then they will go to Jesus, and he will say, 'Go to Muhammad who is a servant, whose sins God has forgiven both first and last.' " (Mishkat, Book XXIII, Chapter XII)

Whatever interpretations Muslim scholars may give to rationalize Koranic passages and traditions dealing with sins of the prophets, it remains a remarkable fact that there is no mention whatever of sin in connection with Jesus Christ. He was truly free from all sins, whether big or small. In this important respect, too, He was a prophet, yet more than a prophet.

The prophets of the Old Testament were conscious of being recipients of direct communications from the living God. Jeremiah confided that a prophet stands in "the counsel of Jehovah" (23:22). According to the testimony of Ezekiel "God spoke to the prophets and they received His words into their hearts and heard them with ears" (Ezek. 3:10). Jesus Christ did not have to depend on seasons of fellowship with God the Father. He was in constant spiritual communion with Him. Everything He did or said was from His Father and according to His good pleasure (John 21:50; 6:28; 10:37; 5:19). He did not need to receive particular revelations from God to convey them to the people. He was the self-revelation of God. Therefore, there were no angels involved coming down from heaven with a given piece of revelation. Jesus Christ as the Word Incarnate himself came down from the kingdom of His Father to redeem the world. As He said:

> And no man hath ascended up to heaven, but he that came down from heaven, even the Son of man which is in heaven. (John 3:13)

He was the bridge between the divine and human, seen and unseen. As such He was truly in contact with both the heaven and the earth. His life teaching, and work, all were self-revelations of God Most High. That is why He spoke and taught with an authority which no mere prophet could ever claim rightfully. When they prophesied, they spoke on behalf of God. Therefore they said, "Thus saith the Lord God." Jesus Christ spoke on His behalf, being one with the Father in heaven (John 10:30). All that His Father taught Him He spoke (John 6:28). Yet when He spoke it was a self-revelation. Hence unlike any other prophet, when He taught people He could say, "But I say unto you" (Matt. 5:20, 22, 28, 32, etc.). He did not speak on behalf of God. He spoke as God in self-revelation.

A noteworthy characteristic of the Old Testament prophet was his predictions. These predictions usually announced the general rules rather than detailed accounts of God's future dealings; nevertheless these predictions involved a disclosure of coming events. It could be said that a teacher without the power to foretell would be no prophet (Deut. 18:21, 22). The words of Jesus Christ are saturated with predictions. These predictions may be classified into six categories as referring to:

1. Individuals
2. His kingdom
3. the material world
4. His own career
5. the destruction of Jerusalem
6. the Parousia or His return and consummation of all things

Many of these predictions are fulfilled already, while the fulfillment of others are yet to be according to the unfolding plan of God to redeem mankind and the rest of creation. It will take considerable space to examine some of these predictions in detail. We summarize the uniqueness and quality of these by quoting from C. P. Grierson:

> If the Gospels be studied with a view to noting those sayings of Jesus which are predictive, surprise will be felt at their number. It will be seen that the parables grouped in Matthew 13 are predictions of the history of the

Kingdom; that His promises not only exhibit His love and power, but also are foretellings of His future action (e.g. Mt 18:20; 28:20). It will be found that His miracles are often prefaced by announcements beforehand of the cure to be wrought (e.g. Lk 8:50; Jn 11:11); that His discourse in Jn 6 is based on a prediction of His own sacrificial death, and that in Jn 14-16 on His foreknowledge of the Holy Spirit's descent. And, further, even in His High-Priestly prayer He shows knowledge of the future by pleading for those whom He foresees as His disciples in the coming age (Jn 17:20); and, if His first recorded word during His ministry is a prophecy of the immediate advent of the kingdom (Mk 1:15), His last word is a prophecy of its spread to the uttermost part of the world (Ac 1:8). His words are saturated with prediction. (*Dictionary of Christ and the Gospels*, Vol. II, p. 436)

Miracles are another feature of some great prophets of the Old Testament. The miracles of Jesus Christ are not an isolated phenomena. They are manifestations of His nature and power in the interest of the salvation of mankind. The Koran mentions several miracles performed by Him. As a matter of fact, it teaches us that Jesus Christ performed some of these miracles even from His cradle. For example, when He was yet a new-born babe, He spoke to the Jews, who intended to accuse His mother, and prophesied about His future mission:

And she made a sign to them (pointing toward the babe). They said, "How shall we speak with him who is in the cradle; an infant?" It said, "Verily I am the servant of God: He hath given me the Book, and He hath made me a prophet, and He hath made me blessed wherever I may be, and hath enjoined me prayer and almsgiving so long as I shall live, and to be dutiful to her that bore me: and hath not made me proud, depraved. And the peace of God was on the day I was born, and will be on the day I shall die, and the day I shall be raised to life." (Sura 19:29-34)

It is important to note that as Jesus Christ was conceived of the Holy Spirit, He was anointed to be the Messiah and a prophet even before His birth. Moreover, He was a born prophet because He spoke from the cradle miraculously and uttered prophecy about His ministry, His death, and His resurrection. The Koran mentions another significant miracle of Jesus Christ from the time when He was still a child:

"Now I have come," he will say, "to you with a sign from your Lord: Out of clay will I make for you, as it were, the figure of a bird: and I will breathe into it, and it shall become, by God's leave, a bird." (Sura 3:49)

This particular miracle is not found in the New Testament, of course. However, its parallels exist in two apocryphal gospels—Gospel of Thomas the Israelite and Gospel of the Infancy. There is some difference in minor details between the Koranic and apocryphal versions, but the essential story is the same. The Gospel of Thomas the Israelite relates:

The child Jesus having become five years old, was playing at the crossing of a brook, and He had collected together into pools the running waters and was making them clean forthwith, and with a single word did He command them. And having made some fine clay, He formed out of it twelve sparrows. And it was the Sabbath when He did these things. There were, however, many other children also playing with Him. But a certain Jew, having seen what Jesus was doing, that He was playing on the sabbath day, went away immediately and told His father Joseph, "Lo! thy child is at the brook, and having taken clay He hath profaned the sabbath." Joseph having come to the spot and having seen, cried out to Him saying, "Why dost thou on the Sabbath do these things which it is not lawful to do?" But Jesus having clapped His hands together cried out to the sparrows and said to them, "Go!" And the sparrows having taken flight, departed twittering. But the Jews, having seen this were astounded and having gone away they related to their chief men what they saw that Jesus did. (Quoted from Tisdall, op. cit., p. 175)

The Arabic Gospel of Infancy relates the same story as follows:

And when the Lord Jesus was seven years of age, He was on a certain day with other boys, His companions about the same age. When they were at play they made clay into several shapes, namely, asses, oxen, birds and other figures, each boasting of his work and endeavouring to exceed the rest. The Lord Jesus said to the boys, "I will command these figures which I have made to walk." And immediately they moved, and when He commanded them to return, they returned. He had also made the figures of birds and sparrows, which, when He commanded to fly did fly, and when He commanded to stand still, did stand still; and if He gave them meat and drink, they did eat and drink. (*The Lost Book of the Bible and Forgotten Books of Eden.* A Meridian Book, pp. 52, 53)

It must be mentioned, in passing, that the apocryphal gospels from which the above quotations have come are pre-Islamic in their antiquity.

The story of Jesus making birds out of clay makes a significant point about His divinity. This comes out clearly in another passage from the Koran:

O Jesus, Son of Mary, remember my favours toward thee, and towards thy mother; when I strengthened thee with the Holy Spirit and that thou shouldst speak unto men in the cradle, and when thou wast grown up, and when I taught thee the Scripture and wisdom, and the Law and the Gospel; and when thou didst create of clay, as it were, the figure of a bird, by my permission, and didst breathe thereon and it became a bird by my permission. (Sura 5:110)

In the above, the word "create" is used in the miracle of Jesus Christ turning the clay bird into a living bird. The power to create life is the exclusive province of God according to the Koran. None except God can create life. In one passage the Koran challenging the idolators reminds them that their idols cannot create:

Those unto whom they cry beside God created nothing but are themselves created. (Sura 16:20. Also, 35:40)

To make the point more pointed the Koran goes on to say:

O mankind! a similitude is coined, so pay ye heed to it: Lo! those on whom ye call beside God will never create a fly though combine together for this purpose. And if the fly took something from them, they could not rescue it from it. (Sura 22:73)

Jesus Christ created a bird out of a clay figure. It happened because He was the Word of God in flesh. Muslim commentators and apologists love to point out that in the relevant verse, it is also said that He performed this miracle of life by the permission of God. It is suggested thereby that the miracle of creation by Jesus Christ had nothing to do with His nature. It happened only because God permitted it. Looking at the situation in the light of the New Testament record, we are reminded that Jesus Christ always obeyed God His Father. He spoke only as His Father taught Him (John 6:28; 12:50). He came to do only the works His Father gave Him to accomplish (John 5:36). He expressed the nature of this relationship between Him and His loving Father in the memorable words:

> I can of mine own self do nothing: as I hear, I judge: and my judgment is just; because I seek not mine own will, but the will of the Father which hath sent me. (John 5:30)

Doing His Father's will perfectly did not mean that Jesus Christ was not the Son of God. As a matter of fact it implies exactly the opposite. On account of His intimate fellowship with His Father and essential unity of nature with Him, the Word of God even after His incarnation, continued to obey absolutely the will of the One who sent Him. No prophet, past or future, could ever dare make the bold statement which Jesus Christ made:

> And he that sent me is with me: the Father hath not left me alone; for I do always those things that please him. (John 8:29)

Jesus never committed a single sin because He always obeyed and loved His Father. This was consistently demonstrated in His teaching life and work. His miracles were no exception to this truth about Him. At the same time they demonstrated His divine power to give and restore life physically and spiritually. It was different with the Old Testament prophets like Elijah or Elisha. When they restored dead persons to life, for example, it was not due to any inherent quality of their own. They were merely human instruments through whom God worked to raise the dead. On the other hand, when Jesus Christ raised the dead back to life, it was a manifestation of His divine power which He shared in common with His Father (John 5:21 26). His divine power was channelled through His humanity to bless people. Elijah or any other prophet whom God used to raise a dead person to life could never say what Jesus Christ said about himself moments before He raised Lazarus, who was dead for four days:

> I am the resurrection, and the life: he that believeth in me, though he were dead, yet shall he live: and whosoever believeth on me shall never die. (John 11:25, 26)

His ability to raise the dead back to life was not a casual demonstration of His spiritual eminence. It was a manifestation of the life divine in Him (John 1:4). He not only raises the physically and spiritually dead back to life, but also the final resurrection of the entire human race will take place on account of Him who said:

> Marvel not at this: for the hour is coming, in which all that are in the

graves shall hear his voice, and shall come forth; they that have done good, unto the resurrection of life; and they that have done evil, unto the resurrection of damnation. (John 5:28, 29)

All the miracles that are attributed to Jesus Christ are summarized thus in the Koran:

> When God saith, "O Jesus Son of Mary, Remember my favour unto thee and unto thy mother; how I strengthened thee with the Holy Spirit, so that thou spokest unto mankind in the cradle as in maturity; and how I taught thee the Scripture and Wisdom and the Torah and the Gospel; and how thou didst create of clay as it were the figure of a bird, by my permission; and didst breathe thereon, and it became a bird by my permission; and thou didst heal one blind from his birth, and the leper, by my permission; and when thou didst bring forth the dead [from their graves], by my permission." (5:110; 3:49)

We learn from the scriptural record that the whole Advent of Jesus Christ was miraculous. Hence miracles cannot be isolated from His unique life. The crowning miracle of Islam is believed to be the Koran. The central miracle of the Christian faith is the Incarnation. The miracles of Jesus Christ, therefore are not sporadic specimens of His power but manifestations of His person. Moreover, His whole career was attended by miraculous events, fifteen of which deserve mention:

1. Annunciation by the angels
2. The Virgin Birth
3. Angels' song
4. Other appearances of angels in the protection of the child Jesus
5. Star of the Magi
6. Voice at His baptism
7. Descent of dove
8. Transfiguration
9. Voices at Transfiguration
10. Opening of the graves at the death of Christ
11. Rending of the veil of the Temple
12. Darkness over land
13. Earthquakes
14. The Resurrection
15. The Ascension

From the Annunciation to the Ascension, the miraculous events and miracles of Jesus Christ constitute an essential part of the Gospel history. We cannot construct a consistent picture of Christ from the Gospels if we leave out the account of these miracles.

The miracles performed by Jesus Christ have been variously classified by scholars. An acceptable classification could be:

A. Miracles on man
B. Miracles on nature
C. Miracles on the Spirit-world

According to the Fourth Gospel, a favorite term used by Jesus Christ for His miracles was "works" (John 5:36; 10:25, 32, 37, 38). He made no great distinction between His ordinary deeds of mercy and the extraordinary acts. He regarded them all alike as done simply and spontaneously in the way of His life and vocation. Again, He did not regard the miracles as highest "works"; they belonged to a lower level of manifestation as compared with His moral and spiritual revelation of God (John 14:11). However, at the same time He qualified His miracles as "the works none other man did" (John 15:24). In all the instances of miracles performed by the Old Testament prophets, it was only God working through them. On the other hand, in the miracles of Jesus Christ God worked directly in His incarnate capacity. Thus Jesus Christ could declare about His miracles;

My Father worketh hitherto, and I work. (John 5:17)

A few notable characteristics of His miracles may also be mentioned here briefly. They were spontaneous manifestations of His life and mission. They always had a high moral purpose. In all of them there is no sign of any ostentatious exercise of power. Rather, He sternly forbade any advertisement of His healings, etc., which aroused public excitement. He also exercised a strong restraint of the use of His supernatural powers. He constantly refused to use them for personal gratification, ease, or convenience. Nothing was done by extraordinary means that could be done by ordinary means. Again, the moral dignity of His miracles was in harmony with His whole life and spirit. They were intended to help the people and succor the suffering. He never used His divine power to hurt or destroy anyone. His actions never issued in meaningless marvels and useless wonders of the sort that appeal to the imagination of the apocryphal writers and storytellers everywhere. Even in those miracles that appear to be far removed from the requirements of mankind a revelation was given of the kind of power which animated and sustained all nature and ordered its course.

The miracles of great prophets of old are also mentioned by the Koran. These "signs" (miracles) are attributed to Noah (23:30), Moses (17:10f; 7:103ff; 27:7ff), Solomon (21:81; 34:12, 14), Jonah (37:142-46), and Jesus (3:45-49; 5:110-115). It is taught, however, that the prophet of Islam was not sent with miracles:

They say, "Why are not signs (aya) sent down to him from his Lord?" Say, "Signs are in the power of God alone, and I am only an open warner" (29:49). "They say, why are not signs (aya) sent down to him from his Lord? Say: God truly misleadeth whom He will, and guideth to Himself who turneth to Him—If there were a Koran by which mountains would be set in motion, or the earth cleft by it, they would not believe." (13:27-30)

And they say, "By no means will we believe on thee till thou cause a fountain to gush forth for us from the earth, or till you have a garden of palm trees and grapes, and thou cause gushing rivers to gush forth in its midst or till thou make heaven to fall upon us in pieces as thou hast pretended; or thou bring God and the angels to vouch for thee; or thou have a house of God, or thou mount up into heaven; nor will we believe in the mounting up until thou send us down a book that we may read. Say, 'Praise be to my Lord'. Am I more than a man, and an apostle?" And what hindereth men from believing, when guidance hath come to them, but that they say, "Hath God sent a mere man as an apostle?" Say, "Did angels walk the earth as its familiars, we had surely sent them a good-apostle out of heaven." (17:92-97)

The only miracle given to the prophet was the Koran:

> And they say: "If only he would bring us a miracle from His Lord!" Hath there not come unto them the proof of what is in the former scriptures? (Sura 20:133)

There is another passage that is relevant here:

> Is it not enough for them that we have sent down unto thee the Scripture which is read unto them? Lo! herein verily is mercy and a reminder for folk who believe. (Sura 29:51)

As the Koran is the chief and only miracle of the prophet, its verses also are called miracles (signs—"Aya"). Hence it is a miracle which consists of many component miracles. But this did not satisfy the Muslim hunger for more miracles. In the passage above we have seen how God complains against the unbelievers who would not be satisfied with the Koran as the only miracle given to the prophet who otherwise was "a plain warner." Like the Muslims of the post-Koranic era the unbelievers of the prophet's time demanded to see some miracles like those performed by the prophets of the Bible—especially the ones by Jesus Christ. The Muslims do believe that the Koran as a whole and in its parts is the one unique miracle granted to their prophet. But in spite of this, they have added to it miracle after miracle. In this way Muslim traditions and storytellers have taken the liberty of bestowing miracles upon their prophet which the Koran never did or sanctioned! Baqillani states the orthodox position on miracles of the prophet:

> What makes it necessary to pay quite particular attention to that Science [known as] "Ijaz al-Quran" is that the prophetic office of the prophet—upon whom be peace—is built upon this miracle. Even though later on he was given the support of many miracles, yet those miracles all belonged to special times, special circumstances, and concerned special individuals. . . . [As against all this] the evidence of the Koran is to a miracle of a general kind [witnessed] in common by men and Jinn, and which has remained a miracle throughout the ages. (Ijaz al-Quran, Cairo 1930 A.D., pp. 13, 36-38)

In this argument what Baqillani has done is to take the doctrine of abrogation applicable to verses of the Koran, and apply it to the miracles attributed to the prophet. There are some verses of the Koran which are believed by Muslims to have been abrogated by others. The abrogated verses, it is claimed, were meant for a given time, person or occasion only. They were not of general applicability and value. Hence they were replaced by those of lasting value. The Koran is considered by Baqillani of permanent value while other miracles associated with the prophet had only a limited and time-bound significance. The chief weakness of this argument and others in the same vein consists in the fact that they go against the teaching of the Koran. Moreover, all miracles except that of the Koran are supported by traditions only. It is an accepted rule that when a tradition goes against the plain teaching of the Koran, it must be abandoned as useless. In the case of miracles of the prophet, not one but a host of traditions need to be discard-

ed. Instead, they are devotedly believed by millions of Muslims. The interesting thing about these post-Koranic miracles is that they kept increasing
in number for quite some time when storytellers and tradition-makers had
the field to themselves. Before enumerating some of the miracles in the tradition only, we must mention some of those which are built around Koranic
verses:

A. The splitting or clefting of the moon. It is built upon Sura 54:1, 2.
Al-Baidhawi says in his commentary on this passage:

> Some say that the unbelievers demanded this sign of the prophet, and the
> moon was cleft into two; but others say it refers to a sign of the coming Res-
> urrection, the words "will be cleft" being expressed in the prophetic preter-
> ite. (Quoted by Hughes' Dictionary of Islam, p. 351)

B. The celebrated night journey built upon Sura 17:1. This is the only
mention of a visionary experience which has been elaborated extensively by
the traditions:

> Praise be to Him who carried His servant by night from the "Masjid
> al-Haram" to the "Majid al-Aqsa."

Abdul-Haqq says that some Muslim divines regard this event as a mere
vision, but the majority hold it to be a literal journey (Hughes' Dictionary,
p. 351).

C. The assistance given to Muslims at the Battle of Badr. This is built
upon Sura 3:120, 121. Accordingly, God is believed to have aided the Muslims by "three thousand angels sent down from on high." It was, obviously,
not a miracle which involved the prophet directly as an instrument but an
expression of divine concern for him and his followers.

Sir William Muir sums up the story about other post-Koranic miracles
of the prophet in his own inimitable way:

> To the same universal desire of glorifying their prophet, must be ascribed
> the miraculous tales with which even the earliest biographies abound. They
> are such as the following: A tree from a distance moves towards the prophet,
> ploughing up the earth as it advances, and then similarly retires; oft repeat-
> ed attempts at murder are miraculously averted; distant occurrences are in-
> stantaneously revealed, and future events foretold; a large company is fed
> from victual hardly adequate for the supply of a single person; prayer draws
> down immediate showers from heaven, and causes their equally sudden ces-
> sation. A frequent class of miracles is for the prophet to touch the udders of
> dry goats which immediately distend with milk; or to make floods of water
> well up from parched fountains, gush forth from empty vessels or gush forth
> from betwixt his fingers. With respect to all such stories, it is sufficient to say
> that they are opposed to clear declarations and pervading sense of the
> Quran. (The Life of Muhammad, pp. 59, 60)

There was a large number of contemporaries of Jesus Christ—both
among His disciples and the outsiders, who recognized Him, without hesitation, as a mighty prophet. But they were quite puzzled when they tried to
fit Him into one of the categories of the former prophets. Such a confusion
of the mind was once reported to Him by the disciples:

> And they said, Some say thou art John the Baptist: some, Elias; and others, Jeremias, or one of the prophets. (Matthew 16:14)

There was no reason for the common people and leaders of the nation to be perplexed about the identity of Jesus Christ if only they had taken the trouble of checking the messianic descriptions in the Scriptures and current traditions about Him. Edersheim points out, from the Talmud, a picture of the Messiah which fits so well the life and ministry of Jesus Christ. "Thus the Messiah was described as pre-existent in the presence of God and destined to subdue Satan. Moreover, the history of the Messiah is compared throughout with that of Moses. Moses was the first redeemer, while the Messiah was the last Redeemer. As Moses was educated in Egypt so the Messiah dwells in Rome (or Edom) among His enemies. Like Moses He comes, withdraws, and comes again. As Moses worked deliverance, so does the Messiah. Though the Messiah was expected to be like Moses, in many respects He was believed to be more than Moses. For example, the redemption wrought by Moses was temporary, while the redemption of the Messiah was to be absolute and eternal. All the wonders and miracles connected with Moses were expected to be repeated in much greater abundance by the Messiah. The ass on which the Messiah was to ride would be that on which Moses had come back to Egypt and that which Abraham used when he went up to offer his son Isaac. It was specially created on the eve of the world's first Sabbath" (Edersheim, *The Life and Times of Jesus the Messiah*, Vol. I, p. 176).

To sum it up:

> The principle that "the later Deliverer would be like the first" was carried into every detail. As the first Deliverer brought down the Manna, so the Messiah; as the first Deliverer had made a spring of water to rise, so would the second. (Edersheim, ibid., p. 176)

On certain occasions the people did remember some of the current messianic ideas and questioned Jesus Christ about them. For example, after the feeding of the five thousand, there were some who witnessed the miracle and said:

> This is of a truth that prophet that should come into the world. (John 6:14)

They recognized in Jesus Christ the prophet-Messiah promised by Moses, for there must be some in the crowd who knew that the Messiah would feed the people miraculously as it happened under Moses. Hence they are found questioning Jesus soon after the great miracle:

> They said therefore unto him, What sign shewest thou then, that we may see, and believe thee? what dost thou work? Our fathers did eat manna in the desert; as it is written, He gave them bread from heaven to eat. (John 6:30, 31)

They, in their spiritual dullness, presumed that the Messiah was to feed them physical bread day by day miraculously as did Moses. They forgot the current tradition that the Messiah was going to repeat some of the works of the time of Moses in a more spiritual and intensified form. Hence in reply to these, His interrogators, Jesus Christ sought to lead them on to the sublime view of the Messiah and His work as compared to Moses:

> Then Jesus said unto them, Verily, verily, I say unto you, Moses gave you not that bread from heaven; but my Father giveth you the true bread from heaven. For the bread of God is he which cometh down from heaven, and giveth life unto the world. (John 6:32, 33)

This sublime offer of the Messiah—the people failed to comprehend and accept despite traditions in favor of it and the fresh enlightenment from Jesus Christ. The only reason for this blindness of the people was a spiritual one. As it is written:

> Therefore they could not believe, because that Esaias said again, He hath blinded their eyes, and hardened their hearts; that they should not see with their eyes, nor understand with their heart, and be converted, and I should heal them. These things said Esaias, when he saw his glory, and spake of him. (John 12:39-41)

The spiritual blindness of the people toward God's Messiah was not something unexpected. It was already predicted by Isaiah who prophesied more about the promised Messiah than any other Old Testament prophet. It is important to note that in the midst of people blinded toward the Messiah, there were still a few—even among the leaders—who believed on Jesus Christ. These were those who could see how their fond traditions about the Messiah and teaching of the Scripture were being fulfilled by Jesus Christ in a strange but profound way. Therefore many of them believed on Him. There were other leaders who had a similar realization about Him, but they did not believe on Him because they were afraid of expulsion from the synagogue (John 12:42).

Having considered some of the traditions about the Messiah during the time of Jesus Christ, let us see what He had to say about himself. Though He had no hesitation in accepting the title of a prophet (Matt. 13:57; Luke 4:24; 13:33, 34), yet He let it be known that He was immensely more than the prophets of old. What manner of a prophet was He then? Once, in the course of a discourse with the people about the Law and Moses, He made a remarkable declaration in order to reveal His identity:

> For had ye believed Moses, ye would have believed me: for he wrote of me. (John 5:46)

In order to find out what Moses did write about Jesus Christ, we refer to Deuteronomy:

> And the Lord God will raise up unto thee a Prophet from the midst of thee, of thy brethren, like unto me; unto him ye shall hearken. (18:15)

To put this crucial and famous prophecy in its proper perspective we must go on with the rest of the relevant Scripture:

> According to all that thou desiredst of the Lord thy God in Horeb in the day of assembly, saying, Let me not hear again the voice of the Lord my God, neither let me see this great fire any more, that I die not. And the Lord said

unto me, They have well spoken that which they have spoken. I will raise them up a Prophet from among their brethren, like unto thee, and will put my words in his mouth; and he shall speak unto them all that I command him. (Ibid. 18:16-18)

On the historic occasion of the giving of the Law, God manifested His glory on Mount Horeb in Sinai, with lightnings, thunderings, earthquake, and sound of trumpet (Ex. 18:18). God wanted to address His people directly in order to communicate to them His commandments (Deut. 4:36). Moses stood between the Lord and the people as an intermediary. But the congregation of Israel could not stand the terrific manifestation of God. They feared for their lives because they had seen the holy majesty of God and heard His thundering voice. That day, despite their mortal fear and trembling, they learned the truth that the living God Most High does condescend to talk with men in their own languages (Deut. 5:24). Fearing for their lives, should the awesome manifestation of the presence of God be prolonged, they requested Moses to be their spokesman before God and His messenger to them. God heard this cry of His people and allowed them to withdraw from His holy presence to their respective tents. He required Moses, however, to stand before Him in order to receive the Law on behalf of the people (5:31). God made this arrangement with a noteworthy wish:

O that there were such an heart in them, that they would fear me, and keep all my commandments always, that it might be well with them, and with their children. (Deuteronomy 5:29)

The children of Israel could not bear the impact of the presence of God on Horeb on account of the hardness and sinfulness of their hearts. They did have a superficial fear of God as they experienced commotion in nature at His manifestation. But that had nothing to do with the true fear of God in their hearts. This is exactly what God wished for. In the historic context of the giving of the Law, God promised Moses that in His good time He was going to raise another special prophet like Moses, and Him Israel was commanded to hear. This prophet was not going to receive the Law inscribed on tablets of stone—indicating the hardness of the heart of the recipients, as did Moses. On the contrary, God said, "I will put my words in his mouth; and he shall speak unto them all that I command him" (Deut. 18:18).

The prophet like Moses was destined to mediate the presence of God to His people in such a way that they could bear it without fearing for their lives. Moreover, God was going to be present directly to speak to His people not just in terms of commandments alone but of life eternal. The contrast between Moses and the Prophet like him is fundamental to the Old and New Covenants of God with His people. It is not a simple matter of the appearance of one particular prophet, in the long line of the Hebrew prophets, more like Moses than others. It is a deep mystery. This truth is depicted so well in the Epistle to the Hebrews:

For ye are not come unto the mount that might be touched, and that burned with fire, nor unto blackness and darkness, and tempest, and the sound of a trumpet, and the voice of words; which voice they that heard intreated that the word should not be spoken to them any more. . . . And so terrible was the sight, that Moses said, I exceedingly fear and quake. (12:18-21)

> But ye are come unto Mount Sion, and unto the city of the living God. . . . And to Jesus the mediator of the new covenant, and to the blood of sprinkling, that speaketh better things than that of Abel. (12:22-24)

The Prophet like Moses mediated the New Covenant between God and man through the shedding of His own precious blood. Formerly God could not communicate directly with His people on account of their sin and hard hearts. The Prophet was God himself who was directly in contact with people with the provision of atonement for their sins by His blood. When Moses communicated the commandments of God to Israel, he was acting just as a middle man. With the Prophet the mediator between God and man is not a third person. It is the humanity of the Incarnate Word of God. When Moses carried the messages of God to the people, he prefaced them by saying, "Thus saith the Lord" or, "God spake all these things" (Ex. 20:1). It was not so with the Prophet. When He delivered His message to the people, instead of saying, "The Lord Jehovah says," He said, "But I say unto you" (Matt. 5:22, 28, 32, 34, 39, 44). Within the short space of one sermon, the Prophet showed His divine authority several times by using the unmistakable words, "I say unto you." Neither Moses nor any other prophet could have spoken with that authority. It would be considered a blasphemy on their part—a man usurping the place of God. But the Prophet spoke with divine authority because He was the Son of God who appeared in flesh to address mankind directly and to redeem them from the power of Satan. Peter in his second sermon after the Pentecost summarized the Gospel of the Prophet in the following words:

> For Moses truly said unto the fathers, A prophet shall the Lord your God raise up unto you of your brethren, like unto me; him shall ye hear in all things whatsoever he shall say. . . . Yea, and all the prophets from Samuel and those that follow after, as many as have spoken, have likewise foretold of these days. Ye are the children of the prophets, and of the covenant which God made with your father, saying unto Abraham, And in thy seed shall all the kindred of the earth be blessed. Unto you first God, having raised up his Son Jesus, sent him to bless you, in turning away every one of you from his iniquities. (Acts 3:22, 24-26)

Jesus Christ was the longed-for Prophet promised through Moses. At the same time He was more than a prophet. He called himself a greater than Jonah or Solomon (Matt. 12:41; Luke 11:31). Though according to the flesh He was born of the father of believers, Abraham, yet He claimed to be greater than he as well as all other prophets who longed to see His day. He said to His disciples:

> For verily I say unto you, That many prophets and righteous men have desired to see these things which ye see, and have not seen them; and to hear those things which ye hear, and have not heard them. (Matthew 13:17)

But the father of believers and the Friend of God was granted a prophetic vision of the Prophet and Messiah of God. The people murmured at

Jesus' claim to give life:

> Art thou greater than our father Abraham, which is dead? and the prophets are dead: whom makest thou thyself? (John 8:53)

He answered them:

> If I honour myself, my honour is nothing: it is my Father that honoureth me; of whom ye say, that he is your God. . . . Your father Abraham rejoiced to see my day: and he saw it, and was glad. (John 8:54, 56)

The Jews claimed Abraham as their father and asked Jesus Christ who He thought He was. He told them that His Father was the same God whom the Hebrews worshipped. As to their father Abraham, he looked forward to seeing the day of the Prophet Jesus the Christ. He was granted to see it—as a prophetic vision, and was pleased at what he saw. We do not know when it happened to Abraham, for the Bible is silent here. However, a very good guess would be a time somewhere between the attempted sacrifice of Isaac and the slaughter of the substitute ram. But he did foresee a glorious vision of the day of Christ. Jesus removed doubts still lingering in the minds of His hearers, about His divinity as the Messiah. We read:

> Then said the Jews unto him, Thou art not yet fifty years old, and hast thou seen Abraham? Jesus said unto them, . . . Before Abraham was, I am. (John 8:57, 58)

Here He used an expression "I am," which was used by God in the case of Moses. When Moses asked the name of God who spoke to him,

> God said unto Moses, I AM THAT I AM: and he said, Thou shalt say unto the children of Israel, I AM hath sent me. (Exodus 3:14)

God, whose name is "I AM," was in Jesus Christ in order to reconcile the world to himself. He appeared in the flesh as the Prophet Messiah the King and High Priest. But He was greater than all prophets, kings and high priests. It was necessary to delineate the Biblical perspective on the Prophet because the Muslims seek to apply the prophecies about Him to their own prophet. By way of a historical background to this belief of the Muslims, it needs to be mentioned that the Koran itself maintains that Muhammad was foretold in the Injil (the Gospels) and Torah:

> Those who follow the messenger, the prophet who could neither read nor write, whom they will find described in the Torah and Injil. (Sura 7:157)

Al-Baidhawi says that Muhammad is foretold both by name and certain description in the Bible (Sale, *Koran*, p. 120, n. 1a). On the basis of the verse quoted above and others containing direct or indirect reference to the same claim, Muslims are convinced that the Hebrew-Christian Scriptures definitely mention the coming of their prophet. Early in the history of Islam, attempts were made to prove this position by quoting from the Bible. But this practice runs contrary to the favorite theory of Muslims about the corruption of the Judeo-Christian Scriptures. If it is supposed that they have been corrupted through and through, then it would be idle for Muslims to look for any references at all to their prophet. The Muslims say that the Jews and the Christians conspired to corrupt their Scriptures in order to reject the claims of the prophet of Islam. In that case, if the Torah and Evangel were alleged to have been corrupted partially, we can be sure that all references to the prophet would be removed first. The alleged corrupters would be expected to be careful, at least, to do away with the most famous prophecy in the mouth of Moses about a prophet like him.

As we have seen before, the Talmud contains a lot of speculation on this prophecy in connection with the subject of the promised Messiah. But this prophecy exists intact even today in the Torah and is taken up in the Evangel (New Testament). For this reason, among others, many Muslim scholars have denied the possibility of corruption in the Word of God contained in the Bible or the Koran. This position, as we have seen already, is quite in harmony with the teaching of the Koran. They have, moreover, searched for Old and New Testament prophecies that might be applicable to their prophet. Attempts to quote definite verses from the Bible date from the middle of the third century of the Muslim era:

> From an un-named work of Ibn Kutaiba, Ibn al-Djawzi in his Kitab al-Wafa quotes several passages of this kind and many others are given about the same time by Ali b. Rabban al-Tabari; these recur again and again in the apologetics and polemics of the following centuries with greater or less completeness. From the Pentateuch the verses Gen. xvi:9-12; xvii:20; xxi:21; Deut. xviii:18; xxxiii:2, 12, play a prominent part in these polemics. (*Shorter Encyclopaedia of Islam*, p. 588)

As it has been shown earlier, according to the Bible the likeness between Moses and the promised Prophet had to do with the two covenants of God with Israel—the Covenant of the Law and the Covenant of Grace. As it is written:

> For the law was given by Moses, but grace and truth came by Jesus Christ. (John 1:17)

The Muslims in their endeavor to apply Deut. 18:18 to their prophet seek to liken him to Moses in spiritually inconsequential and minor details. There is one exception: They say that as Moses was a prophet who brought the Law, so also Muhammad is a prophet to whom a code of law was given. It is obvious to any student of religion that the Ten Commandments given to Moses have no exact similarity with the law received by Muhammad. Moreover, Moses received the Law written by the finger of God on tablets of stone. Whereas Muhammad received all his revelations indirectly through the agency of the angel Gabriel.

Several Koranic laws are a restatement of the laws of Moses, in one form or the other. Those not fitting into this category do not represent a brand new moral insight or an improvement upon the grandeur of the Mosaic code. If a fundamentally new code of laws had been revealed to the prophet of Islam, there could have been a minor justification for comparing his ministry with that of Moses. About the Law of Moses, too, we know that several of its commandments have parallels in the code of Hammurabi. Its uniqueness, therefore, does not connote a totally brand new code of ethics. It is to be found rather in its covenant character—a testament between the living

God, beside whom there is no other God, and His people. According to the clear teaching of the Koran, the prophet Muhammad came to renew the religion of Abraham. But as the Bible enlightens us, the original religion of Abraham did not consist in the revelation of a law to him but in the establishment of a covenant of grace between him and God. God made His covenant with Abraham four hundred and thirty years before the Law was given through Moses (Gal. 3:17). It was not a Covenant of Law. It was the Covenant of Promise whereby God said to Abraham: "And I will bless them that bless thee, and curse him that curseth thee: and in thee shall all families of the earth be blessed" (Gen. 12:3).

This covenant was to be fulfilled in and through the Messiah born of the seed of Abraham. That being the case, the Scripture tells us that the Covenant of the Law of Moses intervened for a very important reason:

> For if the inheritance be of the law, it is no more a promise: but God gave it to Abraham by promise. Wherefore then serveth the law? It was added because of transgressions, till the seed should come to whom the promise was made; and it was ordained by angels in the hand of a mediator. (Galatians 3:18, 19)

In other words, the Law was given to Israel on account of their rebellion against God. It was intended to lead these spiritually immature people, as a schoolteacher, to the Messiah (Gal. 3:24). The religion of Abraham was not a religion of the Law of Moses. It was a religion of faith in the promises of God. Again, it was a religion of faith and not of works as in the case of the Law.

As mentioned above, the prophet of Islam came to revive the religion of Abraham, which is called Islam in the Koran (3:19). At the same time it is claimed that he brought a law as Moses did 430 years after Abraham. Here we are faced with a dilemma because the religion of Abraham was a Covenant of Promise and the religion of Moses was a Covenant of the Law. Therefore, a renewal of the religion of Abraham could not be another code of law after the one given to Moses. To state it succinctly, the Islam of Abraham was a submission to the love and promises of God by faith alone. That is why he is called a friend of God and not a mere slave of His. The Islam based upon a Code of Law demands a submission to the imperious will of God as slaves only. It leaves no room for the love of God and friendship with Him like Abraham (Sura 4:124). The Koran says to the Jews and the Christians that they have no special claim on Abraham because he was neither a Jew nor a Christian (3:67). Without going into this debatable issue it may be pointed out here that he was not a Muslim either in the sense followers of the prophet are Muslims. This Islam is built upon the law and traditions of the prophet. Abraham's Islam was built upon faith alone—upon the promise of God. If the prophet Muhammad came to revive the religion of Abraham, he could not be a prophet like Moses who brought the Law but no renewal of the tradition of Abraham. If he came to bring a law like Moses, then he was poles apart from the way of Abraham—a way of friendship and loving submission to God rather than a mere submission due to fear of punishment or hope of reward under the law.

On exegetical grounds, too, the prophecy about a prophet like Moses can apply only to a born Hebrew. In Deut. 18:15, the expression "a Prophet from the midst of thee, of thy brethren, like unto me" is crucial. It is further reinforced in its proper connotation when God said again, "I will raise them up a Prophet from among their brethren, like unto thee" (18:18). The term brethren here means the Hebrews, not the Arabs. It is also doubtful if the Hebrews (or Jews) as a nation are ever called brethren, or brothers, to the Arabs in the Koran. Moreover, if Deut. 18:18 was a prophecy for the founder of Islam, the Koran, by revelation, could have referred to it specifically and literally, instead of a vague statement like, "Whom they will find described in the Torah" (7:157). As it is now, it is left to the Muslims to try to locate those descriptions of their prophet in an allegedly corrupted Bible.

When Jesus Christ told the Jews that Moses wrote of Him (John 5:46), He was not just hinting at one or two isolated prophecies. He was the fulfillment of both the Law and the prophets in the profoundest sense of the word (Luke 24:44). A moving demonstration of this truth to the disciples took place on the Mount of Transfiguration. Jesus Christ took Peter, John, and James and went up into a mountain to pray. While He was praying His face changed and His garments became brighter than the sun. As the apostles looked at Him intently, suddenly they found Him talking with Moses and Elijah. The topic of their conversation was the approaching sacrificial death of Jesus Christ in Jerusalem. In this vision Moses clearly represented the Law and Elijah the prophets. Jesus Christ, flanked by the two, was the end of the mission of the two. Peter was overwhelmed by this vision as were the other disciples. Not knowing what to do, Peter said in his bewilderment, "Master, it is good for us to be here: and let us make three tabernacles; one for thee, and one for Moses, and one for Elias" (Luke 9:33). While he was yet speaking a cloud covered the whole scene including the disciples. This cloud was a visible symbol of a special but invisible presence of God. Then they heard the voice of God the Father (the Hebrews called it "Bath Qol"), saying, "This is my beloved Son: hear him" (Luke 9:35). As they turned to look again for Jesus, they found Him alone. Then Peter, James, and John were reminded in an unforgettable manner that Moses and Elijah were mere servants of God sent to prepare the way for the advent of the Messiah—the Son of God in flesh. Subsequently, Peter reminisced about this, his profound experience on the mountain:

> For he received from God the Father honour and glory, when there came such a voice to him from the excellent glory, This is my beloved Son, in whom I am well pleased. (2 Peter 1:17)

Jesus Christ, the Prophet like Moses, was testified to by Moses and Elijah. Moreover, "a voice . . . from the excellent glory"—the rarely heard voice of the Father, made it extremely clear that this personage was none other than His own beloved Son in the form of a servant. This verbal support of the Father was only an articulation of His support of His Son throughout His ministry. Thus, the miracles that Jesus Christ performed and the mission He came to accomplish were further demonstrations of the support and approval of His Father. Therefore, there were three witnesses to Jesus the Prophet-Messiah—the Law, the prophets, and the miraculous works He performed in the name of His Father.

Later on, a fourth testimony was added to these after His death and resurrection when the Holy Spirit came to dwell in the hearts of those who believed on Him. This particular testimony is the on-going phenomenon in the church of Christ and its members who are born of God. She is the true church and the real Israel—Israel after the Spirit (cf. 1 Cor. 10:18). According to the promise first pronounced before the Old Israel on the day of Assembly, God raised up a prophet like Moses in Jesus Christ. He came to be such a manifestation of the living God that men and women can approach Him by faith and have fellowship with Him without fearing for their lives or requiring creaturely intermediaries of any kind.

In concluding this section, we must reiterate that the great prophecy concerning the Prophet (Deut. 18:18) was never applied to the prophet of Islam till the middle of the second century (Hijira). By this time Muslims were coming to know the Bible firsthand. They were anxious to substantiate the general hint in the Koran (7:157) as to the description of their prophet to be found in the Judeo-Christian Scripture. It is also important to bear in mind that during the same period, the Muslims began to accuse the Jews and the Christians of corrupting their Scriptures. They discovered that much of the material in the Koran could not be harmonized with its counterpart in the Bible. Moreover, it contained no descriptions of their prophet. Hence an ambivalent attitude toward the Bible began to develop in Islam. It was considered to be corrupted in its present form. Also, it was used to substantiate some of the claims of the prophet.

Chapter 9

Messiah, the Servant

Like the Bible the Koran also dwells upon both the human and divine natures of Jesus Christ. Having spoken of Him as the Word of God who was born of the Virgin Mary miraculously, it goes on to say that He did not hesitate to become a servant in order to accomplish the salvation of mankind. About His role as a servant the Koran says:

> Whereupon the child said, "Verily I am a servant of God; He hath given me the book of the Gospel and hath appointed me a prophet." (Sura 19:30)

As we have seen, Muslim commentators often find it difficult to take literally those passages of the Koran which indicate the divinity of Jesus Christ. But they have no hesitation at all in a literal interpretation of the servant verses in the Christology of the Koran. Moreover, they like to use these either to explain away or to minimize the clear import of those verses which refer to His Godhead. A good example of this policy may be detected in the following remarks of Baidhawi on the passage above:

> These are the first words which were put into the mouth of Jesus, to obviate the imagination of his partaking the divine nature, or having a right to the worship of mankind, on account of his miraculous speaking so soon after the birth. (As quoted by Sale, *Koran*, p. 229, note b)

Jesus Christ is the only person mentioned in the Koran whose biography includes both the divine and human aspects. Therefore, despite all the references to His humanity, He cannot be considered a mere man like other prophets and messengers of God without doing grave injustice to those verses which speak of His divine nature and glory. The Bible shows that the divine and human in Christ spell out the mystery of the Incarnation. In order to accomplish the salvation of mankind, the Word of God adopted the human nature. The Son of God became the Son of man so that sons of man may be adopted into the family of God. In Jesus Christ God came down to transform human beings and lift them up to the dimension of true fellowship and communion with Him. This descent of God in Incarnation meant a humbling of himself in the form of a servant. As it is written:

> Let this mind be in you, which was also in Christ Jesus: who, being in the form of God, thought it not robbery to be equal with God: but made himself of no reputation, and took upon him the form of a servant, and was made in the likeness of men: and being found in fashion as a man, he humbled himself, and became obedient unto death, even the death of the cross. Wherefore God also hath highly exalted him, and given him a name which is above

every name: that at the name of Jesus every knee should bow, of things in heaven, and things in earth, and things under the earth, and that every tongue should confess that Jesus Christ is Lord, to the glory of God the Father. (Philippians 2:5-11)

This is the famous Kenotic passage. When the right time was come in His unfolding plan, God himself appeared in flesh to finish the work of redemption in history. On the basis of his own concept of God, it is hard for a Muslim to take in the mystery that the Lord of all creation should condescend to assume the form of a servant. God uses angels, Jinns, prophets, and other messengers as His servants. How could He himself become a servant? Yet the Koran teaches that God is a Provider (5:18). He cares for mankind bountifully (16:10-18) and feeds the animals (29:60). It is obvious that in this, His providential capacity, God serves His creatures rather than receive service from them. Therefore in a profound sense He is a servant. There is no creature who can take over the work of the divine providence. As a matter of fact, in this context Jesus Christ made an important point when He said: "For whether is greater, he that sitteth at meat, or he that serveth? is not he that sitteth at meat? but I am among you as he that serveth" (Luke 22:27).

When a king sits down to eat and is served by his slaves, he is evidently greater than those who serve him. But on the table of the general providence of God, all His creation sits down to eat while He himself serves them, for He "giveth to all life and breath and all things" (Acts 17:25). Let us also consider the truth that God needs no service for His own benefit. Though we speak of men and angels serving God, yet it is only for the sake of the creation that He uses creaturely instruments. In using a man or an angel God does a favor to His servant. He makes him a participator in His providence. He can and does look after the work of His hands without the help of anyone. But He makes room for granting His chosen servants the privilege of being workers together with Him (2 Cor. 1:6). The Bible teaches us that just as creation and providence belong to God, salvation and redemption of His creation from its present futility also belong to Him alone (Ps. 3:8; Isa. 47:2-22; James 4:12).

The same God who serves mankind in His providence became incarnate to serve in order to save the world. According to the Bible, the Word of God is involved in the creation and sustenance of the world as much as its salvation (John 1:3; Heb. 1:3; John 3:16). God's salvation for mankind is from sin and dominion of Satan into the glorious liberty of His kingdom. This, His kingdom, is based on love—for God is love (1 John 4:16). Hence it calls for an exercise of free will and faith on the part of the sinners to be redeemed. The offer of God's salvation had to be perfected and made available in history so that sinners at all times and everywhere may have a chance. In other words, wherever there is sin in the world, there is need for God's offer of salvation. The Scripture depicts the mystery of God's salvation further in the following words:

Wherefore, as by one man sin entered the world, and death by sin; and so death passed upon all men, for that all have sinned. . . . For as by one man's disobedience many were made sinners, so by the obedience of one man shall many be made righteous. (Romans 5:12, 19)

In order to redeem mankind the Son of God put on the form of a servant. But in doing so He was born of the Virgin Mary by an act of direct creation of God rather than procreation so that the humanity of Jesus was comparable to Adam. As we have discussed it earlier, this truth is affirmed by the Koran also (Sura 3:59). Jesus Christ therefore became a servant related to the human race in a way Adam was related to it. As Adam's disobedience had a race-wide evil effect, so also the obedience of Jesus Christ offers the Good News to all.

The Incarnation meant a voluntary self-abnegation on the part of the Prince of God. This Kenosis (or self-emptying) should make sense to Muslims who believe that the eternal Word of God could be captured within the limitations of the human language and preserved in material books made by human hands. As a matter of fact, all revelation of God to men and angels involves a voluntary self-emptying of God. In order to communicate with His creatures meaningfully, God must act within creaturely limitations. Thus all the self-revelations of God to His prophets meant a Kenosis on the part of Him who otherwise is beyond limit and comprehension. The ultimate Kenosis took place when His Son became a servant to save the world. The Incarnation meant for the Word of God assumption of the form of a servant in His labor of love for mankind. But He went the second mile when, in His role as a servant, He quietly accepted maltreatment, rejection, suffering and death—even the death on the cross. This meekness on the part of Jesus Christ is noted by the Koran:

> The Messiah will never scorn to be a slave of God, nor will the favored angels. Whoso scorneth His service and is proud, all such will He assemble unto Him. (Sura 4:172, Pickethall)

Here the humility of Jesus Christ is lifted up to our attention—He does not hesitate to be a slave of God. It is interesting that another example of such a humility is not taken from the lives of many prophets and saints of God. It comes from those angels who did not rebel against God with Satan and his hosts. According to what the Koran says about the angels, they have a reason to be proud as compared to human beings. They were created immortal and out of a better quality material than man (Sura 38:72-77). They had no right to be proud against God, as Satan was. But they had a justification to be proud in comparison to man whom God chose to be His vicegerent on earth. Hence they could legitimately disdain to serve inferior mortals. But they chose to be humble and become their servants at the command of God.

The willingness of Jesus Christ to become a humble servant belongs in a similar category, as the passage from the Koran states clearly. He is divine by nature, being the Word of God. His humanity also was far superior to ordinary people: He was born miraculously; He remained absolutely sinless, though tempted like us, and performed those miracles which no man ever did. Both in His human and divine majesty, He stood head and shoulders above mankind and angels. Despite this unique dignity and stature, He did not hesitate to become a servant in obedience to God His Father and for the redemption of the world. He humbled himself to the extent of suffering death upon the cross to offer a ransom for many. The only Prince of the king eternal decided to put on the guise of a beggar in order to live with a colony of beggars, sharing their misery and privation eventually to make them rich and free.

> For ye know the grace of our Lord Jesus Christ, that, though he was rich, yet for your sakes he became poor, that ye through his poverty might be rich. (2 Corinthians 8:9)

In His divine nature Jesus Christ was rich indeed. But He chose not to exercise some of His prerogatives and powers during His life on earth in the economy of His plan of salvation. God is limitless in His presence, but by His choice He may manifest himself in a limited way for the good of a man. For example, He spoke to Moses through a burning bush, though He himself is present everywhere. Again, He revealed His will within the limits of the Mosaic Law and human conditions. Though the limitless God may choose to reveal himself in time and space, yet that self-revelation does not make Him less omnipresent. When the Word of God manifested himself within the limitations of the human nature and a body of flesh, He did not become less divine thereby. A manifestation of the sun to humans takes place through a tiny reflection on the retina of the eye—the reflection of a star 300,000 times as big as the earth! This image shows the whole sun while the sun remains itself.

As Jesus Christ emptied himself in the form of a servant, He chose to exercise His divine privilege, glory, and power only to the extent necessary to arouse saving faith among people and to accomplish redemption of mankind. A readily comprehensible example of this, His voluntary poverty, was His experience of hunger. He who fed thousands miraculously would not feed himself that way but depended on natural means like others. This dimension of His poverty is to be found in the Koran also. Referring to Him who was able to bring down a table from heaven miraculously for His disciples (Sura 5:112-115), it says:

> The Messiah Son of Mary, was no other than a messenger, messengers had passed away before him. And his mother was a saintly woman. And they both used to eat food (Sura 5:75).

Because Jesus Christ ate food like other messengers of God, it did not mean that He was just another human being. It only means that He was truly human as He was truly divine. During His days in flesh He remained an obedient servant of God like prophets and servants before Him, nay, even more than they. He became like us in our human nature (Heb. 2:16, 17) in order to establish a truly meaningful contact between God and man. He refused to use His divine power to help or aid himself, but He went about doing good to others thereby. His divine majesty and glory was veiled behind His humanity in such a way that it could be seen properly only by the eye of faith. Every once in a while even the nonbelievers felt the impact of His divinity but they, on account of a lack of faith, never could see what hit them. When a band of soldiers came to arrest Jesus at night, they wandered around in the garden of Gethsemene looking for Him. He stepped up to them and asked whom they were looking for (John 18:4). They said, "Jesus of Nazareth." On hearing that Jesus identified himself, saying, "I am He." As soon as they heard these words, "they went backwards and fell to the ground." Three simple words spoken by Him deliberately to reveal His identity had the impact of a blast on the mob.

In the Old Testament we read about God identifying himself to Moses saying, "I AM." Here the same God in the humble form of a servant named His ancient name to reveal His identity to the would-be captors. They could not bear this sudden but momentary encounter with the glory of the Son of God veiled behind His body of flesh. The truth that Jesus Christ was fully divine even as He was truly human has been expressed succinctly in Colossians: "For in him dwelleth the fulness of godhead bodily" (2:9).

In the beginning God the Father made all things by His Word (John 1:3). Through the self-same Word He sustains and preserves His creation (Heb. 1:3). In and through that very Word, provision was made for the redemption of the world (John 3:16). No mere creature can save, just as no creature can create. Salvation as much as creation belongs to God. At the dawn of creation God foreordained the salvation of mankind and redemption of the rest of His creation from corruption into the regeneration of His kingdom. It is written that we are redeemed "with the precious blood of Christ, as of a lamb without blemish and without spot: who verily was foreordained before the foundation of the world, but was manifest in these last times for you" (1 Pet. 1:19, 20).

The salvation that was foreordained was brought to fruition at a given period of time in history by the Word of God who became flesh and dwelt among us. The good news of His advent was given as soon as the tragedy of sin struck mankind at the source for the first time. God told Adam and Eve, after they had fallen, that He was going to redeem the world through the Saviour born of the seed of woman (Gen. 3:15). Jesus Christ was thus foretold from Adam to John the Baptist (Luke 1:70; Matt. 11:13). The great work He came to accomplish was the work of God as much as creation and preservation of the world. Once during His days in flesh, He healed a man sick for thirty-eight years. It was done on a Sabbath. The Jews who witnessed it began to complain about the violation of the tradition of Sabbath observance rather than to glorify God. Jesus Christ answered their criticism by saying: "My Father worketh hitherto, and I work" (John 5:17).

God does not suspend the work of upholding the universe and preserving His creation even on a Sabbath day. If He did so there would be no humans to observe the Sabbath or Sabbaths to be observed. So Jesus Christ carried on His work of healing and quickening even on Sabbath days, for He was working the works of God the Father who sent Him into the world.

Jesus Christ expressed His spirit of service in a symbolic act which has left its indelible mark on the sacred as well as secular history. On the eve of His betrayal He rose from the Last Supper. Laying aside His upper garments, He took a towel and girded himself:

> After this, he poureth water into a basin, and began to wash the disciples' feet, and to wipe them with the towel wherewith he was girded. (John 13:5)

In the Orient of those days, as even today, it was unthinkable for a teacher to touch the feet of his disciples. The custom was the reverse in many cultures. In the incident narrated by John, the greatest teacher of all time—the Son of God himself—stooped to wash the feet of His disciples, including Judas Iscariot who betrayed Him with a kiss! No wonder Peter was horror-struck to see his Lord getting ready to wash his feet also. He refused to allow this. He relented only when informed of a dire alternative to the washing of his feet:

> Peter saith unto him, Thou shalt never wash my feet. Jesus answered him, If I wash thee not, thou hast no part with me. Simon Peter saith unto him, Lord, not my feet only, but also my hands and my head. (John 13:8, 9)

Jesus Christ summed up the nature and scope of His work as a servant in His own words:

> Even as the Son of man came not to be ministered unto, but to minister, and give his life a ransom for many. (Matthew 20:28)

The service which He came to render to humanity did not consist of a few isolated acts of healing, cleansing, and feet-washing alone. The essence of His unique service was something of an abiding consequence and universal import. The culmination of His ministry to mankind came when He offered His own life as ransom for many. He was not just an ordinary servant of God like many prophets of old. Rather in a very special way He was the Suffering Servant.

Chapter 10

The Servant Role

Among the books of the Old Testament which foretell the servant role of the Messiah and His sufferings, the book of Isaiah deserves special consideration. The titles "Servant" and "Suffering Servant" are given to the One whose call, mission, suffering, death, and exaltation are foretold in Isaiah 53 and related passages. God calls Him "my servant" (Isa. 42:1; 49:3, 6; 52:13; 53:11), and He speaks of himself as "his servant" (Isa. 49:5). There are a number of passages in Isaiah which are called the servant songs. Let us examine the ministry of Jesus Christ in the light of these prophecies.

The Servant Anointed to Bring About Judgment

Isa. 42:1-4 describes the Servant as endowed with the Spirit of God to bring justice or judgment to the nations. This peculiar anointing of Jesus Christ reminds us of the reference in the Koran:

> We gave Jesus son of Mary, clear proofs and we supported him with the Holy Spirit. (2:253, 87)

The Hebrew word translated "judgment" in the passage from Isaiah (42:1) appears to mean "true religion." Thus interpreted the anointing of the Servant with the Holy Spirit is intended to help establish the true worship of God in the world. Jesus Christ, in His conversation with a Samaritan woman, taught about the kind of worship God seeks from His worshippers. The woman was boasting about her ancestral religion—indicative of ancestor worship—rather than a concern with the proper worship of God. She said:

> Our fathers worshipped in this mountain; and ye say, that in Jerusalem is the place where men ought to worship. (John 4:20)

To this tall claim of worshipping God truly in a specified place after the traditions of ancestors, Jesus Christ gave an answer which is valid both for time and eternity. Moreover, it establishes the fundamental distinction between the true religion and the religion so-called which never goes beyond self-worship, demon worship and ancestor worship even when it is carried on ostensibly in the name of God:

> Jesus saith unto her, Woman, believe me, the hour cometh, when ye shall neither in this mountain, nor yet in Jerusalem, worship the Father. . . . But the hour cometh, and now is, when the true worshippers shall worship the Father in Spirit and in truth: for the Father seeketh such to worship him.

God is a spirit: and they that worship him must worship him in spirit and in truth. (John 4:21, 23, 24)

One of the profoundest revelations about the nature of God was shared by Jesus Christ with the Gentile woman from Samaria. He taught her that "God is a spirit." He went on to explain to her the implication of this truth about God and true worship of Him. God the Father seeks those who worship Him in the Holy Spirit and in truth. Who is this Truth? It is Jesus Christ who said: "I am the way, the truth, and the life: no man cometh to the Father, but by me" (John 14:6).

The only way to worship God the Father is through Jesus Christ who is the Truth. The Koran also calls Him the Word of Truth (Sura 19:35). Again, after having entered the only Way, true worship must be carried on in the Holy Spirit who is given in the name of Jesus Christ to those who believe on Him (John 14:26). This is the true religion indeed—a culmination of the faith of Abraham and the prophetic movement which started from him (see Sura 29:27). We remember how Jesus Christ told His Jewish audience that their father Abraham looked forward to the advent of the Messiah in his lineage. He was granted a special favor from God to foresee this Advent. He rejoiced in what he saw and understood in the vision (John 8:56). Jesus Christ did not come just to revive the religion of Abraham. Nor did He appear on the scene to destroy the Law and the prophets related to the faith of Abraham and the divine promise to him. He came, rather, to fulfill it all. This fulfillment brought the ideal involved in the faith and religion of Abraham within the grasp of everyone who believes on Him. They can now worship God the Father in the Spirit and Truth.

The Koran describes the religion of Abraham in the following words:

Whosoever is better in religion than he who surrendereth his purpose to God while doing good and followeth the tradition of Abraham the righteous? God [Himself] chose Abraham for a friend. (4:125)

Two important facets of the religion of Abraham are mentioned here. First of all, he was a friend of God. Secondly, he was totally surrendered to God not only in outer actions but also in inner purposes (Sura 37:97-111). Another passage mentions a third notable characteristic of Abraham's religion: He was devoted to the One true God and hated polytheism (Sura 3:67). Let us, for a moment, consider the monotheism of Abraham. It was not mere unitarianism—a cold intellectual dogma to which a person might become devoted as an ancestral practice. Abraham had a warm-blooded apprehension of the living God. It constrained him to submit to God in love and friendship. A mere unitarian belief in the existence of God with no saving experience of Him may not be better than the belief of devils. The Bible cautions us:

Thou believest that there is one God; thou doest well: the devils also believe, and tremble. (James 2:19)

Satan and his benighted demons believe and know for sure that there is one God and none beside Him. They even tremble at the thought of their coming judgment by the living God Most High. But this unitarian belief by itself has failed to make them followers of the religion of Abraham. The Islam of Abraham called for a total surrender to the one true God in thought, word, and deed. This submission to God is agreed upon by Muslims. But how is one to find out the will of God in one's daily life in order to remain surrendered to Him consistently? The answer is the revealed law of God given to His people—the people of the Book:

> To everyone of you have We given a law (Sharia) and a high road (Minhaj). (Sura 5:48. Also, 45:17)

The Koran recognizes a variety of moral codes given to the Jews and the Muslims. This was done by God purposely. God wanted to try and test His people thereby:

> For each have We appointed a divine law and traced-out way. Had God willed He could have made you one community. But that He may try you by that which He hath given you [He hath made you as you are]. So compete with each other in doing good works. (Sura 5:48)

A revealed law is good insofar as it shows us what God expects of us. But, as the Koran rightly noted, it also is a test for those who seek to remain submitted to God. When we obey these laws, we do good works. When we disobey them, we sin against the law of God, and therefore against God himself. In terms of outer good actions prescribed by a given religious code, we may succeed in doing a few good actions. Here, too, the moral demands of God get mixed up with traditions of men. Often one may be doing a good act, not according to the revealed law of God but after some tradition allegedly built upon it. However, it must be conceded that some good actions according to the law of God controlling the outer conduct may be performed. But God does not look at actions alone. He looks at the heart of a man. The Koranic verse quoted earlier calls for a surrender of our purposes to God (4:125). As the Bible points out:

> For the Lord seeth not as man seeth; for man looketh on the outward appearance, but the Lord looketh on the heart. (1 Samuel 16:7)

In one's endeavor to be surrendered to God in secret thoughts, imaginations and motives, one quickly becomes aware of one's inability to be a godly person all the time. Any conscientious person knows how hard it is to do that which is good in thought, word, and deed; also, how easy it is to do evil. St. Paul articulated this dilemma of an honest seeker after true goodness according to the law:

> For the good that I would I do not: but the evil which I would not, that I do. Now if I do that I would not, it is no more I that do it, but sin that dwelleth in me. I find then a law, that, when I would do good, evil is present with me. For I delight in the law of God after the inward man: but I see another law in my members, warring against the law of my mind, and bringing me into captivity to the law of sin which is in my members. (Romans 7:19-23)

On account of the mystery of sinfulness infecting the human nature, the sort of Islam God requires in His revealed law is not possible for any natural man. As the Bible says, in such a situation no man is justified before God by the works of the law (Gal. 2:16; Rom. 3:20). Whenever a person breaks the law of God in thoughts and intentions of the heart, it is as evil in the sight of God as sinful actions.

Obedience of the law is submission to God (Islam), but its disobedience is exactly the opposite of this Islam. It is a rebellion against God and submission to the lusts and will of Satan. Sin being an alienation from God is also contrary to the Abrahamic ideal of friendship with God. Moreover, it is practical polytheism—a denial of the Unity of God: A sinner worships his own self and its lusts rather than the living God and His will. Also, in sin he unwittingly worships Satan who is called the pseudo-god of this world (2 Cor. 4:4). Thus by breaking the law of God a person becomes an idolater, rebel, and enemy of God. The way to the Islam of Abraham, therefore, is a hard one. A follower of that way through the law finds himself a Muslim at times but a rebel and enemy of God (in thought, word, or deed) most of the time.

The true religion of Abraham, which calls for an unbroken friendship with God through His revealed law, is impossible for man on his own. Jesus Christ came to remedy the predicament involved in this Islam by accomplishing in himself what the law could not do—a reconciliation and love relationship with God that overwhelms the rebellious sinful nature of man. He offered to transform men and women not just into slaves of God or even friends of God but children adopted into the household of God. He opened the way to this ideal involved in the Islam of Abraham by offering in himself an absolute sacrifice for our sins, thereby making us worthy temples of the Holy Spirit who changes us from within. We shall deal with this aspect of the ministry of Jesus Christ in the section on the Suffering Servant. But at this point it is sufficient to bear in mind that according to the prophecy of Isaiah (42:1-4), Jesus Christ came to establish the true religion in the world, whereby in Him a person may worship God the Father in Spirit and in truth.

The Servant as the Light of the World

In Isa. 49:1-6, the Servant announces to distant peoples that He is called of God from birth and kept in readiness for His great and unique mission. He is "Israel" in whom God will be glorified. God has assured Him that it is not enough that He should be God's Servant to restore Israel; He is to be a light to the nations so that the salvation of God may be published to the ends of the earth.

Jesus Christ was born of the Holy Spirit and anointed for His ministry from the conception onwards. Upon this both the Bible and the Koran agree. The Koran goes on to say that He performed miracles and received a revelation while He was yet a babe in the cradle. The Bible unravels the Koranic enigma of how Jesus Christ, despite being the "Word of God" (and the Word from Him), received the Evangel (Gospel) from God? This Evangel was not a written book granted to the child Jesus. The Muslims believe that the Koran was a miracle of their prophet who himself was illiterate. They often say, "How could a person who never knew how to read and write produce a book like the Koran? It must be a miracle from God."

Let us consider this argument in the light of the claim that the child Jesus was taught the Scriptures by God and received the Evangel. A babe in the cradle is bound to be more unlettered than a grown-up person. If the Evangel granted to Christ was a book, then like the Koran this Evangel must also be considered a literary miracle. That would negate the uniqueness claimed by the Muslims for the Koran. Hence the belief that the Evangel granted to Jesus Christ was a book is not only out of harmony with the Bible but also casts a shadow over the Muslim belief in the uniqueness of the Koran.

We have discussed in the preceding that, according to the Bible, Jesus Christ did not receive from God a book called the Evangel. He was the Evangel himself. As Paul expressed it succinctly, the Gospel (Evangel) consists in the good news that "God was in Christ, reconciling the world unto himself, not imputing their trespasses unto them" (2 Cor. 5:19). An angel of the Lord, accompanied by a host of other angels, visited a band of shepherds tending their sheep at night in the fields of Bethlehem. He brought them the most exciting tidings in the history of mankind:

> Fear not: for, behold, I bring you good tidings of great joy, which shall be to all people. For unto you is born this day a Saviour, which is Christ the Lord. (Luke 2:10, 11)

The advent of the Servant of God is the Good News to the whole world because He himself is the source of it. He was announced by the angel as a "Saviour who is Christ the Lord." Jesus Christ was born a Saviour and Lord not only of humans but also of the angels. Even in His form of a servant the Son of God deserved the adoration and worship of angels. He, instead of receiving a written book like some other prophets, was the embodiment of the eternal Book of God which is known as "Umm al- Kitab" (Mother of the Book, Sura 13:39; 85:21).

The passage of Isaiah under review depicts the Servant also as a light to nations. In the Bible, light has been used metaphorically of God. Ps. 104:2 describes Him at creation, covering himself "with light as with a garment." 1 Tim. 6:16 says that He dwells in unapproachable light. His perpetual presence is a sun which never sets so that His people have no need of sun or moon (Rev. 21:23; 22:5). Elsewhere, God is described as light himself in whom there is no darkness (1 John 1:5). It is this light of God that has to do with revelation and spiritual enlightenment of the world. All sources beckoning man to God are in the category of light derived or essential. For example, the human conscience is a God-given lamp which keeps us inwardly enlightened of the truth that we are answerable to God first and then to society. The experience of guilt or moral elation involved in the use of this light within is a sure indication of His government and authority (Luke 11:35, 36; Rom. 1:19; 2:15). All supernatural revelation which is truly of God always touches human conscience for edification.

As we have seen, no man can approach the inaccessible light in which God Most High dwells. At the same time the lost humanity dwells in darkness with only puny lamps of conscience imparting their dim light to enable them at best to grope after God and long for His sunshine. Man by crying in the spiritual darkness around him cannot, thereby, bring about the dawn of the day of divine presence. It is God who must take the initiative to dispel the dark night of the soul by His light. God has done this already. As the Bible declares it:

> God, who commanded the light to shine out of darkness, hath shined in our hearts, to give the light of the knowledge of the glory of God in the face of Jesus Christ. (2 Corinthians 4:6)

When dealing with the subject of revelation, we may distinguish between light *from* God and the light *of* God. A lamp giving its light at night is a light from the sun. A ray of sun directly illuminating a dark place is light of the sun. The light of an oil lamp is light borrowed from the sun ultimately. Similarly, the light from God is like a lamp shining in the spiritual darkness of man to lead him to "the Dayspring from on high" (Luke 1:78). The difference between the light from God and the light of God is brought out in several places in the Bible. We read, for example:

> We have also a more sure word of prophecy; whereunto ye do well that ye take heed, as unto light that shineth in a dark place, until the day dawn, and the day star arise in your hearts. (2 Peter 1:19)

The Old Testament prophecy and the Law have been compared to a lamp as in the passage above and in several other references (e.g., Prov. 6:23; Ps. 119:105). They were only partial revelations from God preparatory to the advent of His full and final revelation—comparable to the dawn of the day and rising of the sun. The Old Testament revelation is a revelation about God, whereas the New Testament documents the revelation of God himself.

The Koran calls God "the light of the heavens and the earth" and goes on to illustrate its own function as a lamp. The celebrated verse of the light goes as follows:

> God is the light of heavens and the earth. The similitude of His light is a niche wherein is a lamp. The lamp is in a glass. The glass is, as it were, a shining star. [This lamp] is kindled from a blessed tree, an olive neither of the East nor of the West, whose oil would almost glow forth though no fire touched it. Light upon light, God guideth unto His light whom He will. (Sura 24:35)

Muslim commentators have attempted all sorts of subtle explanations of the details incorporated in the similitude quoted above. The light described therein as a lamp is interpreted to mean the light revealed in the Koran. This reading of the verse is supported by another verse also:

> So believe in God and His messenger and the light which we have revealed. And God is aware of what ye do. (Sura 64:8)

As compared to God who is "the light of heavens and the earth," the Koran is a lamp. The prophet also is compared to a lamp:

> O prophet! Lo! We have sent thee as a witness and a harbinger of good tidings and a warner, and a summoner unto God by His permission, and as a

lamp that giveth light. (Sura 33:45, 46)

In line with the law and prophets of the Old Testament, one of the shining lamps who witnessed for the dayspring from on High was Zechariah, the father of John the Baptist. In his famous prophetic song (Luke 1:68-78), he foretold that his son would be called the prophet of the Highest and would go before the Lord, as a herald, to prepare His ways (Luke 1:76). According to this word, John the Baptist was sent to prepare the way for Jesus Christ, the Lord Incarnate. Also, the advent of this messianic manifestation of God is called by Zacharias a visitation of the Dayspring from on high (Luke 1:78). Jesus Christ described John the Baptist as a prophet who appeared in the spirit of Elijah in order to prepare the way for Him. Again, He said that of all the prophets born naturally, John the Baptist was the greatest in dignity and prophetic mission—though compared to the Spirit-born he was the least (Matt. 11:11). In spite of such a high estimate of John's ministry, Jesus went on to compare him to a lamp:

> He was a burning and a shining light: and ye were willing for a season to rejoice in his light. (John 5:35)

As a herald of Jesus Christ John the Baptist was the last of the line of the Old Testament prophets. Among these lamps of God leading to the great dawn of the day, John was the brightest light of all. "The Light of the heavens and the earth" made His appearance on the stage of history soon after the conclusion of John's ministry—this was Jesus Christ the Sun of Righteousness about whom the Scripture declares plainly:

> That was the true Light, which lighteth every man that cometh into the world. (John 1:9)

All the shining lamps of prophecy derived their lights from the Sun of Righteousness to whom they bore testimony. Moreover, every normal human being is born with a light within, testifying to God, which is conscience (2 Cor. 4:2). The Word of God is the ultimate source and inspiration of all lamp-like lights to be found in authentic prophecy and moral laws of the human race. Moreover, He is the One who creates a native hunger for God and witness of the conscience to Him in everyone who is born into this world. All these lights, as is the case with a candle or lamp, are only partial and dim revelations of God. They lead men at best, to only a "groping after him to find him" (Acts 17:27).

Jesus the Messiah is never likened to a lamp anywhere in the Bible. The prophet Isaiah, speaking of Jesus Christ, says that just before His advent "darkness shall cover the earth, and gross darkness the people." But this will be the darkest hour before the dawn. So the prophet goes on to say, "But the Lord shall arise upon thee, and his glory shall be seen upon thee" (Isa. 60:2). Having conveyed these tidings of the dawn to Israel, Isaiah concludes his prophecy by relating the Sun of Righteousness to the Gentiles:

> And the Gentiles shall come to thy light, and the kings to the brightness of thy rising. (Isaiah 60:3)

The last prophet of the Old Testament Canon, foretelling the advent of

Jesus Christ, wrote:

> But unto you that fear my name shall the Sun of righteousness arise with healing in his wings; and ye shall go forth, and grow as calves of the stall. (Malachi 4:2)

Prophecy ceased in Israel during the period between the Old and the New Testaments. Throughout this intertestamental time there were no prophets sent from God, nor any angel visitations to His people. Jewish authorities agreed that the voice of prophecy and the Holy Spirit ceased to be known in Israel after Malachi. "Bath Qol"—voice from heaven—replaced them during the silence of God between the two Testaments (see Edersheim, *The Life and Times of Jesus the Messiah*, Vol. I, p. 285). On the eve of the advent of Jesus the Messiah, once again heavens open and all forms of the prophetic activity of the Holy Spirit burst upon the scene in a fresh way. Thus the Holy Spirit, angels, voices from heaven, and prophetic utterances are recorded from the annunciation to the manifestations of Jesus, as Messiah, to Israel.

Zacharias' prophecy about Jesus Christ has already been referred to—he called the advent of the Messiah as rising of the Sun of Righteousness. This prophetic utterance was reinforced by another prophet waiting for the "consolation of Israel" (i.e. the Messiah). It was revealed to him by the Holy Spirit that he should not see death before he had seen the Messiah of God. As Mary and Joseph were visiting the Temple with their child, this prophet, Simeon by name, came in. He took Jesus Christ in his arms and burst forth in a prophetic thanksgiving:

> Lord, now lettest thou thy servant depart in peace, according to thy word: for mine eyes have seen thy salvation, which thou hast prepared before the face of all people; a light to lighten the Gentiles, and the glory of thy people Israel. (Luke 2:29-31)

As it has been observed, all prophets and moral laws, at their best, were only as shining lamps to witness for God. As the sun can properly be seen in its own light, God revealed himself adequately and finally through himself. Hence, the final revelation of God, in which all the partial revelations of old found their fulfillment, took place when the Word became flesh and appeared in history as Jesus the Messiah. It must be pointed out that according to the Biblical perspective the entire Hebrew prophetic movement was in the nature of preparation for the advent of the Messiah. After His manifestation it is no more meaningful to speak of a final prophet in that line of prophecy. This understanding is significant for the Muslim claim as to the finality of their prophet. At least he could not be a final prophet of the line of prophets mentioned in the Old Testament. They were only acting as heralds of the Messiah. This, their ministry, came to a successful conclusion with John the Baptist.

The Koran clearly testifies that Jesus, Son of Mary, was the promised Messiah. After the Messiah is come there is no more need for the Law of Moses or prophecies in the tradition of the Old Testament prophets. It is also noteworthy that the Messiah who appeared among the Hebrews is

128

meant for the whole mankind. This was prophesied across the centuries of the Old Testament, affirmed by Jesus Christ, testified by those who ate and drank with Him, and by the Holy Spirit of God who is granted to all those believing on the Saviour. The first prophecy about the Messiah was given not by a human prophet but by God himself (Gen. 3:15). In this case God acted as a prophet. The fulfillment of that prophecy—having gone through centuries of development through the Old Testament prophets—also was accomplished by God the Prophet-Messiah Jesus.

John the Baptist was sent to bear witness to the dawn of the day of eternity:

> He was not that Light, but was sent to bear witness of that Light. That was the true Light which lighteth every man that cometh into the world. (John 1:8, 9)

After the Sun of Righteousness has arisen in His glory, it will not be wise to walk by the light of a lamp anymore. Now in Jesus Christ God is speaking on His own behalf face to face with all those who approach Him by faith—faith like Abraham's. In Him dwells the fullness of Godhead bodily (Col. 1:19; 2:9). In Him God is seen in His own light. As it is written, "In him was life and that life was the light of men." The life of God and His light go together. But the life of God is the source of His light—eternal glory. It is not a created light like the sun, moon, or other stars, as well as angels—who are created of fire, according to the Koran. The light of Jesus Christ is the effulgence of life divine in Him. He said that as God the Father has life in himself so does the Son. As a result of this life that was in Him, He healed the sick, opened the eyes of the blind, and raised the dead back to life. Jesus Christ said, "For as the Father raiseth up the dead, and quickeneth [makes them alive]; even so the Son quickeneth [gives life to] whom he will" (John 5:21).

We have also discussed His miracle of creating birds out of clay which was a clear indication of His divine life, for according to the Koran pseudo gods cannot create even a fly. When Jesus Christ claimed to be the light of the world, He was not thinking of creaturely light. It is the Light of God. God is called "the Light" (Al-Nur)—it is one of the ninety-nine beautiful names of God in Islam (Sura 24:35). The Bible also teaches that God dwells in unapproachable light and He is Light. Obviously this Light of God is to be distinguished from all created lights. Jesus Christ is the life of God manifested in flesh, and this life also is the uncreated Light for the spiritual enlightenment of mankind (John 1:4). This elucidation is necessary to place the Muslim doctrine of the "light of Muhammad" in its proper perspective. It also is known as the doctrine of the original essence of Muhammad (Al-Haqiqat al-Muhammadiya). The Wabbabis do not believe in it.

The doctrine of the pre-existence of the light of Muhammad (Nur-i-Muhammadi) is not a Koranic doctrine. Under Christian and Gnostic influences this idea first appeared among the Muslim mystics of the third century A.H. From this period onwards it gradually began to dominate popular worship. According to Imam Qastalani, it is related by Jabir ibn Abdullah al-Ansari that the prophet said:

> The first thing created was the light of your prophet, which was created

from the light of God. This light of mine roamed about wherever God willed, and when the Almighty resolved to make the world, he divided the light of Muhammad into four positions: from the first He created the pen (qalam); from the second the tablet (Lauh); from the third the highest heaven and the throne of God (Arsh); the fourth portion was divided into four sections: from the first were created the "Hamalat al-Arsh," or the eight angels who support the throne of God; from the second the "Kursi," or lower throne of God; from the third, the angels, and the fourth, being divided into four divisions, from it were created 1) the firmaments or seven heavens, 2) the earth, 3) the seven paradises and seven hells, 4) and again from a fourth section were created 1) the light of the eyes, 2) the light of the mind, 3) the light of the love of the Unity of God, 4) the remaining portion of creation. (Muwahib-i-Laduniya, Vol. I, p. 12)

According to the author of the "Shia" book of traditions, *Hayat al-Qulub*, the traditions regarding creations from the light of Muhammad are very many. He reconciles their mutual divergences and discrepancies by suggesting that they refer to different eras of creation. He goes on to give his own version of it as follows:

The holy light of Muhammad dwelt under the empyrean seventy-three thousand years and then resided seventy thousand years in Paradise. Afterwards it rested another period of seventy thousand years under the celestial tree called "Sidra al-Muntaha," and, emigrating from heaven to heaven, arrived at length in the lowest of these celestial mansions, where it remained until the Most High willed the creation of Adam. (*Hayat al-Qulub*, Merrick's ed. Boston, 1850, p. 4)

Once again, in regard to the traditions about the light of Muhammad, it is important to remember that they are post-Koranic. There is a wide divergence among them, and the "Shia" traditions do not harmonize with those of the Sunnis. But the fact remains that they believe this light to be a creature. It is not eternal as God and His effulgence. Moreover, this doctrine of the predestined essence of Muhammad as the first creation is carefully distinguished from the doctrine of the uncreated Koran. The Muslim orthodoxy places the latter doctrine above the doctrine of the light of Muhammad. Moreover, this belief must be viewed in the context of the Koran which compares the prophet only to a lamp. But we need to keep in mind that the third century (A.H.) belief about his pre-existence is a phenomenon clearly influenced by Christianity and Gnosticism, and it never equates the light of Muhammad with the uncreated Light of God. Jesus Christ is the Light of God as His Son. The Scripture, therefore, testifies to His divine glory when it says:

God, who gave to our forefathers many glimpses of the truth in the words of the prophets, has now, at the end of the present age, given us the truth in the Son. Through the Son God made the whole universe, and to the Son he has ordained that all creation shall ultimately belong. This Son, the radiance of the glory of God, flawless expression of the nature of God, himself the upholding power of all that is, having effected in person the cleansing of men's sin, took his seat at the right hand of the majesty on high—thus proving himself, by the more glorious name that had been given, far greater than all the angels of God. (Hebrews 1:1-4, J. B. Phillips Translation)

Chapter 11

The Suffering Servant

Continuing with the Servant songs in Isaiah, we come to the significant chapters 52:13-15 and 53:1-10. Here the mysterious Servant of God is depicted in the unusual role of a Suffering Servant. He is to be disfigured, despised and rejected of men. At first the people react to His suffering and death as a token of His rejection by God. But on deeper reflection they come to a movingly profound realization that He did not die for any sin in Him. Rather, He suffered ignominiously, died, and was laid in a felon's grave for the transgressions of the people. The passages under review also hint at the resurrection of the Suffering Servant. In the closing scene, the many whose sins He bore will be appropriated to Him as His spoils of love.

As we have seen, the Koran has no hesitation at all in recognizing Jesus Christ in His role as a servant. But it speaks in enigmas when dealing with His suffering, death, resurrection, and ascension. That Jesus Christ was subject to death like other prophets is clearly indicated in several passages of the Koran. It is written, for example:

> Peace on me the day I was born, and the day I die, and the day I shall be raised alive! (Sura 19:33, Pickethall)

Exactly the same words are used about John the Baptist in Sura 19:15. Therefore, there is no extraordinary significance in the expression used about Jesus Christ, "the day of my being raised up alive." In both cases it implies the general resurrection of the dead. In another passage we read:

> When God said, O Jesus, verily I will cause thee to die, and I will take thee up unto me and I will deliver thee from the unbelievers, and I will place those who follow thee above the unbelievers until the day of resurrection: then unto Me shall ye return, and I will judge between you of that concerning which ye disagree. (3:55, Pickethall)

It is the opinion of many Muslim authorities that Jesus Christ was taken up to heaven alive without experiencing death. They hold that there is a hysteron proteron in the words, "I will cause thee to die, and I will take thee up unto me," and that the copulative does not imply order. In other words, Jesus Christ was taken up to God alive and will die some other time. They suppose that His death will happen sometime when He returns to the earth before the Last Day. Others say that the order of the words need not be changed. They interpret them figuratively, supposing that Jesus Christ was lifted up while He was asleep and that God caused Him to die a spiritual death to all worldly desires. There are yet others who acknowledge that He actually died a natural death, and continued in that state for three hours, or according to another tradition, seven hours—after which He was resurrected and taken to heaven (see Sale, *Koran*, pp. 51, 52, note 1). If the death of Jesus Christ was meant to be a usual occurrence, the Koran did not need to mention some of the unusual details which have baffled Muslims ever since. For example, the expression "Bring thy term to an end" (Mutwaffika) in the quotation above is a perplexing one. It usually signifies death (Sura 2:240). But it is also used of the soul of a person gathered up by God in sleep and then returned when they wake up:

> He it is who gathereth you at night and knoweth that which ye commit by day. Then He raised you again to life therein that the term appointed for you may be accomplished. And afterward unto Him is your return. Then he will proclaim unto you what ye used to do. (Sura 6:60, Pickethall)

The commentator Al-Baidhawi gives five possible explanations of the term "Mutawaffika" as it occurs in 3:55, above. It could mean "achieve thy whole term and tarry till the appointed end," or "take thee from the earth," or "to take thee to myself sleeping," or "to destroy in thee lusts which hinder ascent to the world of spirits," or as some say, God let Him die for seven hours and raised Him to heaven. The fact remains that the death of Jesus Christ is an enigma in the Koran, which Muslim ingenuity, expressed in the numerous commentaries and traditions, has not been able to resolve. The Koran teaches that Jesus Christ, like all mortals, is to taste of death. But it denies that He died upon the cross. It says that at that point God raised Him up to himself. The question left unresolved is, when did He die? At this point the Koran is silent, giving rise to free speculation on the part of Muslim divines. There is one more reference to the death of Christ which needs to be included here:

> They indeed have disbelieved who say: "Lo! Allah is the Messiah, son of Mary." Say, who then can do aught against Allah, if He had willed to destroy the Messiah Son of Mary, and His mother and everyone on earth? Allah's is the sovereignty of the heavens and the earth and all that is between them. He createth what He will, and Allah is able to do all things. (5:17, Pickethall)

Ibn-I-Ishaq says that these words were revealed in reply to Christians of Najran to correct their sectarian differences "in regard to the nature of Jesus" (*Life of Muhammad*, p. 272). The point made in the revelation was that God is living and ever existent, "Whereas Jesus died and was crucified according to their doctrine" (Ibid.). This explanation does not throw any light on the moot question, "When did Jesus Christ die?" The Koran appears to deny plainly that He died upon the cross:

> And because of their saying: "We slew the Messiah, Jesus Son of Mary, Allah's messenger"—they slew him not nor crucified, but it appeared so unto them; and lo! those who disagree concerning it are in doubt thereof, they have no knowledge thereof save persuit of a conjecture, they slew him not for certain. But Allah took him up unto Himself. Allah was ever mighty, wise. (4:157, 158, Pickethall)

It is wrong to say that the Koran denies the incident of the Crucifixion. It only denies that the person crucified on that historic occasion was Jesus Christ. The Jews and the Romans were under the impression that they were crucifying Him. But in that they were deceived. Someone died upon that cross who looked like Jesus Christ. The Muslim scholars take it upon themselves to fill in the gap created by the Koranic statements on the Crucifixion. Some of the most divergent, and often mutually exclusive, theories and stories have cropped up around the theme in the course of centuries following the Koran. Practically all the theories agree that Jesus Christ did not die upon the cross. From this point they take off in different directions of their choice. Various substitutes, who are alleged to have looked like Jesus, have been suggested. But there are a few Muslim scholars who are exceptions to the rule. They grant that Jesus was crucified but assert that He did not die there. Such a position clearly goes against the teaching of the Koran expressed in the well-known statement, "They did not kill him, they did not crucify him." While it allows the validity of the first part of the statement, it rejects the other half of it.

Sayyad Ahmad Khan of India held such a view. He believed that it was Jesus Christ whom they crucified—not someone looking like Him. But He did not die there. He only swooned and was taken down alive after three or four hours (*Religious Ideas of Sir Sayyad Ahmad Khan* by M. Ali, p. 231).

This theory was readily picked up by another Muslim from north India who aimed at being a reformer of Islam but gradually built his claims up to messiahship and prophethood. He took the theory of Sayyad Ahmad Khan and mixed it up with a story, published in his time, about the alleged visit of Jesus Christ to Tibet. The followers of this person even today make a lot of his hodgepodge of a theory about the escape of Jesus Christ from the cross. In view of their propaganda it may be helpful to mention briefly the background to the fiction which their leader Ghulam Ahmad picked up from the press. We cannot do better than quote J. N. Farquhar:

> A Russian, named Nicholas Notovitch, travelled through Cashmere to Leh in Ladak and spent some time in friendly intercourse with Buddhist Lamas of the monastery of Himis. Seven years later he published a book in which he declared that the Abbot of the monastery had brought out and read to him an ancient manuscript, according to which Jesus, in the interval between His visit to the Temple of Jerusalem at the age of twelve and His baptism by John, travelled from Palestine to India, and studied under the Jains, Buddhist and Hindus of those days. (*Modern Religious Movements in India*, New York, 1919, p. 140)

While scholars like Max Muller criticized Notovitch for his fabrications, Prof. Archibald Douglas, of the Government College in Agra, used his summer vacations to journey to Ladak in the hope of finding the MS which the Russian storyteller claimed to have seen. But when he arrived at the monastery and related his tale, the Abbot was wild with indignation at a fabrication which used his name. No such MS existed in the monastery library or indeed anywhere in Tibet. Farquhar goes on to relate:

> The whole story was an impudent lie. Professor Douglas described his

journey in The Nineteenth Century for April 1896; and M. Nicholas Notovitch was recognized to be an unscrupulous adventurer. Yet many Hindus
and Muhammadens still make use of his lies. (Ibid., p. 141)

Ghulam Ahmad took this story and, using the swoon theory of Sayyad
Ahmad Khan, made his own home brew of a theory that Jesus Christ took
His journey to Kashmir not before the opening of His ministry—as in Notovitch story—but after His crucifixion. To further support his theory, he
conveniently found a grave in Sirinagar, Kashmir, which he declared to be
the grave of Jesus. All these speculations have been condemned as heretical
by the Muslim orthodoxy.

It needs to be pointed out here that the earliest Muslim theories dealing
with the crucifixion of Jesus Christ were mainly concerned with finding a
suitable substitute for Him in fulfillment of the description in the Koran,
"Shubbiha Lahu" (His likeness). The later Muslim writers became acquainted with the Bible and benefited from Christian scholarship. They
learned that those crucified did not always die within a few hours. Some of
them used this as an argument to prove Jesus did not die upon the cross.
They disregard the fact that the Roman executioners knew well how to des-
patch a prisoner on the cross even though he may be alive at the time his
body was to be taken down. What happened to the two thieves on either
side of Jesus Christ when their legs were broken by the executioners does
not interest these scholars, nor do they desire to take into consideration the
thrust of a Roman spear through one side of Jesus Christ into His pericardi-
um (John 19:33-35). But such Muslims as Syyad Ahmad Khan and
Ghulam Ahmad theorize about the Crucifixion in a way that is contrary
both to the Koran and the Bible.

The teaching of the Koran that Jesus Christ did not die upon the cross
implies that the entire Christian movement is based on a unique deception
in history. The Romans and the Jews may be alleged to have been deceived
because the one whom they crucified looked like Jesus. But how about the
disciples of Jesus Christ? The New Testament and the history of the Church
testify to the fact that the Christians, of all people, were the first to proclaim to the world, beginning from Jerusalem, that Jesus Christ died upon
the cross to save the world. But the Koran teaches that God rescued Jesus
from the cross and took Him directly to heaven. In that case His disciples'
preaching His crucifixion within a few days of the event becomes a puzzle
to be solved. They could not be accused of a fabrication, for even according
to the Koran they were honest helpers of God (61:14; 3:52). By telling a de-
liberate lie to the world, they would have proved helpers of Satan. Here, the
Muslims might suggest that the first disciples did not preach the death of
their master on the cross and that their testimony to that effect in the Gospels is a later corruption.

But it must be granted that the Bible was sound during the time the
Koran was revealed. To recapitulate what has been discussed at length earlier, the Koran asserts that the Judeo-Christian Scripture existed contem-
poraneously and confirms them (10:38; 2:41). Moreover, Muslims are required to believe in them (42:14, 15; 29:45). Again, the prophet was advised

to consult with those who read the scripture before him if he had any doubt about the revelation sent to him (10:95). If the Bible was corrupted by then, why would God refer the prophet to it? Finally, Christians are admonished to abide by the Gospels:

> Let the People of the Gospel judge by that which Allah hath revealed therein. Whoso judgeth not by that which Allah hath revealed; such are evil-livers. (5:47, Pickethall)

A similar admonition is given to both the Jews and the Christians (74:31; 5:68). How could they be expected to live up to this advice if their Scriptures were corrupted? If a Muslim said that all references to the death of Jesus Christ in the Gospels today are corruption since the time of the Koran, then we have ample evidence to disprove such a theory. We have New Testament MSS that predate the rise of Islam. Apart from the Gospel record the Christian testimony as to the redeeming death of Jesus Christ is consistent and abundant throughout the centuries of the Church history preceding Islam. Add to this the weight of evidence to the same effect from non-Christian sources.

Justin Martyr wrote his *Defense of Christianity* to the emperor Antonius Pius about A.D. 150. He advised the emperor to check the details of the death of Christ in the Acts of the Roman governor of Judaea, Pontius Pilate, during the days of Jesus Christ. Quoting Psalm 22:16 he writes:

> But the words, "They pierced my hands and feet," refer to the nails which were fixed in Jesus' hands and feet on the cross; and after he was crucified, his executioners cast lots for his garments, and divided them among themselves. That these things happened you may learn from the "Acts" which were recorded under Pontius Pilate. (Justin, *First Apology* 35:7-9)

He goes on to say again:

> That he performed these miracles you may easily satisfy yourself by the "Acts of Pontius Pilate." (Ibid. 48:3)

Tacitus in the course of "Roman Annals" (written between A.D. 115-170) mentions the fire of Rome and the Emperor Nero's attempt to put the blame on Christians of the time of Peter and Paul. He gives a brief account of the origin of Christians:

> They got their name from Christ, who was executed by the sentence of the procurator Pontius Pilate in the reign of Tiberius. That checked the pernicious superstition for a short time, but it broke out afresh—not only in Judaea, where the plague first arose, but in Rome itself, where all the horrible and shameful things in the world collect and find a home. (Tacitus Annal XV.44)

About A.D. 52, a writer named Thallus wrote a history of Eastern Mediterranean world from the Trojan War to his own time. This work has disappeared, but excerpts from it have been used by another historian, Julius Africanus, who lived in the early part of the third century.

> Julius Africanus describes the earthquake and the preternatural darkness which accompanied the crucifixion of Christ, and says that Thallus, in

his third book, explained this darkness as an eclipse of the sun. (He also points out that Thallus' explanation was unacceptable because Jesus was crucified at full moon when no eclipse of the sun is possible.) (F. F. Bruce, *Jesus and Christian Origins Outside N.T.*, p. 30)

Though Thallus' original work is lost, yet it contained the earliest known reference to the darkness that prevailed on the day Christ died, outside of the record in the New Testament (23:44-45). As to the death of Christ we have a Syriac manuscript in the British museum which contains a letter written sometime later than A.D. 73 by one Mara bar Serapion to his son Serapion. The writer was in prison when he wrote to his son:

> What advantage did the Athenians gain by putting Socrates to death? Famine and plague came upon them as judgment for their crime. What advantage did the men of Samos gain by burning Pythagoras? In a moment their land was covered with sand. What advantage did the Jews gain from executing their wise king? It was just after that their kingdom was abolished. God justly avenged these three wise men: the Athenians died of hunger; the Samians were overwhelmed by the sea; the Jews ruined and driven from their land, lived in complete dispersion. But Socrates did not die for good; he lived on in the teaching of Plato. Pythagoras did not die for good; he lived on in the statue of Hira. Nor did the wise king die for good; he lived in the teaching which he had given. (Bruce, ibid., p. 31)

Along with the early pagan references to Jesus Christ and His death, we also have a testimony from the rabbinical tradition from the time of Christ. The Tannaitic period of the rabbinic traditions contains one or two references to Jesus Christ. The most important is a "barathia" preserved in the Talmudic tractate Sanhedrin (43[a]):

> Jesus was hanged on Passover eve. Forty days previously the herald had cried, "He is being led out for stoning, because he has practised sorcery and led Israel astray and enticed them into apostasy. Whosoever has anything to say in his defense, let him come and declare it." As nothing was brought forward, he was hanged on Passover Eve. (Bruce, ibid., 56)

The above evidence to the death of Jesus Christ on the cross may be countered by the suggestion of the Koran that both the Romans and the Jews were deceived. They did crucify someone looking like Jesus Christ. But he was not really Jesus—only another person mistaken for him. As we have said before, the Koran does not say whether or not the disciples of Jesus Christ were deceived also like the enemies. But the silence of the Koran at this point is broken by traditions.

Al-Tabari, the well-known historian and commentator on the Koran, reports about a certain Wahab b. Munabih who lived around A.D. 700. This man was a leading transmitter of Judeo-Christian lore to the Muslims. He is perhaps the first on record who made an attempt to bring the Koranic position on the Crucifixion in as close an alignment with the New Testament as was possible for a Muslim. His version of the Passion narrative is reported by Tabari as follows:

> They brought him to the gibbet on which they intended to crucify him, but God raised him up to Himself and a simulacrum was crucified in his

place. He remained there for seven hours, and then his mother and another woman whom He had cured of madness came to weep for him. But Jesus came to them and said, "God has raised me up to Himself, and this is a mere simulacrum." (Bruce, ibid., p. 178)

As an example of growing legendary traditions in Islam on the subject of the Crucifixion, we cite the view of "Thalabi." He wrote the following about three hundred years after Whab b. Munabih:

> When Jesus was brought to the cross, darkness covered the earth, and God sent angels who took position between them (the executioners) and Jesus. The shape of Jesus was put on Judas who had pointed him out, and they crucified him instead, supposing that he was Jesus. After three hours God took Jesus to Himself and raised him up to heaven. (Bruce, ibid., p. 179)

These traditions allow an ignorance on the part of the disciples also as to the person crucified. Jesus Christ himself had to tell His mother and another woman disciple that someone looking like Him was crucified. If two of the followers of Christ were enlightened as to the Crucifixion, it is reasonable to presume that they shared their information with the rest of the disciples also. It would imply that according to traditions, quoted above, the New Testament account of the death of Christ is due to its corruption at the hands of Christians. But any corruption of the Bible cannot be sustained on the basis of the teaching of the Koran, as shown earlier.

This leaves us grounded in a puzzle. A likeness of Jesus Christ was crucified, but the executioners and the Jews thought He was Christ himself. His disciples also had the same belief as recorded in the Gospels. The Koran nowhere states that they too were deceived—only the Jews and Romans were. The Koran came to confirm the Torah and the Gospels. How could it confirm the Gospel account of the death of Christ upon the cross when it says plainly that only a likeness of Jesus Christ was crucified? Before dealing with this intriguing issue let us mention, in passing, that the Koran is not unique in its teaching against the crucifixion of Jesus Christ.

According to the church father, Frenacus (about A.D. 180), a certain Basilides taught that the divine "Nous" appeared in human form. At the Crucifixion He changed form with Simon of Cyrene who had carried the cross. The Jews mistaking Simon for Jesus nailed him to the cross. Jesus stood by deriding the Jews for their error before ascending to heaven (J. B. Lightfoot, *The Apostolic Fathers*, pp. 156 ff.). Mani of Persia who died in A.D. 276 held a similar view. He called Jesus "the son of a widow" and taught that the son of the widow of Nain whom Jesus had raised from the dead was finally put to death in His place. According to another Manichaen document, the Devil, who was trying to have Jesus crucified, fell himself a victim to crucifixion. Photius (A.D. 920-91 circa) writes about an apocryphal book called *The Travels of the Apostles.* In it it was said that Christ was not crucified but another in His place (W. St. Clair Tisdall, op. cit., pp. 184, 185).

Returning to the Koranic treatment of the Crucifixion, it must be kept in mind that the first disciples of Jesus Christ do not appear to be included among those who suffered from a deception. Only those involved in the Crucifixion thought they were killing Christ. Having stated this much, in one passage the Koran seems to include Christians also among those deceived:

> And verily they who disagreed concerning Him, were in a doubt as to this matter, and had no sure knowledge thereof, but followed only an uncertain opinion. They did not really kill Him; but God took Him up unto himself; and God is mighty and wise. (4:157, 158)

Who are those who differed about Jesus Christ and on account of a lack of sure knowledge about Him followed only an opinion? They do not appear to be Jews who were sure that they crucified Him. These Jews are referred to clearly at the end of the verse, "They did not really kill him." In view of the Christological controversies that occupied the attention of the Christian denominations during the rise of Islam, we may quickly identify the group here intended by the Koran. They were its contemporary Christians who demonstrated no sure knowledge about the death of Jesus Christ. They were in doubt as to in which of His two natures He suffered death. This interpretation of the verse is supported by Al-Baidhawi. In his commentary he says:

> For some maintained that he was justly and really crucified; some insisted that it was not Jesus who suffered, but another who resembled him in the face, pretending that the other parts of his body, by their unlikeness plainly revealed the imposition; some said he was taken up to heaven; and others that his manhood only suffered, and that his Godhead ascended into heaven. (As quoted by Sale, Koran (new ed.), p. 94, note 3)

As it has been shown, the two-nature issue was a hot one in the Christological discussions that occupied the attention of Christian denominations during the rise of Islam. Apart from Al-Baidhawi, Ibn Ishaq also confirms that the two-nature controversy, as to its implication for the nativity and crucifixion of Jesus Christ was the moot problem for Christians of those days and that the prophet sought to give a decisive declaration about it. Reporting about a delegation of Christians from Najran that visited the prophet, he writes:

> So they left him and consulted with Aqib who was their chief advisor and asked him what his opinion was. He said, "O, Christians you know right well that Muhammad is a prophet sent [by God] and he has brought a decisive declaration about the nature of your Master." (Op. cit., p. 277)

In another passage also Ibn Ishaq reconfirms the same information. He says that one of the purposes of the Koran was to settle this two-nature dispute among Christians:

> And He sent down the Criterion i.e., the distinction between truth and falsehood about which the sects differ in regard to the nature of Jesus Christ and other natures. (Ibid., p. 272)

In the light of the information from Ibn Ishaq which tallies with what we know of Church history, it is reasonable to believe that the denial of the

Crucifixion in the Koran is Christologically oriented. The Koran aimed to settle the disagreement among its contemporary Christians as to the two natures of Jesus Christ. In regard to the Crucifixion, the Christians were in doubt whether He suffered and died in His human nature alone or whether His divine nature was also involved in some mysterious way. The Monophysite position, as represented by Cyril of Alexandria, maintained that the divine and human natures existed in Christ before the Incarnation. But after it, the two natures fused into an indissoluble unity which can be distinguished only in thought (ERE, Vol. 8, Monophysitism, p. 812). "The united elements of the two natures in the Incarnation form a composite nature, a divine-human hypostasis, and it is to this that all the activities of Jesus Christ are to be attributed" (Ibid., p. 815). Among the orthodox Monophysites there were many who accepted unequivocally the thesis that one of the Holy Trinity suffered in the flesh. The Nestorian position was quite different from this point of view. On the eve of Islam, in the twenty-third year of the Sassanian King Khusro Parviz, the fathers of the Nestorian Church in Persia made an official statement in defense of their Christology, as distinguished from that of the Monophysites. In that credo, referred to earlier, they made the following remarks about the Crucifixion:

> He worked and preached until He was captured and delivered up to His judges and crucified. His human nature felt the pains of torture and death; but His divine nature did not suffer. (G. D. Malech, op. cit., p. 211)

In the case of Crucifixion, the Koran comes closer to the Nestorian position than the Monophysitic stand. It agrees with the Nestorians that the Jews did not kill or crucify Jesus Christ so far as His divine nature was concerned. Hence the Monophysites, who imply that He died even in His divine nature (which they believed was indissolubly linked up with the human), are as wrong as the Jews who thought they killed the Son of God. The Nestorians who taught that Jesus Christ was crucified and died in His humanity only are true to the Scriptures. About His humanity the Bible says, "He was made in the likeness of man" (Phil. 2:7). Again, about His death on the cross we read:

> For what the law could not do, in that it was weak through the flesh, God sending his own son in the likeness of sinful flesh, and for sin, condemned sin in the flesh. (Romans 8:3)

The Koranic expression "Shubbiha Lahum" (4:157) is very close to the Biblical statement, "the likeness of sinful flesh and the likeness of men." To bridge the slight difference between the two, we may make a free translation of the verse in the Koran as follows:

> They slew Him not nor crucified Him but only His likeness of men (or sinful flesh).

This rendering agrees with the teaching of Jesus Christ that the soul of man cannot be killed by men. He said:

> Fear not them which kill the body, but are not able to kill the soul: but rather fear him which is able to destroy both soul and body in hell. (Matthew 10:28)

If the soul of an ordinary human cannot be killed by mortals, how could the Jews ever say they crucified and killed Jesus Christ in His divine majesty? Those Muslims who grant that Jesus Christ was crucified have a problem with "Shubbiha Lahum" of the Koran. The explanation that is discussed here can redeem them of a perplexity involved in their position. Also, it relieves the Koran of the enigma in its teaching about the death of Christ and His ascension.

Chapter 12

Redemptive Death of Jesus, the Messiah

The Koran recognizes that the practice of offering sacrifices is as universal as religion itself. Concerning animal sacrifices, it makes the following observation:

> And whoso maketh valuable offerings unto God, verily they proceed from the piety of men's hearts. Ye receive various advantages from the cattle designed for sacrifices, until a determined time for slaying them: then the place of sacrificing them is the ancient house. Unto the possessor of every religion have we appointed a ritual that they may commemorate the name of God in slaying the brute cattle which He hath provided for them. (Sura 22:32-34)

The measure of piety in the heart of a worshipper is shown by his offering as valuable a sacrifice to God as possible within his means. Al-Baidhawi reports that once the prophet offered one hundred fat camels—among them one which had belonged to Abu Jahl, which had in its nose a gold ring. Umar is known to have offered a camel once for which he had bid three hundred dinars. Baidhawi goes on to comment that the term "mansak" (ritual), in the passage above, means a place of devotion or a sacrifice which draws man to God (Hughes' Dictionary, p. 551). In other words, the Koran considers an animal sacrifice to be an expression of man's hunger for God and a means of seeking His nearness.

The pre-Islamic Arabs offered animal sacrifices to their various gods and goddesses. The prophet of Islam destroyed the idols in the Käaba and elsewhere in Arabia. But he retained the shrine as a center of Islam somewhat in the manner of the Israel of old. Islam has only two great festivals. They are Id Al-Adha and Id Al-Fitr. Id Al-Adha is greater of the two. During the time he lived in the city of Medina, the prophet observed how the Jews kept the great fast of the Atonement on the tenth day of the seventh month. According to a tradition he inquired from the Jews about the reason for the fast. He was informed that it was a memorial of the deliverance, under the leadership of Moses, of the children of Israel from Egyptian slavery. On hearing this, the prophet remarked. "We have a greater right on Moses than they." Therefore he commanded his followers to fast as did the Jews. During this period of his amity with the Jews, the prophet often attended the synagogue, and the Muslims turned toward Jerusalem in prayer. After his estrangement from the Jews, the "Qiblah" was changed from Jerusalem to Mecca. In the second year of the Hijira, both he and his followers did not take part in the Jewish fast. Instead, he instituted the Id Al-Adha. In that connection he adopted the pre-Islamic festival of annual pilgrimage to the Käaba. Offering of animal sacrifices was the concluding ceremony of this festival. The Koran says nothing to connect this sacrifice with the history of Abraham and Ishmael. But it is generally believed by the Muslims that the festival commemorates the willingness of Abraham to offer his son as a sacrifice to God (Hughes' Dictionary, p. 193).

According to the Mosaic Law (in its significance for man's relationship with God), there were two major categories of sacrifices. They consisted of sin offerings and peace offerings. Sin offerings were meant for the priest, nation, and individuals. Guilt offerings belonged to the same class. All these assumed their most characteristic form in connection with the Day of Atonement (Lev. 16). Peace offerings may be taken to include the Passover and all offerings of firstfruits, tithes, and bloodless sacrifices. Sin offerings took notice of human unworthiness to approach God.

Also, it is noteworthy that the offences atoned for by sacrifice were only sins of ignorance or inadvertence and misfortune like leprosy (Lev. 14:9). But for willful disobedience of the laws of God there was no sacrifice (Num. 15:30; Isa. 2:25; 3:14; 1 John 5:16). With every civil penalty there was a sacrifice as well (Lev. 6:5). It signifies that in every crime against man there is a sin against God. Also, it implied the ultimate sovereignty of God in human affairs. Again, the holiness of God was a dominating principle in the Old Testament sacrifices for sin.

In all animal sacrifices a sense of the sacredness of life was expressed by the reverent use of the blood (Lev. 17:11). Sacrificed animals were put to death without inflicting unnecessary pain upon them. It was not their suffering that expiated sin (contrast 1 Kings 18:28). It was the loss of life they suffered that was significant as well as the blood representing life. In a sense the life of the animal was given for the life of the worshipper. It was symbolized when an offerer laid his hands upon the animal to be sacrificed (Lev. 1:4). A similar substitution is indicated in the ransom (Matt. 20:28) paid for the firstborn, although no animal substitute is mentioned (Ex. 13:13; cf. Num. 3:47).

The Jewish Day of Atonement took place on the tenth day of the seventh month on their sacred calendar. Before the destruction of Jerusalem in A.D. 70, it was a day of special sacrifices apart from the usual daily sacrifices. These festive sacrifices of the day consisted in those offered for the high preist and priesthood plus those for the people. The sin offering for the people consisted of two goats. One of them was killed and its blood sprinkled as directed. The other was sent away into the wilderness, bearing all the sins and transgressions of the children of Israel which had been confessed over him and laid upon him by the high priest. This scapegoat was to be sent away into a land not inhabited, bearing the sins of the people. In later Jewish practice, this goat was required to be pushed over a rocky precipice. But Edersheim reminds us:

> It was an innovation in no wise sanctioned by the Law of Moses, and not even introduced at the time the Septuagint translation was made as its rendering of Lev. 16:26 shows. The Law simply ordained that the goat, once arrived in "the land not inhabited" was to be "let go" free, and Jewish ordinance of having it pushed over the rocks is signally characteristic of the Rab-

binical perversion of the type. (Edersheim, *The Temple—Its Ministry and Service*, p. 324)

According to Leviticus 16, the scapegoat was meant for Azazel. Edersheim points out that the word Azazel is derived from a root which means "wholly to put aside" or "wholly to go away." He goes on to make the important observation that the scapegoat was the symbol of the One who was going to bear the sins of the world to put them away finally (Ibid., p. 324).

There is a tradition of an interesting sacrifice offered by the prophet of Islam:

> Ans says: "The prophet sacrificed two rams, one was black, and the other was white, and put his foot on their sides as he killed them and cried, 'In the name of God. God is great.' " (Mishkat, Book IV, Chapter 49)

In this incident the prophet was obviously following the tradition of two goats sacrificed on the Jewish Day of Atonement. But instead of goats he used rams. Again, the scapegoat appears to be represented by the black ram. That the blackness of the ram could symbolize an animal bearing sins of the people is authenticated by a tradition concerning the black stone of Käaba. According to Ibn Abbas, the prophet is reported to have said that this stone came from Paradise. At the time of its descent it was whiter than milk, but due to the sins of children of Adam transferred to it by touch, it became black (Hughes' Dictionary, pp. 154, 155). When the prophet killed both the white and black rams, he followed the practice of his contemporary Jews who killed the scapegoat contrary to the injunction of the Scripture.

It is significant that according to the scriptural prescription, the high priest pronounced the name of Jehovah three times in confession over the scapegoat. The worshippers responded by saying, "Blessed be the Name. Glory of His Kingdom is for ever and for ever" (Edersheim, *The Temple*, p. 310). The prophet, according to tradition just cited, pronounced the name of God over the two sacrificial rams in the manner of the Hebrews of old. This incident belonged, probably, to the period of time when he was friendly toward the Jews.

After his break away from the Jews the prophet shifted fasting prescribed for Muslims from the Day of Atonement to the month of Ramadan. It concluded with Id Al-Fitr. In the place of sacrifice on the Day of Atonement, he introduced "Id Al-Adha" (the festival of sacrifice) to be celebrated yearly on the tenth day of Dhu Al-Hajj and centered in the shrine of Käaba.

The Jews believed that Ashura (the Day of Atonement) was the season when the sacred tablets of the Law were handed over to Moses by God. When fasting for Muslims was moved from Ashura to Ramadan the following revelation was delivered:

> The month of Ramadan in which was revealed the Quran, a guidance for manking and clear proofs of the guidance, and criterion. And whosoever of you is present, let him fast the month, and whosoever of you is sick or on a journey, [let him fast the same] number of other days. (Sura 2:185)

As far as the Jews were concerned, they celebrated the receiving of the tablets of the Law by Moses on the Day of Atonement. This celebration was preceded by days of fasting. The celebration itself was highlighted by the sacrifice of two goats—one of them the scapegoat bearing sins of the people. The prophet turned the Jewish observance into two separate observances for the Muslims. The sacrifice part was linked up with the great sacrifice of Abraham. But confession of sins and bearing of guilt was left out of the picture. This festival of sacrifice came to be considered only commemorative of what was done by Abraham. The Jewish practice of fasting before Ashura was incorporated into the fasting during Ramadan. But it is strange that the confession of people's sins over a scapegoat in the Jewish ceremony was transferred to the believers fasting in Ramadan. Thus the month-long fasting came to be regarded of atoning value for sins committed in the course of a year (see *Shorter Encyclopaedia of Islam*, p. 507).

When the fast of Ramadan and other exercises are believed to be of atoning value, then there should be no need for an intercessor here or in the hereafter. Yet they believe that their prophet will intercede, on their behalf, with God on the Last Day. To clarify this situation it may be mentioned that the intercession of the prophet is expected to be for great sins only, as we have in the following tradition:

> The prophet of God said: "My intercession is for the great sinners of the community." (Abu Daud. Sunna. Bab. 20, Tirmidhi Bab. 2)

In other words, if fasting, prayer, or other ritual exercises are expected to wipe away sins of the Muslims, they could, at best, be minor sins only. Their major sins must wait for the prophetic intercession of the Last Day. Islam also grants the validity of intercession by angels, other apostles and prophets, the martyrs and saints (Bukhari Tawhid. Bab. 24; Ibn Hanbal III 94 Sq, 325 Sq; V 43; Abu Daud Jihad. Bab 26; Al-Tabari. Tafsir III:6 on Sura 2:225; 16:85 on Sura 19:87; 29:91 on Sura 64:48; Abu Talib Al-Makki. Kut Al-Qulub I:39). But of all these possible intercessors, the Muslim generally recognize the pre-eminence of their own prophet. He is considered to be the first to intercede for his community (Muslim Trad. 330, 332 Abu Daud. Sunna Bab. 13).

Muslims usually divide sin into major (Kabir) and minor (Saghir) sins. Such a distinction is based on passages from the Koran. In Sura 42:37, the term "kabir" is already used. The division of sins into the two categories is upheld by the orthodox. But some sects like the Kharidjis or Mutazilis have refused to allow such a distinction (both hold that the consequences of big sins are eternal punishment). Moreover, the orthodox hold that sins are repaired by good works—chief among them being the fast, seeking pardon of God (Istighfar), and repentance.

The Muslim position that their sins (Major) will be forgiven only in the hereafter by the intercession of their prophet is comparable to the Hebrew sacrifices which only "covered" sins of the people but did not remove them finally. This idea agrees with terms used in the Old Testament for "atonement" (Arabic, "Kaffara"), which meant "covering up by a substitute," and the mercy seat as, "the place of covering up." In the words of the eminent Hebrew scholar of the Bible:

> It means the inherent "weakness and unprofitableness of the command-
> ment"; it means that "the Law made nothing perfect but was the bringing of
> a better hope"; that in the covenant mercy of God guilt and sin were "cov-
> ered up," and in that sense atoned for, or rather they were both "covered up"
> and removed but that they were not really taken away and destroyed till
> Christ came; that they were only taken into a land not inhabited, till He
> should blot it out by His own blood; that the provision which the Old Testa-
> ment made was only temporary, "until the time of the reformation"; and
> that hence real and true forgiveness of sins, and with it the spirit of adoption
> could only be finally obtained after the death and resurrection of the Lamb
> of God who taketh away the sins of the world. (Edersheim, *The Temple*, pp.
> 321, 322)

The Old Testament covenant, despite year-round sacrifices culminat-
ing in the sacrifices of the great Day of Atonement, helped only to "cover
up" the sins of the people. For the removal of sin they looked forward to the
advent of the Messiah. Similarly, despite sacrifices and other religious exercises believed to be of redeeming value, the major sins of Muslims are, at
best, covered up till the Last Day. Their guilt remains till then, and forgiveness of their sins is only an eschatological hope.

Id Al-Adha remains the greatest festival of Islam. But it has only a
commemorative value to Muslims. Its celebration enables a believer to
earn reward for good actions, but it is not related to expiation or forgiveness
of sins. In Islam the doctrine of expiation of sins is distinguished from the
doctrine of sacrifice. Sacrifices are confined strictly to Id Al-Adha and
"Aqiqa" ceremony on the seventh day of a child.

It may help our main discussion to recapitulate some salient features of
atonement in Islam. There are two words used for expiation, "kaffara" (to
hide) and "fida" (to ransom or exchange). Muslim theologians choose to
use the terms "kaffara" and "fidiyah" to express expiation to God, while
"divah" and "qisas" for that which is due to man. Expiation, by and large,
carries the idea of restitution for neglected religious ritual and duties like
prayer, almsgiving, fasting and pilgrimage (Sura 5:91, 92; 2:180). Expiation
as restitution to human beings is mentioned in passages like Sura 5:49, 95.
It is worthy of note that in the Hebrew system sacrifice and expiation to
man were related. As it has been mentioned earlier, every penalty for the
breaking of a civil law had an appropriate religious sacrifice. It is not so in
Islam. Again, expiation or atonement for the whole man as a sinner before
the Holy God is not clearly known in the Koran. But faint glimmers of this
important insight for salvation may be detected here and there. There is a
passage in this connection which seems to echo the New Testament parable
of the Foolish Virgins:

> On that day the hypocrites, both men and women, shall say to those who
> believe, "Tarry for us, that we may kindle our light at yours." It shall be
> said, "Return ye back and seek light for yourselves." But between them will
> be set a wall with a gateway, within which shall be the Mercy, and in the
> front, without, the Torment. They shall cry to them "Were we not with
> you?" They shall say, "Yes! But ye led yourselves into temptation, and ye

delayed, and ye doubted, and the good things ye craved deceived you till the doom of God arrived—and the deceiver deceived you in regard to God."

On that day therefore no expiation [ransom] shall be taken from you or from those who believe not—your abode the fire—this shall be your master and wretched the journey thither. (Sura 57:13-15)

In the passage above expiation is used in a moral sense higher than in other related passages. But it remains a restitution made by man to God. Atonement in the Biblical context means an expiation for sins of man made by God. The closest approach to this perspective is the story of the sacrifice of Abraham in the Koran:

And he said, "Verily I repair to my God who will guide me. O Lord, give me a son, of thy righteousness." We announced to him a youth of meekness. And when he became full grown youth, his father said to him, "My son I have seen in a dream that I should sacrifice thee; therefore, consider what thou seest right?" He said, "My father, do what thou art bidden; of the patient, if God please, shalt thou find me." And when they had surrendered themselves to the will of God, he laid him down upon his forehead. We cried unto him, "O Abraham! Now hast thou satisfied the vision. See how we recompense the righteous?" This was indeed a decisive test. And we ransomed his son with a noble victim. And we left this for him among posterity, peace be on Abraham. Thus we reward the well-doers, for he was of our believing servants. (Sura 37:99-111)

The Koran does not specify which of the two sons of Abraham was offered as a sacrifice. Many Muslim scholars have held that it was Ishmael who was the intended sacrifice—"Al-dhabih," and not Isaac. In this group there are authorities like Al-zamkhshari, Al-Baidhawi, Al-Tabari, and Ibn Al-Athir. However, Al-Thalibi expressly states that the "Ashab" (companions of the prophet) and "Tabiun" (successors of the companions), from Umar b. Al-Khattab to Kab Al-Ahbar, believed (in line with the Bible) that the person to be sacrificed was Isaac (*Shorter Encyclopaedia of Islam*, p. 175). Those who believe it was Ishmael who was the intended victim back up their preference with an interesting tradition:

Umar b. Abd-Al-Aziz asked a Jew converted to Islam about the difference of opinion and he answered: "The 'dhabhi' is Ismail; the Jews know this also, but they are jealous of you, they say it was Isaac.' " (Ibid., p. 179)

This tradition could have satisfied only those Muslims who had no direct access to the Bible. The Muslim interest in substituting Ishmael for Isaac is understandable. He is looked upon as the ancestor of north Arabian tribes. It needs to be stated here that Muslim scholars divide the Arabs into three categories: Al-Baida (those who have disappeared), Al-Arabia (the indigenous Arabs), and Al-Mustariba (those Arabicized). Ishmael is regarded as the progenitor of the last-mentioned group. It is claimed that he married the daughter of Al-Muzaz King of Al-Hijaz. From this it is clear that the Arab descendants of Ishmael were a mixed race. The prophet of Islam is considered to be a direct descendant from Ishmael; hence, not a pure Arab.

In the estimate of Muslim scholars, this lack of pure ancestry in their prophet is more than compensated by the greatness of a sacred connection with Abraham through Ishamel. It may be noted that Ishmael is looked upon as a prophet in the Koran (Sura 19:55 ff.; 4:161; 6:86; 21:85; 34:48). That being the case, Muhammad cannot be called the first and the only prophet to the Arabs. According to the Koran, Abraham and Ishamel who built the Käaba were prophets to the Arabs long before the prophet Muhammad—who came only as a reformer and renewer of the religion of Abraham (Sura 74:2; 33:40). But this fact goes against the teaching of the Koran that God had not sent an admonisher to the Arabs before the prophet Muhammad (Sura 32:3; 34:44).

Abraham has been described as "of our believing servants" (37:111). The outstanding characteristic of the religion of Abraham was faith. He believed God absolutely. That led to his unhesitating obedience to God even to his endurance of the extreme trial of a loving father. He was willing to slaughter his own beloved son in sacrifice to God. "This was indeed a decisive test," as the Koran evaluates it. In other words, the whole ordeal was the supreme expression of the true Islam of Abraham. It consisted, first, in his unwavering faith in the living God and His ultimate goodness and faithfulness toward Him. Again, as demonstrated in the historic incident, it meant a total self-surrender to God and love for Him more than anything in the world and more than everybody else.

In the Koranic passage under discussion it is significant that the spiritual attitude and experience of Abraham at the supreme moment in his prophetic life made him righteous in the eyes of God. Thus it is written, "See how we recompense the righteous?" This righteousness, however, did not arise out of obedience to a code of law: The Koran does mention books of Abraham. What those books were and whatever their nature is left to the conjecture of Muslim commentators. The Bible does not say that Abraham received a book or "scrolls" from God by way of revelation. But it is clear even in the narrative of the Koran that the supreme expression of the Islam of Abraham was not dictated by a code of law or a book either. We are told plainly that it took place in response to a dream that Abraham saw (37:102). In tradition, "A good dream is God's favor and a bad dream is that of the devil." Moreover, "good dreams are one of the parts of prophecy" (Mishkat. 21. C. IV). Abraham being a prophet was more under the control of God than ordinary men. His dream regarding the sacrifice to God was not an ordinary dream. As it turned out, it was a vision from God (37:105). In brief, Abraham was declared righteous by God simply because he believed God through a momentous vision and acted accordingly. His was not a righteousness of the law but that of faith. About this true Islam—religion of Abraham—the Bible says:

> What shall we say about Abraham, our forefather according to the flesh? For if Abraham was justified by works, he has something to boast about, but not before God. For what does the scripture say? "Abraham believed God and it was reckoned to him as righteousness." Now to one who works, his wages are not reckoned as gift but as his due. And to one who does not work but trusts him who justifies the ungodly, his faith is reckoned as righteousness." (Romans 4:1-5, RSV)

The only law given to Israel in terms of commandments was the Law of Moses. According to Scripture it came four hundred and thirty years after the covenant promise of God to Abraham (Gal. 3:16). We have mentioned already that in an interesting polemic against its Jewish and Christian contemporaries, the Koran says that Abraham, Ishmael, Isaac, Jacob, and the tribal patriarchs were neither Jews nor Christians (Sura 2:140). In another place, speaking specifically of Abraham, it says:

> Abraham was not a Jew, nor yet a Christian; but he was an upright man who had surrendered and he was not of the idolaters. (3:67)

It is recognized indirectly that the "uprightness," or righteousness, of Abraham was neither based on the Law of Moses nor on a religion called Christianity. His was a righteousness of faith in the living God with whom he entered into a covenant of promise. It is remarkable that after having denied any claim on Abraham on the part of the Jews and Christians, the prophet himself goes ahead to claim him as his own:

> Say: Lo! As for me my Lord hath guided me unto a straight path, a right religion, the community of Abraham the upright, who was not idolater. (Sura 6:62)

The argument used in the Koran to invalidate the claim of Jews and Christians upon Abraham applies equally well to Muslims. If Abraham was neither a Jew nor a Christian, he was not a follower of the prophet Muhammad either. His righteousness was neither of the Law nor of religion consisting of mere ceremonies and dogma divorced from a personal experience of God. The monotheism of Abraham, for example, was not a matter of formal confession and theological reflection alone. It was, for him, a living experience of the living God. Having received the privilege of an intimate faith contact with God, Abraham did not have to be content merely with a repetition of a given formula of the unity of God. He lived by faith, day by day, in the living God and walked with Him.

The animal which Abraham took and sacrificed in the place of his son is described in the Koran as "noble or great." In this connection Sale makes the following observation:

> The epithet of great or noble is here added, either because it was large and fat, or because it was accepted as the ransom of a prophet. Some suppose this victim was a ram, and, if we may believe in common tradition, the very same which Abel sacrificed, having been brought to Abraham out of Paradise; others fancy it was a wild goat, which came down from mount Thabir, near Mecca, for the Mohammedans lay the scene of this transaction in the valley of Mina; as a proof of which they tell us that the horns of the victim were hung up on the spout of the Caaba, where they remained till they were burnt, together with the building, in the day of Abdullah Eben Zobeir. (Sale, op. cit., p. 440)

What made the animal noble and great did not consist in its physical qualities, for a camel is bigger than a ram. It would seem more meaningful to interpret it in terms of the animal being a gift from heaven. When viewed in the light of the Bible, the greatness of the animal sacrificed consisted in its symbolism pointing beyond itself to a fulfillment to come.

There are three unique features of the sacrifice of Abraham that merit consideration. First of all, the animal was provided by God directly. Second, it was a ransom or substitute for the son of Abraham. Finally, the whole incident had a symbolic meaning. Let us deal with these points in some detail. When a worshipper offers a sacrifice to God, it comes, in the last resolution, from God. He takes from what rightfully belongs to God already and offers it back to Him. This important truth is recognized in all sacrifices offered in Islam. According to a tradition, the prophet sacrificed two rams on the day of the Festival of sacrifice and offered a prayer in which he pronounced the formula:

> O God this sacrifice is of Thee and for Thee; accept it from Muhammad and his people. (Mishkat, Book IV, Chapter XLIX)

That God alone provides the sacrificial animal whereby a worshipper may establish contact with Him is plain in all sacrifices. In order to make it absolutely plain, God provided, miraculously, an animal for Abraham to sacrifice instead of his son. Through this incident a supreme sacrifice yet to come was indicated by God—a sacrifice which was to end all animal sacrifices and bring about a reconciliation between Him and lost mankind. Moreover, it was to be a sacrifice provided by God in a sense more profound than the provision of the animal. It was to be the ultimate sacrifice of God to God!

The Koran declares plainly that God ransomed Abraham's son with "a noble victim." The ram provided by God became a substitute for Isaac. We must bear in mind here that according to the narrative, there was no sin committed by Abraham or his son that called for a ransom in the Muslim connotation of the term. Hence the ransom for the son of Abraham was symbolic and not restitutionary of some wrong done by them. It pointed to what God planned to do at the right time by sending His own Son to be a ransom not only for Isaac, Ishmael and Abraham but also for the whole world.

As Abraham journeyed to the place of sacrifice appointed by God (Gen. 22:2), he must have gone through sustained mental and spiritual agony at the prospect of having to kill his beloved son with his own hand. This loving father had to live through the nightmare for three seemingly interminable days. According to the mystery of His salvation for mankind, God allowed Abraham to suffer to the utmost extent possible for a human father. But finally when Abraham stretched forth his hand to slay his son, an angel called and ordered him to hold his hand from harming the son (Gen. 22:10-12). The Koran describes this touching scene in a similar way:

> He laid him down upon his forehead. We cried unto him, "O Abraham, thou hast already fulfilled the vision. Lo, thus do we reward the good." (Sura 37:104, 105)

Through the experience of Abraham as a loving but suffering father, God sought to reveal a deep secret about himself and His beloved Son—His Word. In order to ransom the world from thraldom to sin, God had to pay the greatest price ever. It was the sacrificial and atoning death of His only Begotten Son who became flesh. The suffering of Abraham in connection with the expected sacrifice of his son was a mere shadowy and symbolic indication of the awesome mystery of the suffering of God due to human sin. In revealing this secret of the nature of God, the Bible declares, first, that He is changeless. He is the same from everlasting to everlasting (Ps. 102:26, 27). Yet in a way too deep for human comprehension He suffers on account of the rebellion of man against Him and rejection of His preferred love, for God is love. Moreover, in His transcendence above time and space God knew the further experience of suffering on account of the death of His Incarnate Son upon the cross. It is truly impossible for the human intellect to comprehend God who, despite His changeless nature, has a long-suffering and suffering heart.

It was echoed in the experience of Abraham's attempt to sacrifice his son. But the true quality of divine suffering was manifested in history in and through the life of Jesus Christ. He came as the Suffering Servant— God revealing His suffering and long-suffering in the Incarnation against the background of sinfulness and rebelliousness of a chosen people of God. Isaiah described the sufferings of (God-Man) the Messiah, prophetically:

> He is despised and rejected of men; a man of sorrows, and acquainted with grief: and we hid as it were our faces from him; he was despised, and we esteemed him not. (Isaiah 53:3)

As we read the Gospel accounts of the days of Jesus Christ, we realize how He was destined to be humiliated and to suffer from the manger— where He was born, to the cross—where He died. His sufferings were not entirely unexpected. They were foretold by the prophets of the Old Testament who built upon God's Gospel to Adam and Eve (Gen. 3:15). Therefore, the actual sufferings of the Messiah need not have become a stumbling block to the Hebrews who knew their Scriptures. As it has been pointed out before, the condescension of the Son of God to become the Son of Man was an act of self-humiliation in itself (Phil. 2:6, 7). The Lord of creation and the Lord of angels did not loathe to become "a little lower than angels" by subjecting himself voluntarily to suffering and death on behalf of every man (Heb. 1:9). The Prince of God was not ashamed to call former abject slaves of sin and Satan His own brethren (Heb. 1:11). The historic event of the Crucifixion casts its shadow all across His blessed life. He came in order to suffer and die for the sins of many (Mark 10:45).

During His ministry He faced increasing opposition from the very people who were praying longingly for the advent of the Messiah. As the Scripture says, "He came unto his own, and his own received him not" (John 1:11). He went about doing good. He never lifted even a finger to hurt anyone. Yet there were those who received blessings from Him with one hand and then turned around to strike Him with the other. As it was foretold, they hated Him without a cause (John 15:25). This rebellious attitude and hardness of heart on the part of both His friends and thousands of beneficiaries weighed heavily upon the tender but long-suffering heart of Jesus Christ. After He had tried unsuccessfully to woo Jerusalem for three years or so, toward the close of His ministry, He shed tears of loving concern over its impending doom because it had refused to avail of its finest hour of visitation by the Messiah (Luke 19:41-42). In His great love for the very city where, before long, He was going to be denounced, dishonored and crucified, He burst forth in the cry of a heart bleeding for the people:

> O Jerusalem, Jerusalem, thou that killest the prophets, and stonest them which are sent unto thee, how often would I have gathered thy children together, even as a hen gathereth her chickens under her wings, and ye would not! Behold, your house is left unto you desolate. (Matthew 23:37, 38)

During His sojourn on earth, the sinless Saviour bore patiently the stench of human sin around Him. As He went about healing the sick, opening the eyes of those blind from birth, cleansing the lepers and raising dead back to life, it was not a casual expression of His divine powers. These miracles happened out of the mystery of His bearing the infirmities of the suffering humanity upon himself. As the Scripture states it:

> When even was come, they brought unto him many that were possessed with devils: and he cast out the spirits with his word, and healed all that were sick: that it might be fulfilled which was spoken by Esaias the prophet, saying, Himself took our infirmities, and bare our sicknesses. (Matthew 8:16, 17)

He bore physical infirmities of those whom He healed. But that was a small manifestation of the universal sweep of His atonement. As the sinless Lamb of God, He bore the sins of the world to redeem it.

The animal which God provided as a substitute for Isaac was a prophetic symbol of Jesus Christ. God can forgive sinners against His holy majesty and restore them to a loving fellowship with himself only on account of the atoning death and resurrection of Christ. What Jesus Christ came to do was symbolized in the historic experience of Abraham and Isaac. But more than that, it expressed the will of God from the foundation of the world:

> Forasmuch as ye know that ye were not redeemed with corruptible things, as silver and gold, from your vain conversation received by tradition from your fathers; but with the precious blood of Christ, as of a lamb without blemish and without spot: who verily was foreordained before the foundation of the world, but was manifest in these last times for you. (1 Peter 1:18-20)

God took a calculated risk when He granted man his freedom of the will in a world which was built to accommodate free choices. The incidence of human sin did not take God by surprise. He had made provision for a remedy even before the foundation of the world. Even this provision was not a casual foresight of God. Rather, it was a manifestation of the very nature of God. God is love. But as forgiveness is rooted in the nature of God so also punishment of all sin is the requirement of His holiness and justice.

The Koran uses the names Al-Rahman and Al-Rahim most frequently next to the name Allah. So the famous formula runs, "In the name of God (Allah) the compassionate (Al-Rahman) and the Merciful (Al-Rahim)." He is also known as the Forgiver and Forgiving (Al-Ghaffar, Al-Ghaffur), the One who accepts repentance (Al-Tawwab), the Kind (Al-Rauf) and the Clement (Al-Halim). But along with His qualities of mercy, God is holy (Al-Quddus), just (Al-Adil), the reckoner (Al-Hasib), the destroyer (Al-Muzil), the killer-avenger (Al-Muntaqim).

When a person commits sin, he defies the holiness of God, rebels against His government and rejects His proferred love. Acting according to His justice, God must judge and reckon with such a person. He could not let him go or forgive him arbitrarily. If He forgave without satisfying the absolute demands of His holiness, He would prove to be unjust and acting against himself. God is absolutely free and sovereign in His dealings with His creation, but He is *not* capricious. In His freedom to do what He wills, He never goes against His own nature. Thus though God could do everything, yet certain things are impossible even with Him. For example, God cannot create himself, God cannot commit sin, and God cannot deny himself.

As to the justice, forgiveness, and mercy of God, the Koran contains teaching which is difficult to harmonize. When Muslims began to theologize they faced perplexities in presenting a self-consistent picture of God in the Koran. For instance, over the issue of relating the ninety-nine beautiful names of God with each other and with the nature of God, Muslim scholars split into various contending parties. The orthodox party, finally, decided upon an attitude of tacit acceptance of the Koranic teaching on God without the use of reason. According to them since the attributes of God are beyond the reason of man, they must be accepted as the Koran and the prophet taught, without question. To support this position they quote a well-known verse:

> He it is who hath sent down to thee the book. Some of its signs are of themselves perspicuous (Muhkam). These are the basis of the book, and others are ambiguous (Mutshabih). But they whose hearts are given to err follow its ambiguities, craving discord, craving an interpretation; yet none knoweth its interpretation but God. And the stable in knowledge say, "We believe in it, it is all from our Lord." But none will bear this in mind, save men endued with understanding. (Sura 3:7)

Those who believe in God and the need for His revelation would concede readily that the human mind cannot fully comprehend Him. However, it is expected that when God has condescended to reveal himself to the extent of human capacity and need for salvation, there must be a measure of self-consistency within such a revelation. A revelation that freely contradicts itself will at least leave those whom it is intended to guide and redeem in utter confusion. Moreover, there will be no way for a believer to discern between revelations from God and suggestions from Satan. It would be death of all theology and freedom of discussion within the limits of the revelation of God.

The scholastic theologians of Islam could not quite agree with the extremely orthodox point of view. They were able to read the very proof text used by the orthodox in a different way by a slight change in punctuation. Thus they translated the relevant part of the verse quoted above, as follows:

> None knoweth its interpretation but God and the stable in knowledge. They say we believe in it. (ERE, "God," E. Sale, Vol. 6, p. 301)

In other words, according to the proof text, God and the stable and wise people are considered to be able to investigate all those matters that are dealt with by "ambiguous" verses. Such a qualified use of reason within the bounds of revelation led them to say, in the words of the Koran, "We believe in it." A good example of the kind of problems faced by those who allow the use of reason within the bounds of revelation is the Koran's teaching on the vengeance and forgiveness of God.

God's forgiveness does not appear to be related to His nature. It seems to be a casual choice with Him to guide or misguide people:

> Whom God guides aright, he allows himself to be guided aright, and whom He leads astray, they are the losers. (Sura 7:178)

Again we read:

> If we so willed, we could have given every soul its guidance, but the word from Me concerning evil-doers took effect: that I will fill hell with Jinn and mankind together. (Sura 32:13)

It is noteworthy that in the verses above, God guides or misguides people even before they have a choice to obey or disobey Him. They are benighted not on account of hardness of heart but due ultimately to a choice of God. This understanding of the position of the Koran is supported, for example, by the champion of orthodoxy, Al-Ghazzali:

> He willeth also the unbelief of the unbeliever and the irreligion of the wicked and, without that will, there would neither be unbelief nor irreligion. All we do we do by His will: what He willeth not does not come to pass. If one should ask why God does not will that men should believe, we answer, "We have no right to enquire about what God wills or does. He is perfectly free to will and to do what He pleases." In creating unbelievers, in willing that they should remain in that state; in making serpents, scorpions and pigs: in willing, in short, all that is evil, God has wise ends in veiw which it is not necessary that we should know. (As quoted by Hughes' Dictionary, p. 147)

Al-Ghazzali does not make a distinction between the will of God and the knowledge of God in the matter of salvation. God knows those who are going to hell. But that does not mean that He wills their condemnation. The Bible says:

> The Lord is not slack concerning his promise, as some men count slackness, but is long-suffering to us-ward, not willing that any should perish, but that all should come to repentance. (2 Peter 3:9)

If God wills people to unbelief and then condemns them to hell, it would reduce people to puppets in His hands and true religion to a mechanical performance. But Al-Ghazzali has spoken as best as he could within the bounds of the Koran. The Koran goes on to say that along with misguiding people, God also seals their hearts against good:

> Nay, but God hath set a seal upon them, for their disbelief, so that they believe not save a few. (Sura 4:155; 13:27; 16:93; 74:31)

It is not an indication of those who inherit the land after its people [who thus reaped the consequence of evil doing] that, if We will, We can smite them for their sins and seal their hearts so that they hear not. (Sura 7:100; Also, Sura 9:87, 93; 10:75; 16:108; 30:59; 40:35; 47:16; 63:3)

Despite the recognition that it is God who seals the hearts and eyes of the unbelievers, it is taught that He is "the Avenger." This title of God is not mentioned in the Koran, but the idea is to be found there (cf. Sura 5:95). Again according to another "beautiful name," God is a Reckoner (Sura 4:86; 33:39). To sum up the Koran's teaching on the judgment of God, He is really the One who guides and misguides people, in the last analysis. Those who are unbelievers are doomed to their spiritual plight as their hearts and eyes have been sealed by God who is the Tyrant (Al-Jabbar) and the Haughty (Al-Mutakabbir). Despite this utter helplessness of the unbelievers in the choice of truth, they have to face a reckoning with God the Reckoner and the Avenger, and be condemned. It may be mentioned here that one of the celebrated names of God, "Al-Adil" (the Just), does not occur in the Koran. It is to be found only in traditions. No other name of God used in the Koran represents Him as Just. However, nearest to this concept comes a description of Him as "the best of Judges" (Sura 7:87; 10:110; 12:88; see *Shorter Encyclopaedia of Islam*, p. 34).

In line with what the Koran has to say about the relationship of God with unbelievers and sinners, the traditions also present some utterly deterministic teaching. For example:

When God resolved to create the human race, He took into His hand a mass of earth, the same whence all mankind was formed, and in which they after a manner pre-existed, and having divided the clod into two equal portions, He threw one half into hell, saying, "These to eternal fire, and I care not," and projected the other half into heaven adding, "And these to Paradise, I care not." (Mishkat Al-Masabih Bab. Al-Qadr. Also, Sahih of Bukhari ed. L. Krehl [leiden 1862] I: 342-343)

According to another tradition we learn about Abu Bakr and Umar disputing predestination and the Decree:

"Abu Bakr asserts that God decrees good but does not decree evil, but Umar says that He decrees both alike." Said the apostle of God, "Shall I not decide among you over this with the decision Israfil [the archangel] gave between Gabriel and Michael?" "Did Michael and Gabriel discuss such a thing?" someone asked. He replied, "By Him who sent me with the truth, they were the very first creatures to discuss it. Gabriel took the position of Umar but Michael took that of Abu Bakr." Said Gabriel, "If we two differ about it, will not the inhabitants of heaven also come to differ? Is there not some judge who will give a decision between them?" So they requested Israfil to be the judge, and he gave a decision between them which is my decision between you. "O Apostle of God," they said, "what was this decision?" "It was," he replied, "that the Decree necessarily determines all that is good and all that is evil, all that is harmful and all that is beneficial, all that is sweet and all that is bitter, and that is my decision between you." Then he slapped Abu Bakr on the shoulder and said, "O Abu Bakr, if God Most High had not willed that there be disobedience, He would not have created the Devil."

Said Abu Bakr, "I seek pardon from God. I slipped and stumbled, O apostle of God, but never again will I fall into error about this matter." Nor did he till he was called to meet God. (Al-Sayuti: Al-Laali Al-Masnua [Cairo 1317 A.H., A.D. 1899] I: 131-132)

Abu Hanifa reports another tradition in the same line of thought:

Said the apostle of God, "There is no soul but God has written its entrance and exit and what it will meet." He was asked, "Then what is the point in acting, O apostle of God?" He answered, "Go on acting for everyone is inclined to that for which he was created. If he is for Paradise he will be inclined to the works of the people of Paradise, and if he is for fire, he will be inclined to the works of the people of fire." (Musnad [Cairo 132-A.H., A.D. 1910] p. 5)

Again:

Rafi b. Khadij tells how he asked the apostle of God what he should believe about predestination, and the prophet answered, "You are to believe in God alone, that He has no partner, and that no one shares control with Him over what is harmful and what is beneficial. You are also to believe in heaven and hell, knowing that God created them before He created any other creatures, and that when He did create creatures, He appointed whom of them He willed for heaven and whom He willed for hell, that being pure equity on His part." (Al-Malati: Kitab Al-Tanbih, ed. Sven Dedering [Istanbul 1946] pp. 105-106)

Summarizing the evidence from the Koran and traditions, the mercy of God is acknowledged along with His lack of concern as to the ultimate fate of mankind. God is called the Forgiver, the Forgiving, the Kind and the One who accepts repentance. Also next to "Allah," "Al-Rahman" (the Compassionate), and "Al-Rahim" (the Merciful) are the most popular names of God. There are several traditions that support the kindness and mercy of God. There is one often quoted tradition which says, "My mercy overcomes [or precedes] my wrath" (*Shorter Encyclopaedia of Islam*, p. 36). But in spite of such flashes of light, Islam has to face seriously the whole issue as to how the demands of the holiness of God and His wrath against sin could be satisfied to allow His love, mercy, and forgiveness to flow toward sinners.

The Bible declares that God does not desire that a single sinner should perish but that all be saved (2 Pet. 3:9). But our sins have alienated us from Him (Isa. 59:2). As sinners we come under the judgment of the holy God, for the wages of sin is death (Rom. 6:23). In order that God may reconcile us with himself and be just and true to himself, He made a provision for the atonement of the sins of the world and His forgiveness based upon it (Rom. 3:26). To that point the Scripture says:

God so loved the world, that he gave his only begotten Son, that whosoever believeth on him should not perish, but have eternal life. (John 3:16)

Jesus Christ, the Word of God, incarnate through the Virgin Mary, came to offer himself a ransom for the sins of the world. He is the ultimate and truly effectual sacrifice from "God to God." Also He is the "great and noble sacrifice" (Sura 37:107) provided by God the Father of whom the animal substitute for Isaac was a symbol. Again, He is the one and only sinless Lamb of God who takes away the sins of the world. All animals sacrificed to God as His symbols in the Jewish sacrificial system were required to be physically blameless. Similarly, on Id Al-Idha, animals to be sacrificed must be without blemish. The symbolic connotation of sacrificial victims' freedom from physical defect is fulfilled truly in Jesus Christ who was absolutely without sin. A sinner cannot offer an atonement for other sinners or for himself—just as an animal with physical defects could not be sacrificed for the "covering" of ritual sins in the Old Testament.

Jesus Christ bore the sins of the world and made an atonement for them by His death upon the cross. In the old Hebrew system, sins of the people were confessed and laid upon a scapegoat. It bore their sins in "a land not inhabited." As we have seen, it means that those sins were only put away but not atoned for and finally eradicated. The later Jewish practice to kill the scapegoat, too, was entirely unscriptural, yet it spoke loudly of man's dire need to be rid of his sin and guilt rather than have them "covered" and put away for a season. The ceremony had to be repeated year after year because they did not provide true forgiveness and lasting reconciliation with God. All sacrifices that were made for sins were in the nature of mere "coverings." They covered sins of the people temporarily so that God passed over them till He arranged for their atonement in Jesus Christ.

The Muslims too, bringing sacrifices to God in commemoration of Abraham, offer a ransom for their sins which is in the nature of a "covering" and not atonement. Though the sacrifices on Id Al-Adha are considered only commemorative, some traditions and beliefs about them indicate awareness of a deeper significance of the festival. Thus the shed blood of the sacrifice is regarded as significant:

> Ayisha relates that the prophet said, "Man hath not done anything, on the day of sacrifice, more pleasing to God than spilling blood, for verily the animal sacrificed will come on the Day of Resurrection with its horns, its hair, its hoofs and will make the scales of his actions heavy, verily its blood reacheth the acceptance of God before it falleth upon the ground, therefore be joyful in it." (Mishkat, Book IV, Chapter 42, Section 2)

The blood of the sacrificed animal is believed to reach God. Here is a recognition of the Biblical principle of life for life. When a person sins, he forfeits his life. He is allowed to continue to exist because an animal's life is offered as a substitute for him. This was the case with Isaac who was ransomed with the temporary provision of a ram. For a lack of substitute the firstborn of the Egyptians died. All sinners deserve the judgment of God and death. In the case of Israel in Egypt God passed over when their doorposts were painted with sacrificial blood of animals.

The Passover then and the perpetual Passover observed by the Hebrews subsequently symbolized the true Passover—Jesus Christ (1 Cor. 5:7). God should destroy every person that is born as soon as he commits a sin. This is the categorical demand of His holiness, according to the Bible. But He does not destroy the world full of sinners. On the contrary, He makes His sun to shine upon the good and the evil alike and causes His rain to descend upon both (Matt. 5:45). God does all this and more because He is love. But His holiness demands the sudden destruction of all evil-doers. If God does not so destroy them, it is only because "the Lamb of God was slain from the foundation of the world" (1 Pet. 1:19).

Hence the world continues. All sacrificial systems in the religions of the world are reminders to mankind of the need for an atonement for sin. Therefore the advanced system of sacrifices in the Hebrew religion also provided only a "covering" as a kind of prophetic truth about the Lamb of God that was coming. The atonement for the sins of the world provided before the foundation of the world, promised through the Law and the prophets of the Old Testament and commemorated in the religious sacrifices of the world, was finally accomplished in Jesus Christ through His death on the cross, His resurrection and ascension.

Chapter 13

Sin and Salvation—Islamic Perspective

According to the Bible all problems and ills of the human race are ultimately traceable to its alienation from God who is the true source of sweetness and light, goodness and life. The root of this tragic separation is sin. As it is written:

> Your iniquities have separated between you and your God, and your sins have hid his face from you. (Isaiah 59:2)

In view of this diagnosis, the only prescription for a spiritually meaningful life is redemption from sin and rehabilitation in fellowship with God Most High. But this is something beyond the power of the natural man who is so miserably stuck in the quicksand of sin that the more he tries to extricate himself the deeper he sinks. Salvation is possible only with God.

The Koranic position on the nature of sin and forgiveness consists of strands of teaching. It is difficult to weave them into a harmonious pattern. Man was created by God to be His vicegerent on earth (Sura 6:166). God breathed His Spirit into Adam's body fashioned out of black mud. Then He ordered His angels to fall down prostrate before this new creature (Sura 15:28, 29). However, despite such noble origin and high destiny, Adam was created weak in his spiritual constitution. As the Koran says:

> God will make the burden light for you, for man was created weak. (Sura 4:28)

Al-Baidhawi interprets the text as indicative of an inherent moral weakness in man:

> Being unable to refrain from women and too subject to be led away by carnal appetites. (As quoted by Sale, op, cit., p. 57, note g)

Though the comment leaves the weakness of women out of the picture, it may be taken to include it in view of the generic use of the term man in the text. Evidently, Baidhawi acknowledges a measure of inherited sinfulness in man. But this reading of the Koran about human sinfulness appears contrary to some other passages on the subject. For example, we read about the natural goodness of man:

> So set thy purpose for religion as a man by nature upright—the nature (framed) of God, in which He hath created man ("Fitra"). There is no altering (of the laws) of God's creation. That is the right religion and most men know it not. (Sura 30:30)

The significant term in the text above is "Fitra." It signifies the disposition of a child at birth. Literally, it means, "A kind or way of creating or of being created" (*Shorter Encyclopaedia of Islam*, p. 108). It has been variously explained by Muslim divines. It comes close to the concept of a sort of original righteousness as opposed to the original sinfulness of man in Christian theology. There are traditions to the effect that a child is born naturally inclined toward the true religion—which is understood to be Islam. For example, the prophet is reported to have said:

> Every infant is born according to the "Fitra" (i.e., "God's kind or way of creating"; "on God's plan"), then his parents make him a Jew or a Christian or a Magian. (Ibid., p. 108)

In other words, every child is born a Muslim naturally but is perverted, after birth, by his environment. But this view created difficulties for the Muslim law of inheritance dealing with children of non-Muslims. If they were to be considered naturally Muslims till the age of discretion, they could not inherit from their parents (in the case of their premature death) because the canon law says that a Muslim cannot inherit from a non-Muslim (see Ibid., p. 108). Again, belief in the natural Islam of a child goes against the belief in the sovereign will of God in the guidance and misguidance of mankind:

> Of them are some who listen unto thee, but we have placed upon their hearts veils, lest they should understand, and in their ears a deafness. If they saw every token they would not believe therein; to the point that, when they come unto thee to argue with thee, the disbelievers say: This is naught else than fables of men of old. (Sura 6:25)

On account of several difficulties involved in interpreting "Fitra" as Islam by birth, other interpretations of it have been suggested by Muslim scholars:

> Another view was that being created according to "Fitra" meant only being in a healthy condition, like a sound animal, with a capacity of either belief or unbelief when the time should come. Another was the "Fitra" meant only "beginning" (bada). Still another was that it referred to Allah's creating man with a capacity of either belief or unbelief and laying on them the covenant of the "Day of Alastu" (Sura vii: 172). Finally that it was that to which Allah turns round the hearts of men. (Ibid., p. 108)

The Koranic text which speaks of the "Fitra" can be interpreted in a meaningful way by reference to the creation of man according to the Bible. God created man in His own image. Despite the Fall dating back to Adam and Eve, this image has not been totally erased in mankind. It manifests itself in the natural man's innate hunger for God. Notwithstanding the darkness of his personal and racial guilt and sin, He gropes after God and is restless for Him (Acts 17:27; Ps. 42:1).

Religion is man's search after God, and it is as old as the human race. Philosophers have defined man as a rational animal. Much more appropriately he may be defined a religious animal, for religion is older and more universal than philosophy and science. In this perspective the "Fitra" may be explained as man's inclination toward religion by birth. But this "natural religion" connotes only man's native need and hunger for God.

As we have seen, the burden of the teaching of the Koran about human sinfulness is against its being inherited. But a partial concession to the concept of inherited sin may be seen in its doctrine of predestination. According to this both the believers and nonbelievers are under divine compulsion (Majbur) in their actions. For example we read:

> All things have been created after a fixed decree. (Sura 54:49)
> God misleadeth whom He will and whom He will He guideth. (Sura 14:4)
> The infidels whose eyes were veiled from my warning and had no power to hear. (Sura 18:101)

There are several traditions also about the predestination of all things, including all good and bad actions and guided and misguided people. For example, the prophet is reported to have said about the predestination of the damned and the saved:

> God created Adam and touched his back with His right hand, and brought forth from it a family; and God said to Adam, "I have created this family for Paradise, and their actions will be like unto those of the people of Paradise." Then God touched the back of Adam, and brought forth another family, and said, "I have created this for hell, and their actions will be unto those of the people of hell." Then a man said to the prophet, "Of what use will deeds of any kind be?" He said, "When God createth His servant for Paradise, his actions will be deserving of it until he die, when he will enter therein; and when God createth one for fire, his actions will be like those of the people of hell till he die, when he will enter therein." (From Bukhari and Muslim, as quoted in Hughes' Dictionary, p. 475)

Since there is a predestination involved in good and bad actions and the ultimate destiny of mankind, there is a measure of inherited sin in the unbelievers and the misguided. They are born for hell and their actions are oriented in that direction by a decree of God. But this allowance to the inborn corruption of a part of mankind is different from the Biblical concept of the original sin. The latter involves human responsibility for sin through and through, while the former bases it on the will of God. Moreover, the Bible teaches that all mankind is inclined toward sin, yet all are free to accept God's offer of salvation. As to the issue of freedom of the human will, the Koran favors determinism. In Sura 81:27-29, the will of God is brought into a clear contrast with the free will of man:

> It is but a reminder to the worlds to whomsoever of you chooses to go straight; but ye will not choose, except God, the Lord of the world, should choose.

Even if a person desires to choose God's guidance, he cannot do so without the prior choice of God in favor of his free choice. This is sheer determinism. Contrary to this there is one interesting verse which seems to support freedom of the will clearly:

> The truth is from your Lord, so let him who will, believe; and let him who will disbelieve. (Sura 18:30)

But even in regard to this verse Abbas, an orthodox commentator, refuses to give up determinism. He preferred to read the text as follows:

> Let him whom He will, believe; and let him whom He will disbelieve.
> (See J. W. Sweetman, op. cit., Part I, Vol. 2, p. 157)

As a consequence of the uncertain teaching of the Koran and traditions on the subject of man's freedom as a moral agent, Muslims are divided into various groups. The Mutazilites taught that man earns his good and bad actions and is responsible for them. His punishment and rewards are ordained by God. The Jabbarya believe that man as a moral agent is under a divine compulsion. Hence his acts are found and predetermined through and through. Holding a position between the two extremes the Asharites, represented by the orthodoxy, teach that man acquires his actions, which are originally created and predetermined by God. In this capacity to acquire consists man's moral freedom. As Al-Ghazzali explains it:

> Thus when the two extreme positions are disproved [namely the position that actions are the result of compulsion and the position that they are the result of volition] there remains nothing except the middle road position which asserts that they are voluntary through the will of God by invention and the will of the servant by another connection which is expressed by the term acquisition [Iktisab]. (*The Foundations of the Articles of Faith*, tr. N. A. Faris, p. 79)

Having made a little room for moral freedom reluctantly, Al-Ghazzali hastens back to the all-encompassing doctrine of predestination with strong words:

> He is the source of good and evil, benefit and harm, belief [Islam] and unbelief, knowledge and ignorance, success and failure, orthodoxy and heresy, obedience and disobedience, monotheism and polytheism. . . . He leads astray whom He wishes, He guides whom He wishes. "He shall not be asked for doing but they shall be asked" (Sura 21:23) . . . That "Had He pleased, God would have certainly guided all men aright," and again, "Had we pleased we would have given every soul its guidance." (Ibid., p. 80)

In Islam sin is regarded in terms of a debt. To discharge the debt man owes to God is a virtue, whereas a failure to do so is sin. Hence it is good business to be good. As the Koran states it:

> O ye who believe, shall I lead you to a merchandise which will save you from a grievous woe? To believe in God and His messenger and to fight hard in God's cause with your property and your persons; that it is better for you did ye know? (Sura 61:10-11)
> Verily God hath bought of the believers their persons and their wealth. (Sura 9:112)
> He is not niggardly of the hire of His servants. (Sura 9:122)

The debt which man owes to God may be reduced to three categories: What is owed directly to God, what is owed to the Koran, what is owed to the creatures. The things which a Muslim owes to God are: (A) Acts of the heart—faith, repentance, submission (Islam), and obedience. (B) Acts of the tongue—praise to God, confession of Him, seeking refuge with Him, supplication and prayer. (C) Acts of the person (bodily acts)—ritual worship, ablutions, purificatory acts, attendance at the mosque and fasting. (D) Acts of property—statutory alms and pilgrimage to Mecca. The duties owed to creatures come within the scope of "Din"—code obligatory for the Muslim in his dealings with other Muslims. The whole life of a Muslim is regulated by the code (Sharia). In terms of the "Sharia" a believer comes to be related to God via His creatures.

Morality in Islam is a legal as well as commercial system. It is important for a man to earn merits in this world to be rewarded in heaven. In this connection Sweetman mentions a few examples from traditions:

> One prayer in this mosque of mine (at Medina) is better than a thousand prayers in any other except the holy mosque (Mecca). Both Muslim and Bukhari record the tradition that prayer in the congregation excells prayer said alone by twenty-seven degrees. "The messenger of Allah said, 'whoever recites two hundred times every day the Sura, 'Say He is God alone,' the sins of fifty years will be erased from him, unless he had a debt.' " The prayer with the "miswak" is seventy times better than without it. It is often said that one who recites prayer in the local mosque acquires the merit of twenty-five recitations of the ritual "Salat," in the Juma masjid of his city five hundred, in the mosque at Medina or Jerusalem fifty thousand, and in Kaaba at Mecca one hundred thousand. (Op. cit., p. 198)

Forgiveness of sins is often mentioned in the Koran. Thus we read:

> O my servants who have been extravagant against their souls, be not in despair of the mercy of God; verily God forgives sins, all of them, verily He is forgiving and merciful. (Sura 39:54. Also, 40:1 f.)

There are conditions to the forgiveness of God such as:
1. Following the prophet (Sura 3:29; 57:28; 46:30; 71:4).
2. Conversion to Islam (Sura 9:5; 49:14; 9:12).
3. Forsaking polytheism (Sura 5:78; 33:73; 4:51).
4. Making an expiation of braking the ceremonial law (Sura 5:96-98; 58:3).
5. A reward of good actions (Sura 64:17; 9:100; 30:27).

When all these conditions are fulfilled, even then forgiveness remains an eschatological hope. All major sins can be forgiven only in the hereafter. Moreover, as mentioned earlier, the forgiveness of God depends entirely on His arbitrary will. It is not rooted in His nature nor in the condition of the sinner, ultimately.

The word salvation (Naja) is used once only in the Koran (Sura 40:41). Also, the term is not used generally in Muslim works on theology, although an orthodox sect claims the title "Najiyah"—those who are being saved. The Koran mentions that soon after the expulsion of Adam and Eve from the Garden, God promised to send them a guidance. It appears to be an echo of the Gospel promise contained in Gen. 3:15:

> Guidance shall come to you from me; whoso shall follow my guidance on them shall come no fear, neither shall they be grieved. (Sura 2:38)

This promised guidance from God may be understood as inclusive of the entire human race. But strictly speaking, it is meant only for those who are predestined by God. Since God guides and misguides whom He will (Sura 61:5), the divine guidance is not universal, though it may so appear from some exceptional verses of the Koran. We may compare, for example:

> The truth is from your Lord; let him who will, believe. (Sura 18:30)

With the following:

> Thus make our signs clear to those who consider, and God calleth to the abode of peace (Paradise), and He guideth whom He will into the right way. (Sura 10:25, 26)

Salvation is a gift of God to those who are predestined for it. It is independent of any moral change in the believer himself. It is a "having" rather than "becoming." Thus we read a lot in the Koran about guidance and instruction but very little about regeneration. Salvation is a release in the hereafter from the punishment of sin and not a present freedom from its hold upon the mind and heart of a believer. In one tradition we learn about some Muslims who expressed to the prophet a concern about their evil thoughts. They said:

> "Verily we find in our minds such wicked propensities that we think it even a sin to speak of them." The prophet replied, "Do you find them really bad?" They said, "Yes." He sid, "This is an evidence of faith." (Mishkat, Book I, Chapter I, quoted in Hughes' Dictionary, p. 205)

According to another tradition the prophet went to the extent of showing his anxiety as to the inner purity of his community:

> Sulaiman b. Ahmad related that Ubada b. Nasi said, "I entered to Shaddad b. Awas who was weeping, so I said, 'What makes you weep O father of Abd. al-Rahman?' He answered, 'It is because of something I heard the apostle of Allah say, "What I fear most for my community is their associating anything with Allah and secret lusts." ' " (Quoted in ISLAM: *Muhammad and His Religion*, ed. A. Jeffery, p. 231)

These and similar rare flashes of concern about the purity of secret thoughts and imaginations were not to occupy too much attention of the believers. Muslim theologians explain that the way to salvation consists in due performance of the five duties of Islam: recital of the creed, five daily prayers, fasting (especially during the month of Ramadan), the payment of legal alms, and pilgrimage to Mecca. He who does these things is considered to be in a state of salvation. But whether or not this salvation will be realized in the world to come depends finally on the arbitrary will of God. Along with this ultimate uncertainty goes the disquieting Koranic teaching that all Muslims must face hell first:

> There shall be none of you, but shall approach near the same (hell). This is an established decree with thy Lord. (Sura 19:71)

Explaining the text Sale quotes the opinion of Muslim scholars as follows:

> For the true believers must also pass by or through hell, but the fire will be dampened, and flames abated, so as not to hurt them, though it will lay

hold on others. Some, however, suppose that the words intend no more than a passage over the narrow bridge which is laid over hell. (Op. cit., p. 231, note t)

In Muslim traditions and literature, "Al-Sirat" is used to describe a bridge across the fire of hell, which is believed to be finer than a hair and sharper than a sword. It is beset on each side with briars and hooked thorns. The righteous are expected to pass over it with the swiftness of lightning. The wicked will miss their footing and fall into the fire of hell. As to those Muslims guilty of major sins, the author of "Sharh al-Muwaqif" says:

> Besides those who are unbelievers, all those (Muslims) who are sinners and have committed great sins (Kabir), will go to hell, but they will not remain there always, for it has been said in the Koran (Sura xcix:7), "He who does an atom of good shall see its reward." (As quoted in Hughes' Dictionary, p. 172)

It is evident from these details that all Muslims are believed to pass through hell. The way to heaven for them is paved with hell. Along with this uneasy prospect goes the uncertainty as to divine forgiveness on account of the morally unpredictable will of God. Again, who could be sure of enough good actions which may counterbalance the evil ones to secure a place in Paradise? If the element of intention, which is so important in ritual performances, is also taken into consideration, the security in good actions is reduced drastically. A tradition has been quoted about some believers seeking the counsel of the prophet about evil thoughts and propensities that plagued them. Also, another tradition has been referred to above about the prophet's concern as to the incidence of lust in the community. According to the Koran man was created weak in moral fiber. How could he be sure of a place in Paradise? One quick answer to this question is, by preponderance of good actions. Islam does lay a lot of emphasis on earning merits through good actions to be awarded in the hereafter.

But not much confidence can be placed on ultimate efficacy of good actions either. We have traditions showing the uselessness of good actions to earn Paradise. For example, according to one tradition, the prophet held out the hope that men who accepted the unity of God would go to heaven and for that alone. He was, however, deterred from announcing such a thing publicly. The tradition describes how Abu Huraira was instructed by the prophet:

> Whoever meets thee behind this wall and testifies that there is no God but Allah, affirming it with his heart, give that one the good news of heaven! He did as he was instructed and met Umar, who struck him and led him to the prophet and said, "Didst thou send Abu-Huraira with thy shoes to inform whosoever he meets who testifies from the heart that there is no God but Allah, that there is given him good news of heaven?" "Yes," said the prophet. Umar said, "Then do not act in this way, for I am afraid that men will rely on this alone. So let them perform good works." On this the messenger of Allah said, "Let them do so." (Mishkat Kitab al-Iman. Quoted by Sweetman, op. cit., Vol. 2, Pt. I, p. 205)

Al-Ghazzali holds the position that good works are only added to Iman (faith) but they do not constitute an essential part of it. He writes:

> It proves that good works are not an integral part of belief nor a basic thing for its existence. Rather, they are superaddition (mazid) which augments belief. (Amin Faris, op. cit., p. 116)

Although Al-Ghazzali relegates good works to a secondary status as compared to faith, yet he does not fail to assert the great importance of belief in the balance, judgment of good and bad works, and passage across the bridge "Sirat":

> Again, man should believe that the punishment of the grave is real and the judgment of the body and soul is just and in accordance with His will. And he should believe in the balance with two scales and the tongue—the magnitude of which is like the stages of the Heavens and the earth; in it the deeds are weighed by the power of God, even to the weight of the mote and the mustard seed, in order to establish exact justice. He should believe also that the bridge (Al-Sirat) is real. (Ibid., p. 9)

A belief in the recompense of good and evil deeds by God in the hereafter is considered incumbent by Al-Ghazzali to establish divine justice. This position stands in a bold contrast to the earlier position held by him concerning the sole efficacy of belief and secondary importance of works. This ambivalent attitude toward works is also typical of traditions on the subject. But it was bound to leave a believer, seeking after the assurance of salvation, utterly confused. In view some of the bewildering situations detailed above, we find early Muslims resorting to belief in the sheer grace of God directly or mediated by their prophet. The hope of future forgiveness and Paradise came to rest mainly on the assurance of intercession by the prophet. But this doctrine, though developed quite early in the history of Islam, is not supported by the Koran unambiguously. Intercession occurs here chiefly in a negative context. The Day of Judgment is described as a time when no intercession (Shafaa) will be accepted (Sura 2:45, 254). Also, referring to the opponents of the prophet, who regarded their idols as intercessor, the Koran says:

> They serve not God but what brings them neither ill nor good and they say these are our intercessors with God. (Sura 10:19)
> Say unto God belongeth all intercession. (Sura 39:44)

In several places it is taught that intercession is possible only with God's permission (Sura 2:255). Thus a creature may plead with Him for others:

> No intercession availeth with Him save from him whom He permitteth. (Sura 34:23)

"Shafaa" (intercession) is granted by God within the limits of a covenant (Ahd) relationship:

> Those whom they invoke besides God shall not be able to intercede except those who bear witness to the truth. (Sura 43:86)
> They will have no power of intercession, save him who hath made a covenant with his Lord. (19:87. Also, 21:28)

With the above qualifications, intercession is granted to angels:

> And how many angels are in heaven whose intercession availeth not save after God giveth leave to whom He chooseth and accepteth. (Sura 53:26)
>
> Those who bear the throne, and all who are round about it, hymn the praises of their Lord and believe in Him and ask forgiveness for those who believe (saying), "Our Lord, who embraceth all things in mercy and knowledge; bestow forgiveness on them that repent and follow thy path and keep them from the pains of hell." (Sura 40:7. Also, 42:5)

This allowance for the intercession of the angels in the Koran opened the way for traditions granting the same privilege to the prophet of Islam also. These traditions were based further on a favorable interpretation of Koranic verses like:

> Perhaps the Lord shall call thee to an honourable place. (Sura 17:79)
>
> And thy Lord shall give a reward with which thou shalt be pleased. (93:5)

According to one tradition the prophet was offered a choice by God between two alternatives—the privilege of intercession or the assurance that half of his community would go to Paradise. He chose intercession (Tirmidhi Qiyama Bab 13; Ibn Hanbal IV 404). We have traditions indicating that the prophet exercised the privilege of intercession. According to his wife, Aisha, he often slipped quietly at night, away from her side, to go to a nearby cemetery to pray for the forgiveness of the dead (Muslim Janaiz Trad. 102; cf. Tirmidhi Janaiz Bab. 59). Ibn Hanbal mentions his "salat al-Janaiz" (Musnad IV, p. 170) and explains its efficacy (Ibid., p. 388). Despite traditions dealing with intercessory prayers of the prophet during his lifetime, it must be pointed out that intercession is eschatological in its proper significance. The prophet's intercession on the Day of Judgment is described in a well-known tradition which has been quoted in part earlier. According to this, on the Day of Judgment the believers will search for an intercessor among the prophets beginning from Adam. They will go from prophet to prophet until finally Isa (Jesus Christ) will refer them to Muhammad. The latter will then be told by God, "Rise and say intercession is granted thee." Thereupon he will throw himself before God and intercede several times for the release of believers (from hell) to Paradise. Finally, all will be freed and he will say, "O Lord, now there is only left in hell those who, according to the Koran, are to remain there forever." (Bukhari: Tawhid Bab. 19; Muslim Iman Tradition 19; Ibn Hanbal 1.4; Tirmidhi Tafsir Sura 17 Trad. 19). This tradition in its different forms is used by Muslim scholars as the main authority to limit intercession for them to their prophet. The privilege of "Shafaa" has been bestowed on the prophet by traditions and Ijma (concensus of opinion), whereas the Koran has no direct and clear reference to it (see *Shorter Encyclopaedia of Islam*, p. 512).

The process of allotment of "Shafaa" to the prophet did not stop with him. In course of time traditions granted it to other prophets (Bukhari: Sahih Tawhid Bab 2) as well as holy men and martyrs:

> Three classes will intercede on the day of Judgment, the prophet, the

learned and the martyrs. (Mishkat Book 33 Ch. 12. Also, Abu Daud. Jihad Bab. 26; Al-Tabari Tafsir. III 6 on Sura 2:55)

The privilege of intercession came finally to be bestowed upon all Muslim believers. It is related that 70,000 will enter Paradise through the intercession of one man of the Muslim community (*Shorter Encyclopaedia of Islam*, p. 512).

"Shafaa" is believed to effect a release of all believers from hell. They shall be confined there as a sort of purgatorial preliminary to heaven. However, this belief of the orthodoxy in intercession was hotly contested by the Mutaizila who insisted that none is released from hell once he is thrown into it. Though the orthodox view was reassuring, yet the prospect of going through hell before arrival in Paradise was bound to shake the confidence of many believers in their own salvation. Thus, despite the whole schema and promise of release from hell to Paradise, several among the fathers of Islam are reported to have been in a state of spiritual uncertainty. This insecurity is mentioned even in regard to the prophet. Quoting a tradition from Abu Majah, Al-Ghazzali writes:

> In his prayer the apostle said, "O God, I seek refuge in thee against evil of things I did and things I left undone." He was then told, "Art thou afraid O apostle of God?" To which he replied, "What could make me feel secure when the heart lies between two of the fingers of the Merciful [God]." "And there shall appear to them, from God, things they have never reckoned on." (Sura 39:47). This was interpreted in commentaries to mean that men have done things which they thought were good but [on the day of Judgment] these things appeared in the balance in the scale of evil. (Amin Faris, op. cit., pp. 130, 131)

Before referring to the lack of assurance of salvation on the part of the fathers of Islam, Al-Ghazzali quotes approvingly, "And who can be sure that he is one of those for whom God has preordained good things?" Then he goes on to dwell on the spiritual uncertainty experienced by several believers of old:

> Abu al-Darda used to swear by God saying, "There is no one who feels safe in the belief who is not robbed of it." (Ibid. p. 133)

The fathers used to hesitate in making a firm declaration of their hope of salvation. When asked if they were saved, they used to reply by saying, "If it be the will of God I am a believer." Thus they manifested a lack of assurance of salvation. Al-Ghazzali informs us:

> Yet all the fathers used to refrain from giving a definite reply concerning belief, and were extremely careful not to commit themselves. In this connection Sufyan al-Thawri said, "He who says, 'I am a believer in the sight of God,' is a liar; and he who says 'I am really a believer,' is an innovator." . . . Once upon a time Hasan (al-Basri) was asked, "Art thou a believer?" To which he replied, "If it be the will of God." Thereupon he was told, "O Abu said, why do you qualify your belief?" He answered and said, "I fear saying 'yes,' and then God will say, 'Thou hast lied Hasan.' Then I shall rightly merit His punishment . . . " He also used to say, "I fear that God may find out that I have done something abominable to Him and will consequently

abhor me and say, 'Go away I accept none of thy works.' Then shall the toiling be in vain."

Ibrahim Ibn Adham once said, "Whenever you are asked, 'Are you a believer?' Say, 'There is no god but God.' . . . Alqamah was once asked 'Are you a believer?' To which he replied, 'I do hope so. If it be the will of God.' (Sufyan) Al-Thawri said, 'We believe in God and in His angels, books, and apostles. But we do not know what we are in the sight of God.' " (Ibid., pp. 122, 123)

It may be pointed out that Al-Ghazzali attempts to explain this astounding lack of assurance of salvation and incidence of doubt on the part of the fathers of Islam, as best as he could. One of the reasons he gives goes as follows:

> The fear of the end, for no one knows whether or not he will still have belief at the hour of death. If he should end with unbelief all his previous works will come to naught and fail because [the value of these works] depends entirely upon the good ending. (Ibid., p. 132)

If the prophet's intercession is hoped for and the belief that all Muslims will go to Paradise finally be true, then there should be no doubt at all as to salvation. Moreover, as Al-Ghazzali himself acknowledges doubt disqualifies a person from Islam:

> As to works God said, "The true believers are those only who believe in God and His apostle, and afterwards doubt not; and who contend with their substance and their persons for the cause of God." (Ibid., p. 126)

A doubt and uncertainty as to the future state of salvation may also be due to a lack of the experience of forgiveness of sins in the present. As the Muslims believe that all major sins will only be forgiven in the hereafter, it is easy to see that they are under a necessity to bear the guilt of sins till the Day of Judgment. The hellfire to come is a horrible prospect indeed. But the fire of the hell of guilt in this life is not easy to suffer either.

The mood of uncertainty about salvation coupled with feelings of guilt aroused great fear of the torments of hell among the early Muslims. Popular preachers fed these fears using graphic descriptions of hell in the Koran and their elaborations in traditions. Many stories are related from those days of persons who died of fear hearing a preacher describe tortures of hell awaiting the wicked on the day of resurrection. Others are reported to have wept uncontrollably listening to preachers. Some even swooned away under terror due to remorse. The slightest infraction of the law activated guilt feelings of the believers, leading them to engage in long and painful expiations. Khamas b. Al-Hassan is reported to have wept for forty years just because he once took a piece of clay from a neighbor's wall. Thus a pietistic movement was initiated under the pressure of widespread guilt and fear of torments of hell exactly at a time when material affluence due to military conquests came to the community (see "Ascetism," ERE, Vol. 2, p. 100). Thus we learn:

> Sufyan al-Thawri said, "Only extreme fear enables me to support the burden of devotion."

"Suppose," said Bashir b. Mansur to Ata al-Sulami, "that a blazing fire were kindled, and proclamation made that whoever entered it should be saved?" "I should tremble," Ata replied, "lest my joy might cause me to expire before I reach it." (Ibid., p. 100)

It shows the spiritual desperation of many a believer, in the early days of Islam, to find an assurance of salvation in the present life and its fulfillment in the world to come. We even hear about a class of ascetics among these who in their quest for the experience of salvation and forgiveness were given to much weeping. They were therefore called the Weepers (Al-Bakkaun) (Ibid., p. 100).

We can imagine how the spiritually disturbed in early Islam may have taken to different ways out of their predicament. Some may have sought to drown themselves in the new-found material affluence, leaving their concerns about the hereafter to a benign fatalism. It was believed that when all is said and done every single Muslim will find his way to Paradise. A famous tradition to this effect, from the prophet, has already been quoted. According to that a mere affirmation of the unity of God will suffice to take a Muslim to heaven. A Muslim, therefore, had only to ask for pardon and receive forgiveness thereby:

> An incessant sinner has not sinned that he asked pardon, although he may have sinned seventy times a day, because asking pardon is a cover for sins.
>
> God has said, "Verily if you come before me with sins equal to the dust of the earth, and then come before me without associating anything with me, verily I will come before you with pardon equal to the dust of the earth." (Mishkat, Book X, Chapter II)

This easy way out of moral responsibility and qualms of conscience could not satisfy the thoughtful and sensitive Muslims in those early days or during the intervening centuries on to our own time. There were bound to be those Muslims who, trying the easy fatalistic escape from guilt, found it wanting. We have a tradition which depicts the restlessness of the heart of a believer who tried the easy way to forgiveness:

> Verily my heart is veiled with melancholy, and verily I ask pardon of God one hundred times. (Mishkat, Book X, Chapter III)

Melancholy is a sign of guilt that still needed to be removed. Merely asking pardon of God even 100 times a day did not do any good to the believer. Another tradition warns a sinner:

> Verily when a true believer commits a sin, a black spot is created in his heart; and if he repents and asks pardon of God, the black spot is rubbed off; but if he increases his sins, the black spot increases, so that it takes hold of the whole heart. Then this spot is a rust which God has mentioned in the Quran, "Their hearts become rusty from their works." (Ibid.)

Many early Muslims felt their hearts to be so rusty that they resorted to asceticism and self-renunciation as a measure of relief. The first century of Islam found Muslims possessors of a vast empire in Persia, Mesopotamia, Syria, Egypt, and North Africa. The conquering Arabs lived in garrison cities in seclusion from the conquered people. Theirs was a life of luxury, with concubines and slaves, such as was unknown to their ancestors. This new affluent life-style was supported by taxation of the conquered lands and booty from on-going military campaigns. There were people in the community who disliked the increasing worldliness that was affecting the people in general. They looked back nostalgically to the simplicity of life in Medina during the time of the prophet. They began to protest against the increasing secularization of Islam. To highlight their concern they took to clothing themselves in coarse cloth in the manner of Syrian Christian monks, cloth made of coarse wool called "suf." On that account they came to be called "Sufis" in course of time. They held themselves aloof from the world and took to the study of the sayings of the prophet and biographies of the prophets. They laid the foundation of the religious law of Islam and Islamic sciences. This religious ferment within Islam was particularly intense in Iraq and in the new garrison city of Basra. Hasan al-Basri, the leader of Sufism in Islam, belonged to this place.

The influence of Judaism and Christianity on the growth and development of this mystical movement in early Islam was significant. R. A. Nicholson makes the following observation on the subject:

> Not only can the dress, vows of silence and many other practices of Muslim ascetics be traced to this source, but in the oldest Sufi biographies, besides numerous anecdotes of the Christian monk (Rahib) who from his cell or pillar gives instruction and advice to wandering Muslim devotees, we find unmistakable proof that the doctrines of the latter were, to a considerable extent, based on Jewish and Christian traditions. Quotations from the Pentateuch and the Gospels frequently occur among the sayings attributed to Muhammaden saints; and Biblical stories related from the monastic point of view, were eagerly read, e.g., the popular collection entitled "Al-Israiliyat" which is said to have been completed by Wahab b. Munabih (ob. 728 A.D.) and the still extant Qisas al-Anbiya (Tales of the Prophets) by Thalabi (ob. 1036 A.D.). (ERE, "Asceticism," Vol. 2, p. 101.)

Though there were some outstanding exceptions, yet as a rule this ascetico-mystical movement had its roots among the common people. They embraced the ideal of unworldliness in great numbers and strove to attain it by abandoning society, seeking shelter in caves and cemeteries or roaming in solitary places, deserts, mountains, or monasteries. This phenomenon from the second century (A.H.) was the beginning of the Sufi movement in Islam. Those who chose this path of quest for peace were interested in an experience of God and forgiveness of sins. Knowing God personally was more important to them than anything else that Islam could offer. This, their central concern, included their desire to be free from guilt and sin. One of the leaders in early Sufism, Hasan al-Basri, said:

> This believer wakens grieving and goes to bed grieving, and nothing encompasses him, for he is between two fearful things: between sin which has so possessed him that he knows not what God will do to him, and between his allotted term which so remains that he knows not what mortal thing may strike him.
> The good things have departed; only the reprehensible remains, and

whoever is left among Muslims is afflicted. (From "Hayat al-Awliya" by Abu Nuayym al-Isfhani. Quoted in Islam, ed. J. A. Williams, p. 138)

The ascetical Sufism travelled with the conquering Arabs to the frontiers of the Muslim empire and took root in Khorasan, the eastern province of the newly conquered Persia. Here, besides Christianity, Zoroastrianism, Buddhism, and eventually Hinduism, also began to exercise their influence on the movement in varying degrees. One of the great Khorasani Sufi of the early days was an Arab named Ibrahim Adham. He used to say that he learned true knowledge of God ("Marifa"—Gnosis) from a Syrian monk (see A. J. Arberry Tr. Sufism).

One of the early non-Arab Sufis was a woman called Rabia. She was interested in the love of God above everything else:

Rabia said, "I saw the prophet in a dream, and he said to me, 'O Rabia, dost thou love me?' I said, 'O prophet of God, who is there who does not love thee?' But my love to God has so possessed me that no place remains for loving or hating any save Him." (*Rabia: A Mystic*, by Margaret Smith, p. 99)

Sufism provided the thoughtful and spiritually sensitive Muslims with a retreat from the orthodoxy and legalism of Islam which has stood the test of time in Islamic history. Even with the spiritually less sensitive masses, belief in the forgiveness of sins in the hereafter and reward in terms of Paradise went through some change from its position in the Koran. The Paradise depicted in the Koran is appealing to physical senses and propensities. One of the descriptions of the abode of the blessed goes as follows:

In gardens of delight, a crowd of the former and a few of the later generations; on inwrought couches reclining on them face to face, blooming youth go round about them with goblets and ewers and a cup of flowing wine; their brows ache not from it, nor fails the sense: and with such fruits as shall please them best, and with flesh of such birds as they shall long for; and theirs shall be the "Houris" (heavenly women) with large dark eyes, like pearls in their shells, in recompense for their labours past. No vain discourse shall they hear therein, nor charge of sin, but only peace! peace! . . . Unfailing, unforbidden, and on lofty couches and of a rare creation have we made the "Houris," and we have made them ever virgins, dear to their spouses and of equal age, for the people of the right hand, a crowd of the former and a crowd of the later generations. (Sura 56:12-39. Also, 76:12-22; 55:54-56)

Therein are rivers of water which corrupt not: rivers of milk whose taste changeth not and rivers of wine, delicious to those who quaff it; and rivers of clarified honey. Therein are all kinds of fruit for them from their Lord. (Sura 47:15)

The traditions are also full of descriptions, in minute detail, of the pleasures in Paradise that await Muslims:

Abu Musa relates that the apostle of God said, "Verily there is a tent for every Muslim in Paradise. It is made of one pearl, its interior empty, its breadth 60 'Kos' (a measure of distance) and in every corner of it will be his wives: and they shall not see one another." (Mishkat, Book xxiii, Chapter 13)

Abu also relates that the apostle of God said, "Verily a man in Paradise reclines upon seventy cushions before he turns his other side. Then a woman of Paradise comes to him and pats him on the shoulder and the man sees his face in her cheek, which is brighter than a looking glass, and verily her most inferior pearl brightens the east and the west. Then the woman makes a 'Salam' (salutation) to him, which he returns; and the man says, 'Who are you?' and she replies, 'I am of a number promised by God for the virtuous.' And verily she will have seventy garments, and the man's eyes will be fixed on them, till he will see the marrow of the bones of her legs through the calves of them, and she will have crowns on her head, the meanest pearl of which will give light to east and west." (Ibid.)

Though some Muslim scholars have suggested allegorical interpretations of the delights promised in Paradise, yet the orthodox prefer to take them literally. Both Al-Ashari and Al-Ghazzali admit the literal pleasure of Paradise. But they point out that these will begin only after the resurrection (*Shorter Encyclopaedia of Islam*, p. 88).

From the details that are furnished about the pleasures in Paradise, it is obvious that there is no place for Muslim women. Moreover, thoughtful men were bound to expect more than physical pleasures alone in the hereafter. The natural religion of man, "Fitra," is hunger for God. The human soul cannot rest easy even in Paradise without some experience of God. Therefore, we have also traditions which discuss the possibility of a vision of God in Paradise. For example:

> The prophet said, "When the people who are destined for Paradise enter therein; God Most High will say unto them, 'Do ye wish anything that I can add to you?' They will say, 'Hast not thou whitened our faces, brought us into Paradise and saved us from the Fire?' " Then the prophet said, "A veil will be raised and they will look on the face of God most High and there will be nothing given them more pleasing to them than gazing upon their Lord." (Mushkat Fitan. On the vision of God)

It needs to be pointed out in the above tradition that the vision of God is not granted at the request of the saved. They appear to be quite satisfied with what they had. But God revealed His face to them on His own initiative. However, the believers do realize that a vision of God is the most pleasing experience one could ever have.

The doctrine of the vision of God may be divided into two parts—His vision in this life and in the hereafter. Some Muslim doctors teach the possibility of the vision of God only in Paradise, while others allow it in this world also. The latter position can be supported by reference to the experience of Moses and Muhammad. If it be allowed that Moses saw God when he conversed with Him and Muhammad saw God during his night Journey, then the position is established. There are traditions which do support that both Moses and Muhammad did see God. However, there are also traditions to the contrary. According to one of these:

> Kab replied, "Verily God Most High divided His vision and His conversation between Muhammad and Moses. He spoke to Moses twice and Muhammad saw Him twice." "Then," said Ibn Abbas, "I went to Ayesha and said, 'Did Muhammad see his Lord?' She answered, 'Thou hast said something which makes my hair stand on end.' I said, 'Be easy!' Then I recit-

ed the words, 'He certainly saw some of the greatest signs of the Lord.' She said, 'Wherever are the words carrying you?' " It was only Gabriel. Whoever states that Muhammad saw his Lord, or concealed anything of what he was commanded, or knew the five things of which God Most High spoke, that with Him is knowledge of the Hour of the resurrection and that He sends down the rain and the rest, has told a great lie. But he saw Gabriel. He did not see him in his proper form more than twice, once near the Sidra al-Muntaha, and one in Ajyad. He had six hundred wings and filled the limits of heavens. (Mishkat Fitan. On the vision of God, Tirmidhi's collection)

Whether the vision of God is possible in both the worlds or only in the hereafter may remain debatable with Muslims. However, it is recognized in the relevant traditions that the greatest privilege for man even in Paradise is to be able to see God. This is something fully endorsed by the Sufis who seek to attain to an experience of God in the present life also. But they endeavor to attain this by human devices. Therefore, quite early in its history Sufism stumbled on the rocks of Buddhistic nihilism ("Fana fi Allah"— losing oneself in God) and Hindu pantheism (Baqa bi Allah—finding oneself through identity with God). Moreover, in order to achieve an experience of self-transcendence they began to resort to euphoric drugs, yogic type of meditation, and other auto-hypnotic techniques. But this is the best that natural man can do on his own to try to fill the emptiness of his soul. It is demonstrative of man's inalienable need for a living experience of God here and now and its fruition in the hereafter.

Chapter 14

Emmanuel—The Saviour of the World

Sin and salvation are more profoundly related to each other than is realized in Islam. There can be no salvation in the comprehensive sense of the word without an effective solution of the problem of sin as it concerns both man and God. Contrary to the common misconception, the Bible enlightens us that sin does not exist on account of the law. Rather, the law of God is given because of sin (Gal. 3:19). A violation of the divine law takes place due to the inborn sinfulness of man, which is known as the original sin in Biblical theology. It is a dormant state of human alienation from God. It springs into activity with the first incidence of personal sin and then continues to increase cumulatively throughout a life of rebellion against God. The law does not make a person sin:

> But every man is tempted, when he is drawn away of his own lust, and enticed. Then when lust hath conceived, it bringeth forth sin: and sin, when it is finished, bringeth forth death. (James 1:14, 15)

The law only serves as a means of revealing to a given person his own sinfulness and need for salvation:

> What shall we say then? Is the law sin? God forbid. Nay, I had not known sin, but by the law: for I had not known lust, except the law had said, Thou shalt not covet. (Romans 7:7)

The law arouses the conscience of a sinner to the realization that he is under the judgment of a just and holy God unless his sins are atoned for and he himself is redeemed.

The fundamental sinfulness of the unsaved person is demonstrated not in isolated acts of sin as much as in his life of alienation from God—absence of personal fellowship with Him. Muslims believe that man is good by nature and that every child is born in the right religion, which is Islam. In line with the Koran, Islam must be evaluated in the light of the religion of Abraham. His religion was characterized by a personal and conscious communion with God, so that he is called the Friend of God. The issue of the natural Islam of a child can be determined on the touchstone of Abraham's experience of God. We may, therefore, ask pertinently, "Is a child born with an Abraham-like consciousness of God?" This must be answered in the negative in view of a tradition, already quoted, which says that every child is touched by Satan at birth; therefore he cries. The only exceptions to this universal rule are believed to be the Virgin Mary and Jesus Christ (Hughes' Dictionary, p. 230).

This authentic tradition is in agreement with the teaching of the Koran that man is created weak. If a child is created weak (morally, according to Al-Baidhawi) and touched by Satan at birth, how could he be expected to be a Muslim after Abraham? Moreover, it is important to bear in mind here that Abraham himself was not a born-Muslim. His spiritual experience, as a Muslim, was based on a special covenant revelation of God to him. A child may be called born-Muslim only in the sense that he is not account-able before the law. But he cannot be considered a Muslim in the likeness of Abraham who had an "I-thou" relationship with God. As the Bible teaches us, sin is a condition of personal alienation from God. In this sense every child is born in sin as David confessed:

> Behold, I was shapen in iniquity; and in sin did my mother conceive me. (Psalm 51:5)

Again the Scripture says:

> For all have sinned, and come short of the glory of God. (Romans 3:23)
> What then? are we better than they? No, in no wise: for we have before proved both Jews and Gentiles, that they are all under sin. (Ibid., 3:9)

The only child who was truly born sinless was Jesus Christ, because He was conceived of the Holy Spirit. The Koran recognizes that He was in true communion with God even at birth because He was a born prophet. He spoke from His cradle miraculously to announce His mission and vindicate the honor of His mother. According to the Gospel account, He was the In-carnate Word of God. Hence the question of sin in terms of alienation from God does not even apply in His case.

The sinfulness of the natural man is not just an individual and personal defect. It has a racial background and history which is related in the Bible. We learn therefrom that sin entered the human scene with the rebellion of Adam and Eve against God. They were created in the image of God (Gen. 1:26) with a twofold purpose: they were destined to enjoy an intimate com-munion with Him more than any other creature. Again, they were to rule the earth and subdue it (Gen. 1:28). The task of subjugation implied the presence of an enemy on the scene who had to be overcome by the first hu-man beings. The Koran relates that man was created to be the vicegerent of God on earth (Sura 2:28 ff.). But it says nothing about his creation in the image of God. It may be mentioned here that Al-Ghazzali appropriated teaching of the Bible when he wrote that God created Adam in His own form (Sura) (see *Shorter Encyclopaedia of Islam*, p. 40).

Being in the likeness of God, Adam was granted freedom to choose which was objectively highlighted by the presence of the tree of the knowl-edge of good and evil and the tree of life (Gen. 2:9). The forbidden tree sym-bolized the law of death in alienation from God (Rom. 8:2). It is noteworthy that there was a divine commandment with a warning of death only about this tree (Gen. 2:17; Eph. 2:15). There was no commandment about the second tree because it represented life everlasting and liberty in God (Rom. 8:2). Adam and Eve were growing spiritually. They had only to grow tall enough to be able one day to reach out by faith and partake of the fruit of the tree of their destiny. All went well in the Garden as the first parents of the human race walked with God in the cool of the day in a state of sinlessness (cf. Gen. 3:8, 9). One fateful day, Adam and Eve succumbed to an inner dark urge brought out into the open through the seduction of Satan. It was an inarticulate drive which turned them on to experiment with the forbidden tree rather than the tree of life in the midst of the Garden. Since that time mankind has shown more interest in the knowledge of good and evil under the shadow of law than in the offer of life in the light of the Gospel. Under the prompting from Satan and lure of the forbidden tree, the evil of the hearts of Adam and Eve spelled out an ego-inflation. They desired now to become gods like God and in competition with Him (Gen. 3:4).

It is significant that a similar sin plagued Satan also before he rebelled against God. As it is recorded in Isaiah, Satan said in his pride, "I will ascend above the heights of the clouds; I will be like the most High" (14:14). He, too, aspired to be a god besides the only God Most High. This attempted self-deification spelled out his doom. A similar megalomania captivated Adam and Eve. They sinned against God in their endeavor to deify themselves (Gen. 3:6). It is interesting to note that in our own time many experimenters with euphoric drugs and self-hypnotic techniques experience similar temporary ego-inflations whenever their trips are successful. The sin of Adam and Eve was different from that of Satan because they were tempted, while Satan was not.

The first sin in human history was a rebellion against God based on ego-worship and pride arising out of it. The reason behind sin is pride and self-worship (Sura 2:34, 7:143, 144). Herein also lies the root of idolatry, condemned by the Bible and abhorred by the Koran. Though Islam is against all associationism (Shirk) and idolatry, yet it has not dealt adequately with its source in man—his secret worship of the animal self and the lusts and passions arising therefrom. Without an eradication of the root of sinfulness in man and restoration of a living fellowship with God, there could be no true Islam. This cannot be accomplished by the law. There was a moral law, appointed by God, in the Garden of Eden (Paradise) before the Fall (Gen. 2:7; Sura 2:35). But it did not keep Adam and Eve from sinning against God or to save them after they fell.

The source of the salvation of Adam and Eve and the entire race was revealed by God separately from the law:

> I will put enmity between thee and the woman, and between thy seed and her seed; it shall bruise thy head, and thou shalt bruise his heel. (Gen. 3:15)

The promised One of God was to be born of the seed of the woman in a peculiar way. His advent was intended to be a judgment upon Satan but Good News to mankind. The Koran also contains something of a promise from God after the Fall:

> We said, "Go down, all of you, from hence; but verily there cometh unto you from me a guidance; and whoso followth my guidance, there shall be no fear come upon them neither shall they grieve." (Sura 2:38)

Concerning the interpretation of this text Sale writes as follows:

God here promises Adam that His will should be revealed to him and his posterity; which promise the Muhammadens believe was fulfilled at several times by the ministry of several prophets from Adam himself, who was the first, to Muhammad who was the last. The number of books revealed unto Adam they say was ten. (Op. cit., p. 5, note g)

If the law present in the Garden during the days of innocence of Adam and Eve did not save them, it is futile to believe in its efficacy for salvation in the case of sinful humanity. The Bible separates the law of God from the promise of God. The Good News of a Saviour in Gen. 3:15 was a promise of God and not the law. The law in the Old Testament and its elucidations through the prophets were intended only to reveal the moral nakedness of the chosen people in particular and mankind in general. Again, it was to lead to the fulfillment of God's promise of salvation for all. As St. Paul put it succinctly:

Wherefore the law was our school master to bring us to Christ that we might be justified by faith. (Galatians 3:24)

Neither the law of Moses or any other law can declare a sinner blameless in the sight of God. In Islam, we have seen the secondary character of good works based on the law as compared to faith. It is even recognized in some traditions that a mere belief in the unity of God—without any works whatsoever, can lead a Muslim to Paradise. Also, such a despair in the efficacy of the law to save was reflected in the lack of assurance of salvation among the fathers of Islam and the Sufi revolt against Islamic legalism and ritual observance. As to the weakness of the works of the law to redeem the Bible says:

For as many as are the works of the law are under a curse: for it is written, Cursed is every one that continueth not in all things which are written in the book of the law to do them. (Galatians 3:10)

Breaking of the law of God even in the smallest detail means a violation of the whole Code.

For whosoever shall keep the whole law, and yet offend in one point, he is guilty of all. (James 2:10)

There is no justification for a sinner through the law. As soon as he conscientiously attempts to live up to the law of God, he soon discovers the hopelessness of keeping it in all points.

There is no reason for utter despair as to salvation on account of the demand of the law. Though every sinner is under a curse on account of his failure to live up to it (Gal. 3:10), yet there is good news for him. According to this Gospel (Good News) of God:

Christ hath redeemed us from the curse of the law, being made a curse for us: for it is written, Cursed is every one that hangeth on a tree: that the blessing of Abraham might come on the Gentiles through Jesus Christ: that we might receive the promise of the Spirit through faith. (Galatians 3:13, 14)

Jesus Christ, through His atoning death upon the cross, fulfilled the demand of the law upon sinners and through himself opened the way for them to the presence of God the Father. Now it is possible for a redeemed of His to testify:

> Having therefore, brethren, boldness to enter into the holiest by the blood of Jesus, by a new and living way, which he hath consecrated for us, through the veil, that is to say, his flesh. (Hebrews 10:19, 20)

The appearance of the Word of God in flesh, His unique ministry and atoning death upon the cross was limited in time and space. But He came to be the Saviour of the world. Hence His incarnation and crucifixion are not the last words about His mission. It also included His resurrection from the dead on the third day, ascension to the right hand of God the Father, and promise of His return one day.

Jesus Christ began His ministry in flesh necessarily from a given part of the earth and at a given time. During those days He could have healed, saved, and blessed only a limited number of His contemporaries who came into contact with Him. Due to His incarnational limitations, He could not have reached all people everywhere and at all times. In that situation He first spoke of a limited scope of His ministry. Thus He said:

> I am not sent but unto the lost sheep of the house of Israel. (Matthew 15:24)

His mission concerned immediately the Hebrews who had been prepared by God through the centuries of their history for the advent of the Messiah. According to the Old Testament prophecies, the Chosen Servant of God was to launch His work of redemption, beginning from Israel (Mic. 5:2) to the uttermost parts of the world (Isa. 11:10). In line with the growing sweep of His ministry, Jesus Christ, even during His own lifetime, chose to preach to the Gentiles and journey to Samaritan cities—something which He originally forbade His disciples to do. Here was a progressive expansion of His messianic ministry foretold by the prophets of the Old Testament. The ultimate goal of its outreach was the whole world—Jews as well as Gentiles.

About the worldwide scope of His ministry Jesus Christ made the significant statement:

> And other sheep I have, which are not of this fold: them also I must bring, and they shall hear my voice; and there shall be one fold, one Shepherd. (John 10:16)

Along with this prophetic authentication of His universal ministry, we remember His great commandment to the disciples after His resurrection:

> Go ye therefore, and teach all nations, baptizing them in the name of the Father, and of the Son, and of the Holy Ghost. (Matthew 28:19)

The particular and universal dimensions of the ministry of Jesus Christ, according to both the Old Testament and His own teaching, must be kept in a proper balance and perspective. They embody not only a fulfillment of prophecies regarding the total ministry of the Messiah, but also they are indicative of a great truth about His past and current reality. As we have observed, during the days of His flesh, the saving outreach of Jesus Christ was naturally limited in time and space. Therefore, He could not have blessed people everywhere and at all times. In order to be the Saviour of the world, He looked ahead to His crucifixion, death, resurrection and ascension. The life and light which the Saviour brought in himself for mankind was first tested, tried, and demonstrated in the crucible of human existence. To that intent the Word of God:

> Took not on him the nature of angels; but he took on him the seed of Abraham.
>
> Wherefore in all things it behoved him to be made like unto his brethren, that he might be a merciful and faithful high priest in things pertaining to God, to make a reconciliation for the sins of the people. For in that he himself hath suffered being tempted, he is able to succour them that are tempted. (Hebrews 2:16-18)

After having inaugurated the kingdom of God in and through His incarnation, Jesus Christ sought to universalize it by transcending the limitations of His physical body. About this, the Temple of the Logos (the Word), He once promised the Jews a great sign in support of His messianic claim:

> Then answered the Jews and said unto him, What sign shewest thou unto us, seeing that thou doest these things? Jesus answered and said unto them, Destroy this temple, and in three days I will raise it up. Then said the Jews, Forty and six years was this temple in the building, and wilt thou rear it up in three days? But he spake of the temple of his body. (John 2:18-21)

In order to establish a redemptive contact with His people in the wilderness, God suggested building of the Tabernacle to Moses. This tent was made according to a pattern revealed to the prophet. It contained symbols of the presence of God. When Israel ceased from wandering and settled down in the Promised Land, the Tabernacle was replaced by the temple in Jerusalem. The second temple, during the time of Jesus Christ, had all the ceremonies of the days gone by, but it was divested of the visible symbols of the presence of God. Edersheim informs us:

> Confessedly the real elements of Temple glory no longer existed. The Holy of Holies was quite empty, the Ark of the Covenant with the Cherubims, the Tablets of the Law, the book of the covenant, Aaron's rod that budded, and the pot of manna, were no longer in the sanctuary. The fire that had descended from heaven upon the altar was extinct. What was far more solemn, the visible presence of God in the Shekinah was wanting. Nor could the will of God be now ascertained through the Urim and Thummim, nor even the high preist could be anointed with the oil, its very composition being unknown. Yet all the more jealously did the Rabbis draw lines of fictitious sanctity and guard them against all infringement. (*The Temple*, E. Edersheim, pp. 61, 62)

God rejected the temple in Jerusalem made by human hands in favor of a glorious Temple made by himself. This happened when the Word of God himself became flesh and dwelt in Israel. Jesus Christ prophesied about the Jews destroying the temple of His physical body as He looked forward to setting up a universal temple, whereby the true worshippers could worship the Father in Spirit and truth without any physical barriers (John 4:23). He proposed to raise up this cosmic temple in three stages.

The Lamb of God, bearing the sins of the world, shed His blood of atonement upon the cross (1 John 2:2). The law stipulated that it is the blood that makes atonement (Lev. 17:11). Moreover, the Bible says that blood is the bearer of life (Gen. 9:4). The shed blood of Christ made the absolute atonement on the cross—after which no more animal sacrifices are needed by those who approach God. Also, it indicated release of His incarnate life from the limitations of a physical body in order to be made available universally. After His crucifixion, Jesus Christ died and was buried like a grain of wheat that falls into the ground. A short time before His betrayal, He used this meaningful figure of speech to explain to His disciples the purpose of His impending death:

> And Jesus answered them, saying, The hour is come, that the Son of man should be glorified. Verily, verily, I say unto you, Except a corn of wheat fall into the ground and die, it abideth alone: but if it die, it bringeth forth much fruit. (John 12:23, 24)

According to His prophetic promise, on the third day after His death, the Grain of Life Eternal rose again from the dead and was lifted up to the right hand of God the Father. Thus Jesus Christ of history became "Jesus Christ, the same yesterday, today and forever" (Heb. 13:18) through His death, resurrection and ascension. Now, as God the Father is everywhere so also His Son, in His role as the Saviour of the world, is omnipresent. In this, His glorified reality, He promised His immediate disciples and through them all others to follow:

> For where two or three are gathered together in my name, there am I in the midst of them. (Matthew 18:20)

A true disciple of Jesus Christ is never alone. On account of the presence of the Holy Spirit in Him, he is always a majority of two. In the fellowship of other disciples he becomes at least a group of three; beyond that it might be any number. But in all instances the glorified Lord Jesus Christ is always present with His own. He reiterated this blessed assurance a little differently during His final post-resurrection appearance to the disciples:

> And lo, I am with you alway, even unto the end of the world. (Matthew 28:20)

He is with His own in this world till the end of the age. After that His own will be with Him in His Father's kingdom forever and ever.

The broadcast of the love of God in Christ was made about two thousand years ago from the land of the chosen people and the prophets. But after His crucifixion, death and resurrection, He was universalized, being lifted up on the (radio) waves of the presence of God the Father. Thus this divine broadcast encircles mankind and permeates the whole universe. Therefore, now He can be experienced by a recipient who is linked with Him by faith like a radio set tuned to a broadcast. As a radio set is a witness of the presence of the radio world, so also a true disciple is a witness of his glorified Lord and Saviour Jesus Christ. The first disciples who ate and drank with Him were His witnesses in a twofold way: They witnessed His physical resurrection and left a record of their experience for posterity. Also, they became the first witnesses of His universal and continued presence in the world, after the Holy Spirit came upon them on the day of Pentecost (Acts 1:8; 2:4; 5:32). In this sense all true disciples (past, present, and future) are His witnesses to the world, while they in turn witness inwardly the presence of God the Father and the Son through the Holy Spirit.

As we have discussed in the preceding, man is born religious in the sense that he needs God as much as his necessary physical food. But on account of his sinfulness and sin, he is separated from God. Religion has been defined as man's search after God. The Bible tells us that the natural man cannot find God by a lot of searching (Job 11:7, 8). He, at best, feels after Him like a blind man in the darkness of his sins (Acts 17:27). In order to redeem man from his futility, God took the initiative. This is the Gospel of Jesus Christ. In contradistinction to religion, the Gospel may be described as God's down-reach for man. In Christ God appeared in history not to condemn lost sinners but to save them. As the Saviour announced:

> For the Son of man is come to seek and to save that which was lost. (Luke 19:10)

In His search after sinners He is present everywhere. Only the sinners need to become aware of the Good Shepherd and hear His call. This happens when the good news about Him is proclaimed, by those who know Him, under the power of the Holy Spirit. That is why the Scripture rejoices in those who carry the Gospel from the Mount of fellowship with Him to the world. St. Paul wrote in memorable words:

> How then shall they call on him in whom they have not believed? and how shall they believe in him of whom they have not heard? and how shall they hear without a preacher? And how shall they preach except they be sent? as it is written, How beautiful are the feet of them that preach the gospel of peace, and bring glad tidings of good things! (Romans 10:14, 15)

As the Gospel is preached, the Holy Spirit of God moves upon many hearers, convicting them of their sin and convincing them about righteousness—being rightly related to God in Christ (John 16:8). Soon a sinner hears inwardly, through his aroused conscience and inspired common sense, the gentle Saviour saying:

> Behold, I stand at the door, and knock: if any man hear my voice, and open the door, I will come in to him, and will sup with him, and he with me. (Revelation 3:20)

At that crisis moment a sinner has but to repent of his sins and his style of life without God. Then he needs to surrender himself (Islam) to the Saviour by faith. He readily receives such a penitent soul by forgiving his sins, cleansing him, and filling him with an experience of His presence. God the Father and Son enter the spirit of a man through the Holy Spirit. From that blessed time onwards he becomes the living temple of God Most High. This experience of salvation and reconciliation with God is meant for the present life (John 3:12). Jesus Christ called it "being born again" or "being born of the Spirit" (John 3:3, 5). A Spirit-born person is human by his nature but a child of God by adoption. He is assured of this fact in his life by the Holy Spirit who is also called the Spirit of adoption (Rom. 8:15). Therefore, with confidence he looks forward to the world to come for the fruition of the life already begun in him.

The phrase "face (wajah) of God" occurs frequently in the Koran. Two most important texts about it are Sura 2:115 and Sura 28:88. Men act out of a desire to see the face of God (Sura 13:22). They seek the face of God (Sura 6:52; 30:38 ff.). In the traditions also the greatest happiness for believers in Paradise is expected to be a vision of God. As we have seen, it has been debated among Muslim scholars whether this experience of seeing the face of God is possible in this world or only in the world to come. The Bible carries the Good News for all Muslim seekers after the face of God that Jesus Christ is the image of the invisible God (Col. 1:15). In order to "see" the invisible God, a person needs to look at His face who became incarnate. Through a living-faith encounter with Him, one can see God in the present life. As it is written:

> For God, who commanded the light to shine out of darkness, hath shined in our hearts, to give the light of the knowledge of the glory of God in the face of Jesus Christ. (2 Corinthians 4:6)

To anyone desiring to know what the invisible God is like, the divine answer is, "He is like Jesus Christ." Moreover, the living presence of this Mediator between God and man can be experienced here and now. On the basis of that, a redeemed person looks forward to the perfect revelation of God in the world to come. As it is testified by Paul:

> For now we see through a glass, darkly; but then face to face: now I know in part; but then shall I know even as also I am known. (1 Corinthians 13:12)

In brief, one who comes by faith to Jesus Christ can see the face of God as through a mirror in the present life and then look forward to seeing Him directly and abiding in Him forever.

The Christian experience is a foretaste of the powers of the world to come (Heb. 6:5) and the experience of peace which passes all understanding and joy unspeakable and full of glory. A Christian is freed from guilt and other powers of hell that plague godless humanity in the present life. In the hereafter he fears no hell either. When he finishes his journey here, he goes straight to the presence of the Lord Jesus Christ to remain with Him forevermore. Unlike the belief about Muslims crossing hellfire, no true Christian will ever come anywhere near it.

The living experience of God in Jesus Christ is transforming and unique in its nature. A born-again person comes to know Him in a tri-personal dimension, which corresponds with the divine revelation in the Bible. He perceives the breath of the presence of God deep within himself, with himself, and yet above and way beyond himself. As we learn from the Scripture, God the Father and the Son dwell in a believer through the Holy Spirit (John 14:23; 1 Cor. 15:45; 2 Cor. 3:17). Again, both the Father and the Holy Spirit are present in the Son who walks hand in hand with a true

Christian (1 Cor. 1:9; 1 John 3:6). Finally, the Son and the Spirit watch over the redeemed in the Father who is above all (Eph. 4:6; John 20:17; Matt. 6:9). The revelation of God in the Bible, along with its authentication in Christian experience, leads us to consider briefly the Koranic position on the unity of God.

The earliest suras of the Koran dwell more prominently on the omnipotence of God rather than His unity. But on the whole, the unity of God as opposed to polytheism and "Shirk" (associating creatures with the Creator) is an important part of its teaching. In this regard it claims to reinstate the pristine monotheism of Abraham and other prophets of the Hebrew tradition, including Jesus Christ (Sura 2:136). According to Muslim theologians, the name "Allah" signifies the nature of God, while His ninety-nine names indicate His attributes. The teaching of the Koran about God and His attributes raises the difficult problem of their relationship to His essence. In theological terms the question may be asked, "Are these qualities inherent in the nature of God or are they extraneous to Him?" If they are considered outside His nature, then to attribute the ninety-nine beautiful names to God will amount to "Shirk" (Associationism), which is the unpardonable sin in the Koran (Sura 31:13). On the other hand, if these qualities belong to the divine nature, the absolute unity of God, which is the chief cornerstone of belief and theology in Islam, is removed. Granting the proposition that the attributes of God are essential, there arise several problems which may be divided into three categories:

1. The problem involved in relating the qualities of God to His nature. If they are essential, then we have one nature of God and ninety-nine names. Thus, as hinted above, we cannot maintain the Muslim concept of the absolute inner unity of God. Moreover, the picture turns out very much like the Christian doctrine of the Holy Trinity. One of the earliest Christian apologists to Islam, John of Damascus, explains this point as follows:

> They call us Associators because, they say, we have introduced a companion for God when we call Christ "Son of God" and "God." . . . But since you say that Christ is the Word of God and Spirit, how can you revile us as associators? For the Word of God and the Spirit are inseparable from Him in whom they exist. If therefore the Word is in God, it is clear that it is God. But if it is outside God, then according to you, God is without a word and without mind. (Quoted by L. E. Browne, *Eclipse of Christianity in Asia*, p. 129)

As Muslims believe in one God with His ninety-nine qualities, it should be easy for them to consider the Biblical teaching about the one God in three persons in whom the divine qualities are inherent. When we say God knows, there must be someone known to Him eternally. Thus the knower, the known one and knowledge existed within the self-same God. The Bible tells us that God is love (1 John 4:8). This implies an eternal truth within the Godhead in terms of the Lover, Beloved, and the relationship between the two. It is expressed by the Father, Son, the Spirit of love.

2. The issue of relationship between the various attributes of God. Some of them are contraries. For example, the Koran says that He guides as well as misguides. Again, among the names of God we find "Al-Khaliq"

(the Creator) and "Al-Mumit" (the Destroyer). Life and death are obviously contraries and therefore difficult to imagine as coherent in the divine nature.

3. The problem of relationship between the attributes of God and creation. The term monotheism signifies belief in the one and only God and opposition to all polytheism (belief in creatures who are deified). In this sense Islam is as much monotheistic as Christianity and Judaeism. But the Muslim belief in the absolute unity of God goes beyond. It denies all multiplicity in the divine nature. Allowing this, it is easy to look upon the entire creation as against the fundamental nature of God—His unity, about which Sweetman writes:

> When the terms of unity—"wahid," "ahad," and "mutwahid"—are used of Allah they signify, according to expositors, He who is one in Essence, having no like nor peer nor second. He is the One in Attributes beside whom there is no other. He is also utterly simple, unsusceptible to division into parts and having no double. Ibn Athir and the Lisan al-Arab would make the terms signify that He has always been alone. Of the strange name for God in Sura of the Unity namely, "As Samad," Lane says it means the Being which "Continues or continues forever after His creatures have perished." (Sweetman, op. cit., p. 17)

The thought that the absolute unity of God is opposed to all manner of multiplicity is supportable from a famous text of the Koran:

> And cry not unto any other god along with God. There is no God save Him. Everything will perish save His countenance. (Sura 28:88)

In the text idolatry is condemned with the argument that ultimately all creatures will vanish out of existence except God. This line of thinking leads to the conclusion that ultimately both Paradise and hell also will pass away. It leaves no promise of life everlasting for the creature. On the foundation of this absolute unity of God, the Sufis built their doctrine of ultimate annihilation in Him. Though some Buddhist influence may have operated in their speculations, yet it is noteworthy that the belief in the unity of God proved the main inspiration for their doctrine. R. A. Nicholson points out:

> The gnostic contemplates the attributes of God, not His essence, for even in gnosis a small trace of duality remains: this disappears only in "fana al-fana," the total passing-away in the undifferentiated Godhead. The cardinal attribute of God is unity, and the divine unity is the first and last principle of gnosis. (*The Mystics of Islam*, p. 79)

In the absence of belief in the mediator between God and creation, Muslims have been struggling to satisfactorily reconcile the two opposite poles of divine transcendence and immanence. Thus in terms of a devotional relationship with God, the Sufis have managed to lose themselves in pantheism, while other Muslims have sought satisfaction in practical Deism. At the same time, the gap between the two extreme positions has been filled by the cult of the prophet and saints and martyrs. But these intermediaries being human cannot mediate adequately between God and creation. Hence under the stress of the need for a more than human mediator, traditions, devotional literature, and popular belief have almost deified Muhammad. This cult, of course, is contrary to the plain teaching of the Koran about him (Sura 3:144; 47:19; 13:27). The "Shia" Muslims have deified their Imams. But all deification of the creature is a sin condemned in the Koran. The only Mediator between God and creation is His Word—the Son. He became the Son of man in order that sons of man may obtain everlasting life and be adopted into the family of God. Without this Mediator mankind will always be under a spiritual constraint either to deify creatures or changing:

> The glory of the uncorruptible God into an image made like to corruptible man, and to birds, and four-footed beasts, and creeping things. (Romans 1:23)

Another major problem pertaining to monotheism in the Koran arises from its teaching about the heavenly "Mother of the Book." It is a book containing all revelations that angels bring down to the prophets of God. The Koran claims to be a copy of this original with God. God deletes out of it what He wills and establishes what He wills (Sura 13:19). It is also a record of all things and a book of decrees (Sura 6:38; 17:58). It cannot be determined from the Koran if this heavenly document is eternal. But Muslim orthodoxy regard it so. If it be granted that this "Preserved Tablet" is eternal, then we have two eternals—God and the Book. This jeopardizes monotheism as well as divine unity. Al-Ghazzali and others solved this difficulty by locating the source of all revelations (The Tablet) in the essence of God (Amin Faris, op. cit., pp. 6, 75). This approach, however, is very close to the Biblical teaching about the Logos (John 1:1, 2, 9). It is no wonder, therefore, that under the influence of the Christian doctrine of Logos, the Koran came to acquire the impress of the two-nature theory. We remember that this line of thinking was evolved by Christians in explanation of the person of Jesus Christ. The Bible provides a satisfactory answer to the relationship between the source of all revelation, the Son (or the Word), and God, the Father. This explanation is based on the revelation of the Word himself in flesh and a record about Him written and preserved by those who originally communed with Him (1 John 1:1-3).

Let us consider now the sort of tritheism that has been exposed and criticized in the Koran. It accuses some Christians of holding the following belief:

> O people of the Scripture do not exaggerate in your religion nor utter aught against God save the truth. The Messiah, Jesus Son of Mary, was only a messenger of God, and His Word which He conveyed into Mary, and Spirit from Him. So believe in God and His messengers, and say not "Three"— cease (it is) better for you God is only one God. Far it is from His transcendent majesty that He should have a son. (Sura 4:171. Also, 5:77)

On a cursory glance at the text it may appear that the doctrine of Trinity has been criticized therein. As to the meaning of the expression "Say not three," we may seek clarification from the Koran itself:

> And when God says, "O Jesus, Son of Mary." Didst you say unto man-

kind: Take me and my mother for two gods besides God?" (Sura 5:116)

It is plain, therefore, that the Koran seeks to condemn a tritheistic doctrine consisting of Jesus Son of Mary, His mother Mary and God. Moreover, it is mentioned specifically in the verse above that Jesus Christ never taught such a horrible thing to mankind. Thus the balance of the verse goes on to register His reply:

> Be glorified! It was not mine to utter that to which I had no ought. If I used to say it, then thou knewest it. Thou knowest what is in my mind.

The Koran bears clear testimony to the fact that Jesus Christ never taught a tritheistic heresy to His disciples or other people. What He did teach about God is recorded in the Bible:

> And Jesus answered him, The first of all commandments is, Hear, O Israel; The Lord our God is one Lord. (Mark 12:29)

The accusation of the Koran embodied in the expression "say not three" could only apply to those heretical Christians who wandered away from the teaching of their Lord. Again, it must be reiterated emphatically that the Koran does not imply the proper dogma of the Holy Trinity in its condemnation of a false tritheism consisting of Allah, Mary, and Jesus Christ.

Muslim commentators and scholars usually make the mistake of applying the statement "say not three" against all Christians. In this they do something not sanctioned by the Koran, as shown by Sura 5:116. Moreover, they go beyond the Koran in equating a false tritheism with the Christian doctrine of Trinity. As a result, they are quite confusing in their interpretation of "say not three." If they had remained faithful to the guidelines in the Koran, their interpretations would not have lent a wrong sanction to the widespread misunderstanding among Muslims that Christians believe in three Gods. As an example of a confusing interpretation of "say not three," let us hear from al-Baidhawi:

> "Say not there are three," that is, "Do not say there are three Gods," namely, Allah, and al-Masih and Maryam; or "Do not say God is three," meaning that there are three *Aqanim* or Essences—*Ab* (Father), *Ibn* (Son), and *Ruh al-Quds* (Holy Spirit), and interpreting it thus: *Ab*, the *Zat* or essence; *Ibn*, the *Ilm* or knowledge; and *Ruh al-Quds*, the *Hayat* or Life of God. (Al-Baidhawi quoted in Hughes' Dictionary, p. 234)

It is obvious from the quotation above that having interpreted "say not three" faithfully in the light of the Koran, Al-Baidhawi takes the liberty to apply the criticism to the doctrine of Trinity. In doing this he shows some acquaintance with interpretation of the doctrine current among Syrian Christians. Thus he uses the term *Aqanim* (plural or *Aqnum*). But it appears that he did not quite appreciate the Christian connotation of the term. Sweetman has delved into the history of this important term used by eastern Christians in their theological discourses about the Trinity and Incarnation. He sums up his research by informing us:

> Finally, as to the propriety of using the term *aqnum* in the language areas Arabic or influenced by Arabic, whatever the history of this word might have

been it comes to the Christians of the Middle and Near East and North India with only one application, i.e., for the Person of Christ or for the Persons of the Holy Trinity. . . . So let us remember that this word is primarily a Scriptural word, which cannot be said even for *persona*, appropriate to the differentiation between the Father, Son and Holy Spirit and valuable to preserve the self-revelatory acts of God and to do justice to the reality of the Incarnation. (Op. cit., Part I, Vol. 2, pp. 236, 237)

The statement of Jesus Christ in the Koran denying that He taught the tritheism of Allah, Mary and Jesus, must have puzzled Muslim scholars as to two things: First, how did this tritheistic belief originate? Second, where were these tritheists? As to its origin they must have indulged in fanciful theories rather than check up on the history of the Church. Furthermore, it was easy for them to identify tritheists condemned by the Koran with Christians as a whole. In doing so they failed to make allowance for the existence of true Christians properly taught by their Lord according to Sura 5:116. Moreover, they confused tritheism with the doctrine of Trinity, taking them to mean practically the same thing. A good example of the phenomenon surmised here is found in *Al-Insan al-Kamil* of Abd. al-Karim Ibn Ibrahim al-Jili.

It is said that when the Christians found that there was at the commencement of the *Injil*, the superinscription, "In the name of the Father and Son," they took the words in their natural meaning, and (thinking it ought to be *Ab*, father, *Umm*, mother, and *Ibn* (son)) understood by *Ab* the Spirit, by *Umm*, Mary and by *Ibn* Jesus; and on this account they said, "*Salisu Salasatin*," i.e., (God is) the third of the three (Sura 5:73). But they did not understand that by *Ab* is meant God Most High, by *Umm* the Mahiyatu al-Haqqaiq, or "essence of Truth" (Quidditas veritatum), and by *Ibn*, the Book of God, which is called the *wujud al-Mutlaq*, or Absolute Existence being an emanation from of the Essence of Truth, as is implied in the words of the Koran, Sura 13:9, "And with him is the *Umm al-Kitab*," or the Mother of the Book. (As quoted in Hughes' Dictionary, pp. 464, 647)

In the quotation above Jili identifies the Son with the "Mother of the Book"—a point discussed earlier. Also, he presents a fanciful reason for Christians misunderstanding the Trinitarian sentence in the New Testament and reduces it to tritheism of the kind condemned in the Koran. If we refer to the history of the Church, we do not need to give imaginary explanations for the Koranic reference to some Christians who had a tritheistic belief in God. It has been surmised by some Christian scholars that the reference under discussion might have applied to a few obscure hereitcal sects. Usually collyridians are suggested as a possibility (Hughes' Dictionary, p. 234). But the authority on which even the existence of this sect could be granted is Epiphanius about whom Gerock writes:

Epiphanius does not relate anything definite concerning the sect, and the long chapter devoted to this heresy contains next to nothing save controversy, in which the author seems to delight. Even had such a sect existed at the time of Epiphanius in Arabia, it is far from probable that, consisting only of women, it would have continued three centuries until the time of Muhammad and became so extended that Muhammad could mistake it for Christian religion. (Gerock, cited by S. M. Zwemer, *Moselm Doctrine of God*, p. 89)

Instead of making a scapegoat of some obscure heretical sect, it may be recognized that the widely popular form of the religion which Harnack called *Christianity of the second rank* is the most probable source of the tritheistic tendency condemned in the Koran. As it has been shown, this degenerate type of Christianity exalted the Virgin Mary to a divine status, though the official doctrine of the Church did not support it. But some outstanding Church fathers by their devotion to the cult of Mary lent support to the heterodox thinking of the lay people. There were some fathers at the Nicene council who were extreme in their Mariolatory. They even went to the extent of asserting that there were two gods besides God the Father— the Virgin Mary and Jesus Christ. This unofficial thinking in favor of the cult of Mary is exactly like the tritheism rejected by the Koran. We remember also as to how, at the Council of Ephesus, Cyril of Alexandria introduced the doctrine of *permutatio nomenium*. According to this, "Everything held true of the Son may be said to a great extent of the mother, because without her there would be no God-man" (Harnack, op. cit., p. 316). Nestorius protested in vain, "Don't make the Virgin into a goddess" (Ibid., p. 316). It has been mentioned that Cyril was popular with those to whom the cult of Mary and Monasticism were dear. The Koran criticizes Mariolatory. Also it rejects monasticism as an invention of some Christians and not sanctioned by Jesus Christ (Sura 57:27). Would it amount to taking too much for granted if these Christians are identified with the cultic heirs of Cyril? They were strong in lands around Arabia except Persia, where their influence was intermittent.

It may be conceded that the Koran justifiably criticized the tritheism and idolatrous practices of those Christians who were devoted to the cult of Mary and that of saints and martyrs. They were as much Associators (Mushrikun) as the pagan contemporaries of the prophet. One main point needs to be clarified in this discussion of the tritheism rejected by the Koran. It deals with the apparent denial of the divinity of the Messiah. Thus the Koran says:

> They surely disbelieve who say Lo! God is the Messiah, Son of Mary. The Messiah himself said: O children of Israel worship God, my Lord and your Lord. Lo! whoso ascribeth partners to God, for him God hath forbidden Paradise. (Sura 5:72)

It is repeated in several other verses that the Messiah son of Mary is only an apostle of God and not Son of God. This sonship is understood in the sense the pagan Arabs believed that God had sons and daughters:

> Yet they ascribe as partners unto Him the Jinn, although He did create them, and impute falsely, without knowledge, sons and daughters unto Him. Glorified be He and high and exalted above [all] that they ascribe [unto Him]. (Sura 6:101; 16:57; 37:149; 53:21)

From the references cited above it becomes clear that the Koran's distaste for calling the Messiah (Son of Mary) the Son of God is to be understood in terms of the creaturely aspect of the Incarnation. Here we are reminded of the Koran describing the Messiah as like Adam in the sight of God. In other words, when the Word of God descended into Mary, the child who was thus born was directly created as Adam who, too, was the direct creation of God. It may be better expressed in the words of Nestorius who said, "He who was born of Mary was a man who truly was our Saviour" (Bazaar of Heraclides, p. 201). By the term "man" Nestorius meant the human nature of Jesus Christ who is also divine:

> Consubstantial with the Father is Christ: this is true, for in the divinity He is eternal. Consubstantial with us [is He] naturally: this is true; for He too was a man as we also are. (Ibid., p. 391)

The Koran echoes Nestorian Christology as, along with the declaration that Jesus Christ was the Word of God conveyed into Mary, it insists also on His humanity which must not be deified. Nestorius referred to His humanity as the likeness of a servant (Ibid., p. 63, 70). In His human capacity He came as a Servant. In His humanity He is not the eternal Son of God, only in His divinity.

The Koran is silent as to the proper Dogma of the Holy Trinity. But it does show some of its influence indirectly which may be mentioned, in passing.

The "Bismillah" (the invocatory sentence in the Koran) suggests the Trinitarian influence. It speaks of *Allah, Rahman* and *Rahim*. The Syrian Christians employed the term "Rahmana" for Jesus Christ (H. Hirschfeld, *New Researches into the Composition and Exegesis of the Quran*, p. 68). In this regard they did the same as the Jews in speaking of God. The prophet had some difficulty in adopting this name for Allah. This incident is recorded in the Koran:

> When it is said to them: Bow down before al-Rahman, they say: Who is al-Rahman? Shall we bow down to what then biddest? (Sura 25:60)

To this objection against the name for God which was used both by the Jews (see H. W. Stanton, *Teaching of the Quran*, p. 23) and the Christians, the oracle came:

> Call upon Allah, or call upon al-Rahman, by whichsoever you will invoke Him. (Sura 17:110)

In other words, to the prophet's mind, Allah and Rahman were identical terms. He preferred to use the former more often in the interest of his mission to the Arabs.

A remarkable feature of the chapter in the Koran named after Mary is the employment of the name al-Rahman for Allah no less than eighteen times. Sprenger held the opinion that the word stands for Christ (Hirschfeld, op. cit., p. 68). But Hirschfeld doubts this since "Maryam herself places her hope in al-Rahman before Jesus was born" (Ibid., p. 23). Without bothering to examine the relative merits of the two opinions, it is sufficient, for our purpose, to point out that the prophet used al-Rahman in connection with Mary and the virgin birth narratives. This indicates his awareness of the Syrian Christian background of the name al-Rahman—in which case it was employed for the divine nature of Jesus Christ.

After the name Allah, al-Rabb is most frequently used of God in the Koran. "It seems to stand in the relative position of the Jehovah of the Old Testament and kurios of the New Testament" (Hughes' Dictionary, p. 141). Hirschfeld thinks that al-Rahman in the Koran is only "a synonym for Allah or Rabb" (Op. cit., p. 68). Briefly, since after the name Allah, al-Rahman and al-Rabb are the two most frequently used designations of God in the Koran, it is easy to suppose that the prophet had some knowledge of the Jewish and Christian doctrines of God. He criticized the tritheism involved in Mariolatory, but made no comment upon the proper doctrine of Trinity. On the other hand, he used freely al-Rahman, which had a Trinitarian significance for the Syrian Christians. Its conspicuous presence in the chapter on Mary is all the more significant in this regard.